S0-AJI-062

GRINDER, DELOZIER AND ASSOCIATES

1077 Smith Grade

Bonny Doon, California 95060

All articles © Copyright 1991 by Bretto, DeLozier and Grinder.
Printed in the United States of America. All rights reserved.
This book or parts thereof may not be printed without
written permission of the publisher.

Library of Congress Catalog Card Number 88-82414
ISBN #0-929514-02-5

We dedicate this book to

Sylvia J. Topel

*"You have touched me deeply and so whenever
I hear the wind in the trees and feel the sun
on my face, I shall remember you and be glad."*
— *Sylvia J. Topel, Moscow, 1990*

And so in this same way, my friend,
we shall remember you
for you have touched us deeply
and we are glad

TABLE OF CONTENTS

FOREWORD
by
John T. Grinder

It is a genuine treat for me to write the opening for this casebook. Some of us are fortunate enough, indeed, that within our own lifetime we can witness the consequences of something which we have had a hand in creating. This casebook is an example of such an event. In the reports which follow the reader will find much that represents the personal and professional commitments of the writers who are also principle actors in the drama, and yet running through the entire array of stories, there is a common thread which links them together — a thread which is commonly known as Neuro Linguistic Programming (NLP).

An acquaintance of mine recently gave me, as a gift, a book called *Angels Fear*, authored by Gregory Bateson and Mary Catherine Bateson. The book was a gift on several accounts. I had feared that I had received the last of the guidance and tutelage of a man who I consider to be one of the geniuses of our century — Gregory Bateson — yet here before me, through the efforts of his able daughter, was new material — his voice once again instructing and challenging me. Many thanks to Mary Catherine Bateson for rescuing her father's unfinished manuscript and making it available to the world. The second sense in which this book was a gift is that the manuscript is relatively rough and unfinished. These qualities — the lack of polish, its only partially completed state, the various false starts, the intellectual cul-de-sacs and so on — reduce its effectiveness, perhaps, as a document at the level of the content which Gregory was seeking to elucidate, but increase its value at the level of process. Here are the tracks in the damp earth, here are the scratches at the base of the piñon, here are the sections of prairie grass still bent, slightly deviating from the wind-blown attitude of its associates — all messages which demand the attention of the tracker—all signals which together form in the active, restless mind of the stalker a vivid, dynamic, and indeed compelling image of the great cat which passed this way not so very long ago. The manuscript reveals in a surprisingly transparent way the thinking of this great man in a manner which his completed and polished works do not. That most relentless tracker of them all — Death — found Gregory in July 1980 before he could return to the manuscript and sweep the path clean of the traces of how he thought through the material which is its subject. Thus, this document makes apparent what is opaque in his finished writing — the quality of movement of his thinking process — arguably his most important contribution.

The partially completed building, the opening run through of a theater group, the initial rehearsals of an orchestra working to make a new composition part of its repertoire, all offer the astute observer deep insight into the underlying processes which yield the satisfaction of the finished edifice, the magical quality of an opening night, the electricity of a debut performance.

Angels Fear is Bateson's unfinished symphony. May it inspire many more! *Leaves Before The Wind* has some of the same qualities to recommend it. The articles which constitute this casebook are reports by involved and committed practitioners of the art of Neuro Linguistic Programming. These reports are not detached, dispassionate representations of the finest work these practitioners are capable of, but interim reports by participants fully engaged in the use of a technology (NLP) to make a difference worth making in the quality of life.

The purpose of this casebook is to inspire the reader to excel in the application of NLP in his and her life experiences. The transparent quality of the description (at least to the trained NLP practitioner) allows the reader to enter into the perceptual position of the writers/actors and to appreciate both what the specific practitioner perceived, thought, and did, and more importantly what the practitioner *might* have perceived, thought, and done, but did not.

If the casebook works as intended, each of the reports actually represents a class of experience — a class defined by what actually happened plus all the variations of what could have happened as worked out by the participating reader. Like Gregory Bateson, the writer/actor offering their descriptions here would with hindsight have played with variations on the theme reported — removing this inelegance and smoothing out this transition — but have left transparent and available for your inspection the processes they used in responding to the opportunities each case represents. We thank them and ask that you use the material to stimulate and refine your own applications. The offerings here range from a Pulitzer Prize winning composer's hypnotic induction with an audience to assist them in achieving the appropriate appreciative state of active listening, to the application of a sensory acuity exercise to an industrial factory setting to reduce physical injuries at the human/machine interface, to an attention-fixing maneuver by an emergency room physician. This enormous range of contexts offers the reader a wide scope within which they can appreciate applications of the same body of patterning — patterns of excellence identified and coded by NLP modeling. If the reader finds him or herself changing and finishing the various reports to make them more satisfying or aesthetic, then the casebook will have served its purpose well.

CONTRIBUTORS

Stephanie Rachel Alt, M.S.
479 Pacific Street, Suite #3
Monterey, California 93940
Certified Master Practitioner, NLP
Certified in Hypnosis Grinder, DeLozier & Assoc.
(408) 373-4298 (work)
(408) 675-0156 (home)

Stephanie Rachel Alt currently has her private practice as an educational consultant/counselor on the Monterey Penninsula. Working with individuals, couples, and families, utilizing her training in Neuro-Linguistic Programming, Hypnosis, and Family Systems approach, she is successful in assisting her clientele effect change and improve the quality of their lives.

She has extensive training and experience in both education and medical environments. Her work has encompassed developing and directing programs, training and supervising students and staff, and working as an adjunct consultant with medical staff, social workers, psychiatrists and teachers. She is currently in the process of writing an innovative psychology text and developing accompanying educational materials..

Norma Barretta, Ph.D., Clinical Psychologist
Phillip Barretta, M.A., M.F.C.C., Psychotherapist
The Southern California Center for NLP
Executive Directors
2075 Palos Verdes Drive Noth, Suite 200
Lomita, California 90717-3726
(213) 326-5545

Norma Barretta and Phillip Barretta have between them, over 40 years of professional experience in the science of helping others to help themselves. With the extraordinarily elegant techniques of Neurolinguistic Programming, progress and growth are rapid, evolutionary experiences. Professional, individual, and family counseling are available, with the emphasis on preserving the resources within to alter old patterns and create the opportunity for developing the patterns of excellence. The Barrettas offer unique training opportunities in a wide range of classes, seminars, and workshop experiences designed to open the path to operating effectively. The Barrettas are licensed psychotherapists and certified trainers of NLP, holding the personal endorsement of NLP's co-developer, John Grinder. They are internationally acclaimed as two of the most effective Neurolinguistic Programmers and trainers. Their dedication, flexibility, and irrepressible good humor make the learning process both joyful and inspirational.

Steven F. Bierman M.D.
143 8th St.
Del Mar, California 92014
Diplomate, American Academy Family Practice
Diplomate, American College Emergency Physicians

Dr. Bierman is currently the Assistant Director of the Emergency Department at Scripps Memorial Hospital, Encinitas, California. He is board certified in Emergency Medicine, Family Practice, and Medical Hypnosis. In his professional life he works to blend traditional allopathic techniques with nontraditional alternative modalities, including NLP and hypnosis. In his private life, he enjoys sunsets and moonsets over the Pacific with his wife, Helen, and his daughter, Clea, from their home in Del Mar, California.

Cecile A. Carson, M.D.
20 Brighton Street
Rochester, New York 14607
(716) 271-5650

Cecile A. Carson is a Clinical Assistant Professor of Medicine and Psychiatry at the University of Rochester Medical School in Rochester, New York. She is an internist and specialist in Behavioral and Psychosomatic Medicine. She did Practitioner training in NLP with Bandler and Grinder in 1982, then hypnosis and modeling training with Grinder, and metaphor training with David Gordon. Recognizing the importance of somatic change work, she trained extensively with Scout Lee, completing the Master Practitioner and Trainer requirements in the Excellence Principle Utilizing NLP. She has been teaching workshops and training courses in NLP, as well as integrating NLP principles in health care and medical education. She has most recently developed a curriculum in nonverbal communication for medical residents based on NLP techniques, and is writing a text based on this material.

Michael Colgrass
583 Palmerston Avenue
Toronto, Ontario
Canada M6G 2P6

Michael Colgrass, after graduating from the University of Illinois in 1956, went to New York City where he freelanced as a percussionist with such groups as the New York Philharmonic, Broadway's *West Side Story*, Stravinsky's Columbia Recording Orchestra and myriad modern music concerts, films and recordings, including third stream performances with Dizzy Gillespie and the Modern Jazz Quartet.

In 1967 he stopped playing in order to compose and has been making his living exclulsively as a composer ever since. In 1974 he moved to

Toronto with his wife Ulla and his son Neal. His works have been played by all the major symphony orchestras in the United States and Canada and many in Europe as well. He has won numerous awards, including an Emmy Award for the documentary film, "Soundings: The Music of Michael Colgrass" (1982), and in 1978 he won the Pulitzer Prize for Music.

Describing Colgrass' music in the New York Times, critic Harold Schonberg said, "Mr. Colgrass is something of a maverick. He will use serial textures, but will mix them with jazz, or outright romanticism, or dissonance à la Ives. He also has evolved a distinct sort of miniature style that is extremely personal and poetic."

His expanding interest in all the arts led him to study mime, acting, dance and theatre directing. He began giving workshops in these skills for musicians in 1971, and the workshops excited so much interest that professionals outside the arts began to attend them. Colgrass' techniques attracted the developers of Neuro-Linguistic Programming — the study of learning and communications — who made him a trainer in their workshops. He now teaches many of these NLP techniques in his Excellence in Performance workshops.

Janus Daniels
Investment Productivity Associates
Suite 2-1A, 100 Memorial Drive
Cambridge, Massachusetts 02142

In 1988 Janus experienced, learned, and began seeing clients for I-factoring with Bill Kennedy Ph.D., who invented the process. I-f, a model for individual and organizational identity and creativity, integrates well with NLP since it performs best when outcome frames don't. It has been restricted to use in high investment business consulting. He wants to offer his resources, including I-f, to more people seeking to better themselves and the world. He has begun with the Boston Shakespeare Company, sharing the hope of peace through art.

Hilda Cole Espy
Box 328
Delaware Water Gap, Pennsylvania 18327

Hilda Cole Espy is a writer who has painted occasionally all her life, but paints often since moving to Delaware Water Gap in 1982. After being assistant to the publicity director at Harper & Brothers Publishers she joined the publicity department of CBS during the heyday of radio and interviewed stars of the era. She became Kate Smith's advance publicity agent on a coast-to-coast personal appearance tour in the great gilt-trimmed vaudeville and movie palaces of the time. Smith was billed as

"The Songbird of the South," and Espy arranged for her induction into the Sioux tribe at Sioux City, Iowa, as "The Songbird of the Sioux," an event that was broadcast by CBS on a national hookup. Later, she joined Fred Waring and his Pennsylvanians as advance press agent on two nationwide tours and worked with the organization through its famous Chesterfield series, broadcast nightly from the Vanderbilt Theater in New York. Following marriage and children she wrote short stories and articles for *Ladies Home Journal, McCall's, Redbook, Cosmopolitan* and *Collier's.* Later she joined the staff of *Woman's Day* as a feature writer and editor of the "What Goes On Here" department. One of her cover stories related the training and adventures of Peace Corps Volunteers and was later used by the Peace Corps as a recruiting booklet. After travelling and living in all five Central American republics she wrote about the areas for the travel section of the New York Times. Hilda was publicity chairman of Americans Concerned for Tomorrow, a nuclear freeze group. Her paintings have been shown at the Dutot Museum and exhibits sponsored by the Monroe County Arts Council.

Arun V. Hejmadi, Ph.D., M.S.W.
PAX Physiotherapy Services
2519 Garden Way
Colorado Springs, Colorado 80918
(719) 598-4410

Arun Hejmadi is a versatile professional who thrives on innovation. He earned his MSW in 1981, switching careers after earning a Ph.D. in Chemical Engineering in 1970, working in industry, and teaching at the University of Michigan. With Patricia Lyall, he developed Autogenic Metaphor Resolution (AMR), an interactive method for working with the mind-body interface. They received the 1986 Annual Holos Award for their work. He has applied AMR in working with many functional and stress-related illnesses. He has worked in community mental health psychiatric hospitals, and an HMO. In 1980, he developed a program for minority students at the University of Michigan which significantly improved grades and retention among minority freshmen engineering students. He is currently a Co-director of Pax Institute, and Clinic Director of Counseling Care of Colorado.

Michael Kollar, Ph.D.
27 Gamecock Ave., Suite #203
Charleston, South Carolina 29407

Dr. Michael Kollar is a licensed Counseling Psychologist offering individual, marital, and family therapy, sex therapy, and hypnotherapy. He is consultant to the Special Weapons and Tactics Team of the Charleston Police Department, a police negotiations team trained to communicate with hostile people in life-threatening situations. He also consults with local and national agencies and companies on a wide variety of subjects from mental health to industrial safety. Dr. Kollar received his doctorate in Educational and Counseling Psychology from the University of Tennessee. He completed his Master's degree in Counseling and his B.S. in Psychology at Western Carolina University. He is a Certified Sex Therapist and Certified Master Practitioner of Neuro-Linguistic Programming. He has presented numerous professional papers at mental health conferences on NLP, Human Sexuality and Hypnosis and has published several papers on related topics. Dr. Kollar has taught for Western Carolina University, the American College of Obstetricians and Gynecologists, the Citadel, the College of Charleston, and the University of Tennessee. He is a member of the American Psychological Association; American Association of Sex Educators, Counselors and Therapists; and a Clinical Member of the American Association for Marriage and Family Therapy.

Patricia J. Lyall, B. S., R.P.T.
PAX Physiotherapy Services
2519 Garden Way
Colorado Springs, Colorado 80918
(719) 598-4410

Ms. Lyall has been a physical therapist since 1965. She was introduced to NLP in 1978 by Dr. Stan Woollams, and completed practitioner certification with NLP of Colorado in 1980. The AMR approach initially evolved as a process for resolving her own physical difficulties — allergies, headaches, gastritis. With Dr. Hejmadi, the approach was refined and formalized for work with individual clients, then further developed and integrated with medical and stress research to create a teaching model. Their paper, *Beyond Stress Management: Autogenic Metaphor Resolution*, received the 1986 Annual Holos Award, presented by Dr. C. Norman Shealy and the Holos Institutes of Health. Ms. Lyall is currently a co-director with Dr. Hejmadi of PAX Physiotherapy Services and PAX Institute in Colorado Springs, Colorado. She is involved in individual and group treatment and in teaching workshops for clients and professionals on the AMR approach to resolving functional disease, chronic pain, and anxiety and post-traumatic stress disorders.

Thomas E. Malloy
Department of Psychology
University of Utah
Salt Lake City, Utah 84112

Tom Malloy is on the psychology faculty at the University of Utah, specializing in cognition, statistics, methodology, and iconoclastry. He also teaches Freshman Writing in the University Writing Program. Working with John Grinder, he is currently writing a book about walking from Leningrad to Moscow carrying a photograph of the earth.

Judith A. Marriott, B.A., M.A., S.R.N., D.R.C., M.A.C.P.C.Ps., J.P.
Psychologist in private practice
Eastwood, New South Wales, Australia

She has specialized in hypnotherapy for the past ten years, often using NLP techniques in conjunction with hypnosis and counseling. She has lectured extensively and published a number of articles on hypnosis in therapy. In addition to holding a master degree in psychology, she is a rehabilitation counselor and a registered nurse. She is currently assistant editor of the Australian Journal of Clinical Hypnotherapy and Hypnosis.

Diane Marshall, Ph.D.
1415 Pullan Avenue
Cincinnati, Ohio 45223

Diane Marshall is a graduate of Murray State University. She received a master of music in voice from the University of South Florida and doctor of musical arts in choral conducting from the Cincinnati College-Conservatory of Music. After ten years of teaching vocal music in the public schools of Alabama, Florida and North Carolina, Dr. Marshall was associated with the St. John's Unitarian Church and Cincinnati Symphony Orchestra in Cincinnati, Ohio. She has maintained a private voice studio for twelve years. Dr. Marshall is presently engaged in artistic applications of NLP in the field of music in San Francisco, California.

Eric Oliver
P.O. Box 1278
Friday Harbor, WA 98250

Eric Oliver has ten years experience in the field of human communication. He spent four years counseling individuals and families with substance abuse difficulties before moving into the communication education field. He still maintains a small private practice. He ran MetaSystems, a personal and professional development concern out of Minneapolis, with clients from every profession, including customers from such organizations as Honeywell, Control Data, and Sperry-Univac (Unisys). For over three years he has been getting attorneys in Minnesota acquainted with Other-Than-Conscious-Communication under the auspices of the State Board of Continuing Legal Education. He has spent the last three and one-half years studying with Dr. Dave Dobson on San Juan Island in Washington State. He is a member of the National Association of Neuro-Linguistic Programming, and spends the majority of his time these days delivering seminars on Dr. Dobson's Other-Than-Conscious-Communication approach. He is also editing a book on the subject due out early next year.

Linda Shapiro, M.S.
4 Copper Beech Circle
White Plains, New York 10605

Linda Shapiro, M.S. is a psychotherapist/touch healer in private practice in White Plains, New York. She is known for her work in crisis intervention and her success with chronic pain sufferers.

In addition to counseling children, single parents, couples and families, her professional career includes leading workshops on Healing, teaching adult education classes, writing, and doing oral histories of New York's elderly.

Ms. Shapiro holds a B.A. in literature from Bennington College, a Master's degree in Human Development/Counseling from Bank Street College and is Master certified in Neuro-Linguistic Programming. In January '91, she completed The Training Program in Alcohol and Chemical Dependency Counseling for Health Care Professionals provided by the National Council on Alcoholism and other Drug Addictions/Westchester.

She is married to actor George Guidall and has two daughters, Keren and Mia.

CHAPTER I

HYPNOSIS AND NLP

Preface to
HYPNOSIS AND NLP
by
Charlotte C. Bretto, M.S.

We claim to be modelers and that Neuro Linguistic Programming is a set of patterns which provide the practitioner with skills in building explicit models of complex human behavior. What this means is that we build maps of these complex patterns of behavior and these maps then allow other people to learn and use these behavior patterns. Dr. Milton H. Erickson, the father of modern hypnosis and its offspring, brief strategic psychotherapy, was a master clinician who used hypnosis because it was a model par excellence of influence in communication. Although extremely complex, Dr. Erickson's behavior while inducing and utilizing hypnotic states had distinctive patterns. The patterns, as discerned by Grinder and Bandler, are presented in previous books.

In this section, Hypnosis and NLP, practitioners of Ericksonian Hypnosis and NLP demonstrate the application of some of the behavioral patterns in different contexts: an emergency room in a hospital, family therapy, and psychotherapy practice in Australia. When reading this section you can, from third position (a detached observer), recognize the phases of hypnosis-induction, utilization, and future-pacing with ecology — as well as specific verbal and nonverbal techniques. The use of presuppositions, embedded commands, and sentence fragments is combined with special uses of voice tempo, tonality, and matching (pacing) physiological behaviors (such as the client's breathing rate and location). In addition, the NLP practitioner will recognize the familiar patterns of the outcome frame, reframing, and anchoring, to mention a few. From first position (through your eyes, ears and internal sensations) and second position (through the eyes, ears and internal sensations of the clinician and client(s), consider what you as the practitioner might have done differently and the possible results of these interventions.

Perhaps more important to consider are the frames, premises, presuppositions, or assumptions from which Ericksonian hypnosis operates. Hypnosis is conceptualized as an experientially absorbing interactional sequence that produces an altered state of consciousness wherein self-expressions begin to happen automatically (i.e., without conscious mediation).[1] Bierman's work with Arthur in Case 9 is an example. Erickson believed that the mechanism by which a problem is maintained is also the mechanism of solution. The client's well developed symptom circuitry is used to increase their personal power by expanding their range of behavioral possibilities. As you read notice how the practitioner uses the same language the client uses to describe the problems and solutions during the induction and utilization phases.

Another major premise underlying this view is that the value of an experience depends primarily on its context.[2] A good example is in Marriott's work with Susan, Case 1, where by exploring an interaction from three different perceptual positions Susan accessed the very neurological circuitry in one context which provided the necessary resources for achieving her desired solution in another context. After all, Bateson suggests that context fixes meaning and that without context words and actions have no meaning at all.

In the psychotherapeutic field Bateson says we not only walk into and create something which we will call a context, but that we also come with stories — not just a supply of stories to deliver to the therapist but stories built into our very being. These stories represent our well developed circuitry. He also states in *Mind and Nature* that "behavior" is in fact those stories projected into "action." Marriott's work with Lisa in Case 3 demonstrates how we can use the client's 'story' during the induction phase of hypnosis; the Barrettas' work with the Smith family, Case 1, demonstrates how we can use the client's 'story' during the utilization phase of hypnosis. In addition, the Barrettas provide information on how to construct and use metaphor for leading to the client's desired outcome. In recent audio tapes of an early Bateson lecture, he stated that the root 'meta' and 'trans' are the same. 'Meta' is the Greek word for the Latin 'trans'; a metamorphosis is a transformation, and a metaphor is a transform.

Erickson's approach was also one of cooperation. An approach is a way of going about tackling a problem and may be relevant to more than one subject. For example, an 'experimental approach' might be taken to the problems of physics, psychology, agriculture, and many other subjects.[4] The hypnotist's use of the client's patterns of expression verbally and non-verbally constitutes the basis of the induction and utilization phase of trance. This approach emphasizes that trance always occurs in a relationship context, in which neither hypnotist nor subject can be considered independently of each other.[5] Beirman's work in Case 5 demonstrates this approach in an even larger system, including the boy's mother, in order to accomplish the necessary trance state for the work at hand. To this extent the approach is cybernetic.

Cybernetics is the theory supporting "General Systems Theory." The word, cybernetics, comes from the Greek word meaning steersman. Plato used the word in making an analogy between the helmsman steering a ship and a statesman steering the 'ship of state'. For Ashby, a leading theoretician in the 1950s and 1960s, cybernetics deals with "all forms of behaviors in so far as they are regular, or determinate or reproducible".[6]

Bateson argues that the mind–body problem which has plagued philosophy for hundreds of years, viewed cybernetically, seems to be wrongly posed.[7] In a cybernetic analysis of the process in which a person thinks, acts, and modifies subsequent behavior in the light of preceding acts, all these items, including the acts themselves, may be seen as information processing. Bateson argues that the total self-corrective unit which does this processing is not, however, the human being, but a system whose boundaries extend beyond the human body. The system is a network of information transmitting pathways including some external to the actor; and in this view, mind is not simply associated with the human body but is imminent in brain, plus body, plus environment.[8] The central concept 'system' embodies the idea of a set of elements connected together which form a whole, thus showing properties which are properties of the whole, rather than properties of the component parts. The taste of water, for example, is a property of the substance of water, not of the hydrogen and oxygen which combine to form it.

The word 'thinking' in 'systems thinking' implies thinking about ourselves and the world outside ourselves, very much in the way envisioned in the following passage by Einstein:

> What, precisely, is 'thinking'? When at the reception of sense impressions, memory pictures emerge, this is not yet 'thinking.' And when such pictures form series, each member of which calls forth another, this too is not yet 'thinking.' When, however, a certain picture turns up in many such series, then — precisely through such return — it becomes an ordering element for such series. Such an element becomes an instrument, a concept. I think that the transition from free association or 'dreaming' to thinking is characterized by the more or less dominating role which the 'concept' plays in it.[9]

Systems thinking, then, makes conscious use of the particular concept of wholeness captured in the word 'system,' to order our thoughts. A 'systems approach' then implies using the product of this thinking to initiate and guide actions we take in the world. Ericksonian hypnosis is 'a systems approach' to communication. A systems approach takes a broad view which tries to take all aspects into account, and which concentrates on interactions between the different parts of the problem.[10]

Think beyond this section and these applications and consider the possibility of using the premises of Ericksonian Hypnosis and NLP Modeling as tools for living in this time which has been referred to as 'the Systems Age.'

REFERENCES

1. Gilligan, Steven G. Therapeutic Trances: The Cooperation Principle in Ericksonian Hypnotherapy. New York, New York: Brunner/Mazel Publishers, 1987.

2. Ibid.

3. Bateson, Gregory. Mind And Nature A Necessary Unit. New York, New York: Bantam Books, 1979.

4. Checkland, Peter. Systems Thinking, Systems Practice. New York, New York: John Wiley & Sons Ltd., 1981.

5. Gilligan, Steven. Op. Cit.

6. Ashby, W.R. An Introduction To Cybernetics. London, England: Chapman & Hall Ltd., 1956.

7. Bateson, Gregory. Op. Cit.

8. Checkland, Peter. Op. Cit.

9. Schlipp, P.A. (Ed.) Albert Einstein: Philosopher-Scientist. LaSale, Illinois: Open Court, 1949.

10. Checkland, Peter. Op. Cit.

HYPNOSIS IN THE EMERGENCY ROOM
August 1, 1987
by
Steven F. Bierman, M.D.

ABSTRACT

Ten cases are presented illustrating the applicability of hypnosis to a broad range of medical emergencies. In all cases, the Emergency Physician served both as treating physician and as hypnotist. The method employed for trance induction is outlined, and criteria for bedside determination of trance discussed. The previously unreported phenomenon of the non-manipulative reduction of a dislocated shoulder by means of hypnosis is detailed. Hyperventilation syndrome is also treated hypnotically. In addition, several cases are described in which anesthesia/analgesia is achieved using hypnosis either alone or in concert with other modalities.

INTRODUCTION

Hypnotic phenomena, such as anesthesia and analgesia, have long been subjects of scientific study and documentation. (1,2). Yet, despite their promised efficacy, direct clinical application to medical emergencies has only rarely been reported. (3,4). In the few cases that do appear in the literature the hypnotist has often been a consultant and not the Emergency Physician.

Most likely, this paucity of published reports reflects the general belief that hypnosis requires considerable time, a quiet place, and an operator free from distractions. The following cases, however, all occurred in the routine course of events in a moderately busy (1000 patient-visits/month) urban Emergency Department (ED). They do not represent a series in sequence, but rather selected cases intended to display the spectrum of conditions in which hypnosis may be useful. In all cases, the author was both Emergency Physician and hypnotist.

METHOD

The method for inducing hypnotic trance was fundamentally identical in all cases. Initially rapport (used here in a technical sense) was established between physician and patient by mirroring as much as possible, without being obvious, the patient's behaviors, beliefs, physiology, etc. (5,6). The patient's attention was then "unlimbered": that is to say, loosened up, distracted from the chief complaint and directed to other sensations and awarenesses. For example, reference might have been made to similar past episodes, to last night's sleep, to other areas of the body, the borders of the painful area, etc. Then, the suggestion: "I wonder if you can (patient's first name) close your eyes and allow yourself to recognize certain other sensations . . . such as . . .?" From this point on, the hypnotist generally delivered his phrases in synchrony with the patient's breathing rhythm. Perceptions just outside of consciousness were then catalogued (e.g., one's breathing, the sensation of the bed sheets upon one's legs, distant sounds, the shifting patterns of light and shade upon one's closed eyelids, etc.). During this phase, suggestions for rest and a gradually increasing sense of comfort and security were often interspersed. Further absorption was then achieved by means of metaphors and images. In children, for instance, a fantasy of Disneyland or some other favorite place was elaborated. By then, trance had usually begun to develop. Suggestions designed to effect the desired therapeutic outcome were then embedded into the context of the ongoing metaphors and images.

ASSESSMENT OF TRANCE

Presently, there are no physiologic parameters of trance that can be assessed rapidly and unobtrusively at the bedside. However, there are certain recognizable changes that occur regularly as one enters trance. These changes are listed in Table I. In cases 1 and 10 below, it will be noted that arousal occurred spontaneously with the achievement of the desired therapeutic result. In all other respects, however, the criteria listed in Table I were fully met by the cases presented.

Table I

BEDSIDE CRITERIA FOR DETERMINING TRANCE-STATE
I. Symmetrical facial flaccidity
II. Altered facial vascularity (usually pallor)
III. Generalized immobility
IV. Responsiveness to prescribed behaviors
V. Relative absence of non-prescribed behaviors
VI. Lag phase (usually 15-30 seconds) between suggestion and response

Case 1

Walter, a 36 year old male with a history of recurrent shoulder dislocations, complained of intense pain in the left shoulder following an accident. Physical findings were consistent with an anterior dislocation of the humeral head, without neurapraxia.

No medications were given, despite the patient's report that four previous episodes of the same had invariably required Demerol.

Instead, a trance was induced under which various unsuccessful attempts at mechanical reduction were made. At length, two techniques of indirect suggestion were employed. First, a metaphor was elaborated wherein a bowling ball was pictured ". . . rolling in comfort and ease into the pocket." Second, an embedded command in which the key words were marked out by means of selectively altering the hypnotist's tone of voice. (5).

Thus, " . . . allowing me to *shoulder* the responsibility, as you continue to settle *down*, all the way *down, into the proper place*." (The indirect suggestion being . . . shoulder . . . down . . . down . . . into the proper place . . . .) As these suggestions were given, the affected shoulder was merely supported in a neutral position. Approximately 15 seconds after delivery of the embedded command, the shoulder clunked into anatomic position (later confirmed by x-ray), and the patient spontaneously roused.

Two weeks later, the patient reported a faster and more comfortable convalescence than on all previous occasions.

Case 2

Jason, a 7-year-old boy, was brought to the ED with multiple abrasions of the left upper and lower extremities, following a bicycle accident. After a physical examination confirmed the absence of other injuries, trance was induced. Levitation and catalepsy of the right upper extremity were elicited and sustained throughout the treatment. A metaphor was then used concerning the "tubular arms and legs" of a bicycle that began brand new and become "scratched and injured." But, it was explained, those tubular limbs were "without feeling, because they *don't need to feel anything*"; so their owner could easily "*lift* a *hand* to have them cleaned *up* in perfect comfort." (Again, the technique of embedded commands.) Profound hemianesthesia resulted.

The ED nurse then accomplished a thorough cleansing and debridement of multiple partial-thickness abrasions without disturbing the boy. He was subsequently aroused and reported having felt no discomfort.

Case 3

Thomas, a 54-year-old male, complained of perianal pain and swelling. Physical examination revealed a thrombosed external hemorrhoid requiring enucleation. Demerol (100mg.) and Phenergan (25mg.) were administered by intramuscular injection.

A simple Neuro-Linguistic Programming (NLP) technique was then used, in anticipation of injecting a local anesthetic.

Considerable experience with this procedure has convinced the author that parenteral analgesia alone will not provide sufficient pain relief. Accordingly, an "anchor" stimulus (visual, auditory or kinesthetic) is first associated with a state of rest and comfort. Repetition of the anchor stimulus at the time of injection then recalls the associated mental state.

Injections are thus rarely perceived. (6). Unlike most cases in which this technique is used, a sustained trance ensued.

Suggestions were promptly given for deepening and maintaining the trance. Then, as the anchor stimulus was being repeated (in this case, touching the left elbow), 0.5% Marcaine anesthesia was injected locally at four points. The anal wink reflex occurred with only two of the four injections. The fourth needle insertion resulted in the patient momentarily lifting his head and opening his eyes. However, his gaze remained unfocused, and moments later he returned to his previous position. The remainder of the procedure was uneventful: the patient remained in trance throughout.

The patient roused upon command, and reported — on a scale from one to ten, ten being the most extreme pain — having felt a "-30" during the entire episode. He had no recollection of the injection.

Case 4

Denise, a 24-year-old female under considerable emotional stress, presented herself to the ED with classic symptoms of hyperventilation syndrome. The diagnosis was confirmed by history and physical examination. Trance was induced, and suggestions were given for her to "allow herself to experience a certain amount of coolness." Later, she was directed to observe that with each breath she could become a little more cool. "Now nobody likes to be cold. And so you are discovering how to breathe just enough to stay cool, just cool, under all conditions . . . and isn't it nice to know . . . that you can work out your problems . . . however much time it takes . . . in cool and comfortable contemplation . . ." And so forth.

Suggestions were initially delivered at the pace of the patient's breathing, and then gradually slowed. The patient's breathing pattern followed the hypnotist's lead, gradually normalizing.

Her symptoms soon resolved, and she was roused and discharged feeling greatly improved.

Case 5

A two-year-old boy was brought by his mother to the ED on account of a head injury. On physical examination the sole finding was a 2 centimeter long scalp laceration. The child was neurologically normal. However, both mother and child were agitated and crying. Initial attempts to induce trance were directed at the child without success. It was noted, however, that during the induction attempt, the mother's blink reflex and facial muscle tonus had altered (signs of developing trance).

Subsequent suggestions were directed, as it were, through the child to the mother. The latter promptly entered a trance state; and the child followed his mother's lead.

Injection, debridement, and suturing of the wound were then accomplished without noticeable discomfort to the boy, who remained quiet and immobile throughout the procedure. Both subjects were thereafter roused, and discharged from the ED.

Case 6

Melissa, a 12-year-old girl, was brought to the ED after a fall.

There were no physical abnormalities other than a scalp laceration which required suturing. However the patient adamantly refused any procedure involving a needle. In the course of explaining that a needle would not be necessary, trance was induced. Melissa was then directed to "fully enjoy watching a comfortable scene from her past." Meanwhile, the wound was thoroughly cleansed, debrided, and sutured without the use of local anesthesia.

On arousal, the patient reported her amusement at having been able to "watch a movie" while her medical needs were being attended to painlessly.

Case 7

Randy, a 9-year-old boy with chronic asthma, was brought to the ED complaining of shortness of breath. On introduction to the Emergency Physician, he blurted: "I don't want a shot!"

Physical examination revealed a slightly pale, afebrile child with bilateral expiratory wheezes. He had a history of responding well to subcutaneous epinephrine.

Trance was induced, and epinephrine 0.25cc (1:1000) administered subcutaneously. The boy was then roused and given the appropriate dose of an oral theophylline preparation. His clinical condition gradually ameliorated. Approximately 30 minutes later trance was again induced, and a second injection, this time Susphrine, administered. On arousal, the patient was told he had already received two injections, and would require no more. In disbelief, the boy created an unusual disturbance by repeatedly exclaiming, "I got a shot, and I didn't even feel it!"

The patient was discharged on oral theophylline, his lungs clear to auscultation.

Case 8

Kristin, a 6-year-old girl, was brought to the ED with a classic Colles' deformity of the right forearm. After a brief examination confirmed the absence of neuro-vascular impairment, trance was induced.

The patient was then instructed about what would transpire during her brief visit to the Radiology Department. She was assured that she would remain safe and secure, and that her father (who had brought her to the ED) and the doctor would always be near. She was told that she "could continue to enjoy a deep, restful sleep" no matter where she went or what other people said. She was then conveyed by wheelchair to Radiology.

An unrelated emergency intervened, and the Emergency physician was unable to accompany the patient. Nevertheless, the father reported that she remained apparently "asleep" throughout the various manipulations necessary to obtain adequate films.

Orthopedic consultation was arranged, and the patient was aroused. (Note: It was felt necessary to arouse the patient prior to her seeing the specialist, since no arrangements had been made in advance concerning the use of hypnosis.)

In the following two cases, the presence of confounding factors make it difficult to designate the precise effect of the hypnotic encounter.

Case 9

Arthur, an 84-year-old man with a history of paroxysmal atrial fibrillation, arrived in the ED complaining of an irregular heart beat. Atrial fibrillation was diagnosed by EKG and physical examination. No other abnormalities were noted. Serum electrolytes and arterial blood gases were within normal limits. He was in no distress.

The patient reported having had a similar episode at another hospital some years earlier. He explained that just prior to his transfer from that hospital's ED to the medical floor, he had converted spontaneously to normal sinus rhythm (NSR). His subsequent work-up had reportedly been normal.

While awaiting laboratory results, it was decided to try hypnosis. Trance was induced. The patient was then directed to recall all aspects of his condition and circumstances just prior to his previous conversion to NSR: the bed he was in, how he felt, what he saw, heard, his emotions at that time, the odors, and so on. In addition, a description was given of how unconscious regulatory functions can come under conscious control. For example, "before mentioning it . . . you were probably not aware of the rate of your own rhythmic breathing . . . which you might now . . . consciously . . . begin to slow down . . ." Embedded suggestions to regulate heart rate were also interspersed, as trance was maintained and deepened. Gradually, the patient's respiratory rate slowed from 18 to 10 per minute, and his heart rate from 130-140/minute to 100-110/minute.

The patient was then instructed to fully experience the completion of his resurrected memory, that is, to relive his own spontaneous conversion to NSR. He was told he could do so at whatever time seemed most appropriate to him: he could, ". . . return to this restful place (i.e. trance) whenever you feel the need."

After some time, the rhythm remained unchanged. The patient was therefore aroused. Digoxin 0.150 mg. was administered intravenously. An hour later, still no change. A cardiologist was called. While awaiting his arrival, the patient voluntarily relapsed into trance. Moments later, the rhythm converted to NSR. The patient aroused spontaneously as the cardiologist arrived, and reported: "I did it. I went back there and did just what the doctor said to do!"

Case 10

Michael, an 11-year-old boy, was brought to the ED having suffered a left elbow dislocation. X-ray and physical examination confirmed a posteriorly displaced ulna, without neurovascular compromise. Orthopedic consultation was obtained. During the orthopedist's examination, the elbow was gingerly manipulated through no more than 10 degrees range of motion. No traction or forcible maneuvers were applied. The orthopedist requested an IV be established prior to his efforts at reduction. He then indicated he would return shortly.

Because of the patient's avowed fear of needles, the NLP technique previously outlined in Case 3 was used. The IV was thus established without any discomfort to the patient. During the procedure, it was noticed that Michael exhibited certain hypnotic readiness; trance was induced. Metaphors and suggestions for relaxation, and relaxation only, were delivered.

As the orthopedist returned, the patient was aroused.

Repeat examination at that time revealed complete anatomic reduction of the left elbow.

DISCUSSION

These cases illustrate that even in the often hectic setting of the Emergency Department, hypnosis can be readily employed by the Emergency Physician to reduce pain and suffering.

Three cases are cited in which hypnosis is used as the sole form of anesthesia (Cases 2,6,7). As such, it is effective not only for simple injections, but also for complex debridement and wound closure. Hypnotically induced pre-injection anesthesia (i.e., anesthesia used prior to the instillation of local xylocaine) is also demonstrated (Case 5). In all cases, it should be noted, trance confers the additional benefits of relaxation and immobility effects especially advantageous in suturing small children.

Hypnosis can also be used in concert with other forms of anesthesia. In Case 3, for example, the usually excruciating experience of perianal injection is rendered painless by a combination of trance, parenteral analgesia, and Neuro-Linguistic Programming.

Case 8 reconfirms earlier reports that hypnosis can effect profound analgesia in fractures and dislocation. (4). Further, it introduces the assurance that in such cases, the hypnotist need not be present continuously. Erickson was aware of this, and offered specific advice on how to approach such situations. (7).

The application of hypnosis to medical emergencies, however, extends beyond the realm of pain relief. In Case 4, for example, hyperventilation syndrome is treated effectively using hypnosis.

There is no claim here that calm and quiet talk might not have been equally effective, only that by assuring compliance through trance the desired end was arrived at quickly and efficiently.

Skeletal muscle relaxation is also achieved hypnotically, and to a degree sufficient to have allowed the non-manipulative reduction of a dislocated shoulder (Case 1) and, a dislocated elbow (Case 10). To the author's knowledge, no such cases using hypnosis have ever been reported.

Finally, in Case 9, there is the suggestion that such "autonomic"

functions as heart rate and rhythm may also be amenable to hypnotic intervention.

In addition to these intended therapeutic effects, one consistent conse-
quence of the hypnotic encounter is enhanced physician rapport with both
patient and parent, arising largely out of the technique itself, which requires
that the operator establish a pattern of semblance between himself and his
subject. (5). Such a relationship not only serves to obviate future
misunderstandings, but also quite conceivably strengthens the physician's
capacity to effect healing.

Since Charcot's pronouncement in the last century that children cannot
be hypnotized, many have held to that erroneous notion. In fact, children
are highly susceptible to hypnosis. One recent report documents hundreds
of cases in which hypnotherapeutic interventions were effective in the pediatric age group. (8). Case 5 further illustrates that, provided the operator
is flexible, trance can be induced in patients as young as two-years-old.

Patients in the ED are particularly disposed to trance. Erickson pointed
out that confusion is an essential element of many hypnotic inductions. The
disturbances that prompt ED visits generally constitute such a storm of
confusion that trance is accepted as a safe haven. Moreover, the ambient din
of the ED serves to highlight the distinction between "internal" and "external" processes, also conducive to trance. The author's experience with
hundreds of patients indicates that in many cases trance can be induced in
the time it takes to utter no more than a half a dozen sentences. The usual
time required is 5-10 minutes, no more than is necessary to cautiously ad-
minister, say, intravenous morphine.

SUMMARY

The cases presented demonstrate the applicability of hypnosis to a broad
range of medical conditions. They illustrate clearly that the process of trance
induction can be performed by the Emergency Physician in the course of
his usual business.

Hypnosis need not be excessively time consuming, especially in the ED,
where patients are predisposed to trance.

BIBLIOGRAPHY

1. Hartland J: <u>Medical And Dental Hypnosis.</u> London: Bailliere, Tindal, and Cassell, 1971 (Second Edition)

2. Hilgard ER, Hilgard JR: <u>Hypnosis In Pain Relief</u>. Los Altos, Calif, William Kaufman, 1975

3. Wain HJ, Amen DG: "Emergency Room Use of Hypnosis." General Hosp phych 8, 19-20, 1986

4. Goldie L: "Hypnosis in the Casualty Department." Br Med J 2:1340-1342, 1956

5. Grinder J, Bandler R: <u>Trance-Formations</u>. Moab, Utah, Real People Press 1981

6. Grinder J, Bandler R: <u>Frogs Into Princes</u>. Moab, Utah, Real People Press, 1979

7. Erickson MH, Rossi EL: <u>Hypnotic Realities</u>. New York, Irvinton Publisher, 1976

8. Kohen DP, Olness KN: "The Use of Relaxation-Mental Imagery (Self-Hypnosis) in the Management of 505 Pediatric Behavioral Encounters." Developmental and Behavioral Pediatrics 5 (No.l), 21-25, Feb. 1984.

NLP TECHNOLOGY AND HYPNOSIS
by
Judith A. Marriott, B.A., M.A.

As a counselling psychologist and hypnotherapist in private practice, I find it essential to utilize various techniques according to the individual client personality, needs and responses to precipitate change. As Milton Erickson (Haley 1973) showed in his approach to therapy, planned assessment and strategy are not always the answer, theories do not always fit. Therapy is done with the individual by using information in the best way to get results.

Many of the difficulties encountered in life are related to getting along with other people, not only in the social or work situations, where one may function adequately but in sustained and intimate relationships such as those of marriage and family involvement. To assess these difficulties it is often helpful to examine the power structure in a relationship or situation as well as the existing patterns of behavior.

Personality cannot be isolated from interpersonal situations. It is not possible to speak of an individual's personality without in the same breath saying or implying something about the person's relationships with other people. For instance, shyness, friendliness, hostility, ambition, alienation, etc., do not make much sense outside the social situation (Sullivan 1955). As well as stressing social determinants of personality, Sullivan specified certain capacities with which an infant begins life, including 'tension' and 'symbolism', both being bases for later experiences. There is a primitive desire for contact which is in turn the basis of later needs for tenderness, love and intimacy.

As the infant gradually learns to classify events and to anticipate good and bad experiences, i.e., those which increase or relieve tension, the developing child builds a self-system in the context of social rewards and threats to security, learning to use something akin to Freud's defense mechanisms to remove threatening aspects of the self from conscious consideration.

Very early in life, then, anxiety is associated with social disapproval and insecurity, and it is not an unreasonable assumption that the early caretaker wields an influence which may set patterns of behavior throughout the lifetime of the person.

To alleviate tension, the child needs to strike a balance of power in a relationship. To avoid feelings of 'helplessness' where the child does not receive his or her perceived share of love and attention by fair means, he or she must gain it by other means, i.e., a deviant or inappropriate way. If a sense of power is not developed along adequate lines, then a sense of helplessness may become incorporated in the person's conception of their self-worth or self-esteem.

However, all is not lost. Two phases of development are mentioned by Winnicott (1978): first, development is a matter of inheritance of the maturational process and only occurs in a facilitating environment which is first absolutely and then relatively important; that is, the course of the development can be described in terms of absolute dependence, relative dependence and toward independence; and second, development is also concerned with the accumulation of living experiences. Mead (1934) points out that the self is a process — it can never be fully defined, processed or measured, for as soon as we talk of 'I', it has become a 'Me'. We are not, then, passive creatures shaped by external forces, but constantly active in social interaction creating and recreating ourselves as the flow of experiencing changes and evolves all the years of our lives. Change, then, can be affected through experience, and inappropriate defense patterns learned in childhood phased out.

In dealing with crises in the relationships of life in therapy, it seems important to assess the power structure within those relationships — the way balance is achieved, whether it is flexible or rigid. Although hypnosis is based on a voluntary relationship (the procedures are imposed not on an unwilling person but upon someone who SEEKS OUT this type of relationship (Erickson, 1973), power is *perceived* to be in the hands of the hypnotist. People will, however, often resist the direction offered and there is a necessity to motivate them towards cooperation, and often to deal with resistance. Hypnotic 'power' must often be manipulated and used indirectly: past resources revived (regardless of their context); or new ways of looking at old situations encouraged. Such evolution of the client may be achieved through the processes of NLP technology, where the shift from present to desired state, generalized as future-pacing, is effected and enhanced in the hypnotic state.

In the following case histories, hypnosis combined with NLP technology is used to effect change in a variety of individuals by allowing them to see present defense patterns — and where appropriate to be aware of their roots in childhood — and through reframing and restructuring to modify inappropriate behavior, to observe and reinforce the change as their perception of themselves in the situation (and therefore in their world) moves from emotional helplessness to a belief and attitude of equality and power.

Case 1

Susan, aged 34, is single and a successful freelance writer. For the last five years, she had been emotionally and physically tied to John, a married man. She wished to sever the relationship and get on with her life. Her desire was to marry and have a child, and she felt that time was running out. The relationship with John was, she realized, obsessional and without future. It restricted her and held her back from getting to know other men.

She related an incident which brought home to her the need to rid herself of this relationship. She had attended a party recently and was deep in conversation with Dan, an "attractive and witty" man who she knew was attracted to her and had been for some time, when John arrived on the scene. John immediately and possessively cut Dan out of the conversation and led Susan off to a secluded corner of the room where they stayed together for the rest of the evening. This was typical. Susan knew Dan had been embarrassed, but felt compelled to go along with John and accede to his wish for her exclusive company. She knew that any arrangement John made with her to meet later would just as likely be canceled or simply not kept, depending on plans made by John's wife, and in fact such a date to meet after the party proved to be no exception. This was especially annoying as Susan had canceled a date she had previously made with Dan in order to meet John.

Susan was first allowed to rest in the hypnotic state to reduce tension, and then asked to replay, in her mind, the incident described above in four frames: first as herself; second in the role of Dan; third as John; and finally to stand aside and watch the incident as if merely an observer. As a result Susan immediately became aware of John's carelessly arrogant manner and his way of apparently losing interest if she so much as greeted a friend, causing her to become anxious and attentive to him. This insight triggered feelings of anger and a tactile anchor was immediately attached to that emotion by a touch to the shoulder.

She was then asked to restructure the incident: "see what happens if you excuse yourself from the exclusive company of John and wander about the room greeting other people." Doing so gave her a feeling of *strength* and *power*, which was immediately combined with *anger* by the same tactile anchor.

She was then asked to imagine future situations where she might hear from or see John and to take the anger/strength/power resource into those situations to reject him. The strength of the resource was tested by having Susan lift her right arm against the unexpected pressure of the therapist's hand while envisioning the situations, to create a symbolic paradox forcing her to act as instructed, but against the 'will' of the hypnotist — and proved to be powerful. Suggestion was then given that . . . "seeing or hearing from John would trigger this angry strength, giving you the power to sever this relationship." This in turn was tested and reinforced by visual imagery in which she met John and walked away, combined with the tactile anchor, i.e., her shoulder was touched; and in addition an auditory stimulus was thrown in — hearing his voice on the phone — with the rejecting strength of the tactile anchor for good measure.

Finally, she was asked to recall a time when she had experienced total *freedom and relief*. Her recall was that of completing final examinations at school, and this resource was combined via the previous imagery to the tactile anchor, tested as before, and the session terminated.

At her next session three weeks later this client reported that the obsession with John was over. For a number of days after the first therapy session fury had consumed her as she recalled the times she had allowed John to manipulate her; the fury had subsided into rejection of any thought of John by shifting her attention elsewhere when he came into her mind. She had refused to speak to him on the phone, and had "cut him dead" at a function they had both attended. Finally her attitude to him became indifference, "as if he doesn't really exist." Best of all she was increasingly aware of a genuine friendliness and outgoing manner in her dealings with the men she came into contact with socially. This was already producing interesting results. No further intervention has been necessary.

DISCUSSION

The hypnotic state to enhance relaxation and imagery as well as increase suggestibility was used with reframing and restructuring to objectify feelings and to access the strength — in this case anger — required to break free of an obsessional and potentially destructive relationship. Visual and auditory 'triggers' were used with suggestion to access this resource feeling which in turn served to trigger the idea of freedom and relief, itself accessed from an appropriate time in this client's past experience, becoming a future-pacer for new behavior as her emotional helplessness in the situation was transformed to an attitude of equality and power in turn reinforced by responses from the environment, i.e., attention from other men in whom she saw potential for achieving her goal, that of marrying and having a child.

Case 2

Gavin, twenty-seven, and Margaret, thirty-six, presented themselves for marriage counseling. The marriage was in its second year and the couple had lived together for approximately a year before the ceremony. A month before the marriage was formalized, Margaret had met up with an old flame and had seriously considered marrying this man instead of Gavin, who had waited anxiously on the sidelines while Margaret made up her mind between the two of them.

Margaret's previous marriage had been dissolved after three years, without issue; Gavin had never had a relationship with a woman until he met Margaret. Neither wanted children and Gavin had undergone a vasectomy two years ago to ensure there would be none. Both had similar family histories except that Gavin was a country boy and Margaret had been brought up in the city. Both were only children with adequate but undemonstrative working mothers and achievement-oriented fathers. Both sets of parents were living, their marriages intact.

Their relationship had been excellent at first but since then the marriage had become more and more stressful for both. Gavin expressed the problem in the relationship as, "Margaret doesn't give me the affection I need." Margaret said, "Gavin is too intrusive and demanding of me."

Initially, it was ascertained that they loved each other and that there was a genuine desire to make the marriage work. Without these elements there would be no point to entering into therapy. The following individual differences were noted:

a) When 'down,' Gavin liked to be cheered up and 'brought out' of himself while Margaret preferred to be left alone when feeling out of sorts. Each treated the other as they would wish to be treated themselves; consequently both were frustrated and disrespected.

b) Gavin felt the need to reach a conclusion in an argument, while Margaret withdrew from arguments altogether.

c) Gavin liked to try new things sexually and enjoyed love-making at night. Margaret wanted to relax at night, preferred making love in the morning, and was also more conventional.

d) Gavin was a logical thinker, while Margaret relied a great deal on intuition.

It was noted that Gavin was extremely attentive and vigilant of his wife during their first consultation. In addition it was observed that while Gavin was in the consulting room, Margaret would not allow herself to enter the hypnotic state, but when seen alone, she quickly entered into a deep and 'passive' state.

Gavin, on the other hand, was an excellent and 'active' subject who could achieve hypnosis whether alone with the therapist or in the company of his wife.

During the one and only private consultation with Margaret, she commented that she accepted Gavin as he was and, "he must do the same for me." She realized that his continual criticism and fault finding was a result of his insecurity about her which was unfounded. As a child, she said, she had hungered for affection and had coped with rejection by withdrawing into herself. She added that she had learned a lot from her previous marriage and that people must be free to be themselves within a relationship, she was *not* prepared to enter therapy to, "change my ways for Gavin." She said she wanted a husband who was an equal, not a son.

In the relaxed state of hypnosis, using visual imagery and a tactile anchor (a touch to the hand) a warm feeling was accessed on recalling the relaxed, confident Gavin of their first few months together, especially their first encounters where he had instructed Margaret in scuba diving, and reframing him as such into the present. She felt "more at ease than I've felt in a long time" after the session, and a cassette tape was provided for her to use at home to help reduce her stress level. She was discharged without making any further appointments.

Gavin, in his initial private consultation, said he realized he would probably have to make the necessary changes, but did not see why he should have to, "if she wouldn't." He too had craved affection in his childhood. He had been prone to childhood illnesses which kept his mother home from work to look after him.

After four consultations with Gavin, he was taught self-hypnosis by association of the relaxed state anchoring, and his focus shifted from Margaret to himself. As he gained confidence in his abilities and power through the hypnotic situation so he gained confidence in his power in the relationship. To this end, paradoxical suggestion was used; "although I tell you to remain in hypnosis . . . at the count of three, you will find that your own control is such . . . is so complete that you will easily overcome . . . that instruction . . . and awaken fully . . . despite my instructions to the contrary . . ." In addition, imagery was used with tactile anchoring to reframe situations illustrating his present associations with his old patterns of behavior, i.e., it was demonstrated that his 'depressions' of today related to the 'illnesses' of his childhood in his efforts to gain attention. He was able to access the same insecurity from the past and was consequently able to see how tension and anxiety increased when Margaret did not comfort him (e.g., "stay home from work" as his mother had). He saw for himself his inappropriate and 'childlike' behavior.

Subsequently, tactile, auditory, and visual anchors were used to transfer resources of strength, calmness, confidence and interest from his weekend job (teaching scuba diving to beginners) to other areas of his life, both daily work and social situations to demonstrate how HIS words, HIS actions could cause a desirable response in another person (a vital skill which he was *already using* when teaching beginner scuba divers). In this way his own sense of logic was triggered and he responded to the future-pacing by experimenting with different behaviors at work and in social situations. As he found responses positive it followed almost automatically that he experiment at home. This of course was reinforced by Margaret's positive responses to him as his own sense of personal power increased.

Three weeks were allowed between Gavin's second and final sessions to test consolidation of future-pacing. On his final consultation he reported that positive changes had taken place. His vigilance had ceased and Margaret was actually approaching him sexually at times. "It's as if I've grown up," he commented, "just because of my changed attitude, she is acting differently towards me."

DISCUSSION

In this relationship the power structure was obviously out of balance. All the communication in the world between two people is useless if it is directed only to "how we should meet others' needs," especially if those needs are inappropriate and untenable to the partner. Margaret admitted she was not without problems but knew she would change — by relaxing without feeling threatened — if Gavin acted differently. Her desire not to enter therapy was accepted by the author for three reasons:

Firstly, it could be used to show Gavin the ball was in his court. Only *he* had the power and resilience to make the necessary changes.

Secondly, it alleviated the considerable stress Margaret was experiencing by removing the 'blame' from her. Threatened as she was by a sense of intrusion and violation which could destroy the relationship, she needed time to herself. Gavin's need was related to his own insecurity and therefore insatiable. In Berne's analogy she continually strived to act the 'adult' to Gavin's 'child,' but he was not able to alter his response to match hers and hence became more and more demanding in his anxiety; and the strain was telling on his wife who was an essentially private person. Using NLP technology confirmed that change in him would trigger warm response from her.

Thirdly, he was younger than she and this was his first relationship. His development, then, must be through this relationship. The 'old flame' episode prior to the marriage had evoked insecurity in him, and he needed to be shown appropriate behaviors which would relieve tension rather than increase it.

The problem was in his perception of the relationship, and as therapy progressed he stopped searching for signs of rejection and took up his interrupted movement toward independence. He learned to take an active rather than a reactive part in the partnership.

By using hypnosis in conjunction with NLP, resistance was dealt with by redirecting it in the reframing and restructuring process. Motivation to cooperate was achieved by subtle means and future-pacing followed as a matter of course as feelings of personal power and desired response from the environment logically trigger each other, simultaneously allowing independence and freedom as the limitations from the past are eliminated.

Case 3

Mild degrees of dissociation are not uncommon in everyday life. Most people have experienced absentmindedness, or have lost themselves in thought, in music, in a book and so forth. Less common is the dissociative reaction which interferes significantly with everyday life. One form of this is the somnambulistic trance. In contrast to simply walking and talking in one's sleep, the somnambulistic trance involves the carrying out of complex and meaningful activities and conversations during the sleeping state which are not recalled in the waking state.

The feelings of helplessness in a person prone to somnambulistic trance are understandably considerable, especially when awakened in the process of undertaking some behavior for which there is no recollection of having begun, nor for what reason; or more sinisterly when experiencing the situation of waking in the morning, after what seemed a reasonable night of sleep to find one's feet dirty and muddied clothes and shoes in a pile on the floor beside the bed and realizing one has been out "— but where? — and what did I do?" As the conscious ego appears to be totally unaware of the somnambulistic activity it seems reasonable to treat the dissociated state as a separate entity when attempting to uncover details of the somnambulistic trance activities in therapy. This is not dissimilar to communication with various 'parts' within the person in the NLP technology; and indeed it would then seem feasible to integrate the two ego states using an anchoring and collapsing technique similar to that described by Cameron-Bandler (1978) in the attempt to achieve full association/memory of that particular incident and, hopefully, ameliora-tion of the recurring problem. Such a procedure is illustrated in this case report. Only one therapy session was required and the client was in hyp-nosis for exactly thirty minutes.

Lisa, an attractive twenty-one-year-old, requested help in locating a ring. She had left it in its box on her dresser since the day she purchased it a week ago although she had been intending to put it away in a safe place. On Tuesday morning she had woken with the ring uppermost in her mind, with a strong feeling that it was not in the box. On investigating she found that the ring was indeed missing. It was now Friday and she had searched to no avail, even asking various people if she had given it to them for safe-keeping. She was becoming more and more anxious, the thought of the ring constantly on her mind. It then occurred to her that she may have "done something with it in my sleep" as she had often done "strange things" while asleep. Her history revealed recurrent som-nambulistic episodes since childhood. She gave examples of several times when she had woken fully dressed sitting on the balcony or in the garden drinking coffee or smoking a cigarette, and on one memorable occasion she had woken to find herself walking down the street in pajamas while on holiday in Asia. She was always completely amnesic regarding the somnambulistic state. Lisa's mother had also been prone to somnambulism when younger.

Lisa presented as an attractive young woman, casual and intelligent. She admitted to habitual procrastination, absentmindedness, and forget-fulness which she coped with by getting others to remind her of appoint-ments and so forth.

Although this client had never been hypnotized for therapy previous-ly, she was at ease and her expectations positive.

The induction used was based on a mediational technique described by Meares (1979). She was instructed to breathe deeply and to exhale slowly several times . . . to notice the relaxed feelings . . . in "your legs . . . arms . . . back . . . chest and abdomen . . . relaxed feelings in . . . your mind . . ." The subject's right arm was then lifted by the wrist and held in a horizontal position; as contact was slowly released, the arm re-mained elevated without support (Matheson & Graham 1979). The following suggestion was then given: "Soon your right arm will get heavier . . . it will begin to lower . . . itself . . . slowly . . . as soon as the hand touches the arm of the chair . . . and the arm relaxes against . . . the chair . . . you will find yourself in that state-of mind . . . you were in . . . on Monday night last." As her arm came to rest, she was asked, via a change from past to present tense to "... recall the thought in your mind ... the thought you have in that state of activity ... what is the thought?" (a change from past to present tense).

Lisa: (frowning) The ring is not in a safe place. It must be moved to a safe place.

Therapist: What will you do about it?

Lisa: My mind is blank. I don't know.

Therapist: That's fine ... ok ... as you breathe, you drift deeper and deeper ... and you feel that familiar lightness in the right arm ... as the arm ... begins to lift ... off the chair, to float higher and higher ... and you drift ... deeper ... deeper as the arm floats ... and all the while the thought stays with you, growing stronger ... the ring is not in a safe place ... it must be moved to a safe place ... that thought ... is all there is ... (In this way, the thought which triggered the original action becomes the anchor for the dissociated state.)

Therapist: (When the arm had reached shoulder level) Soon ... in just a moment ... your arm will begin to drift down towards the arm of the chair ... and the arm relaxes against it ... as it does so ... you will be ... that part of yourself which acts while you sleep ... (As the arm came to rest on the chair, she was touched on the hand providing a reinforced tactile anchor for the state.)

Therapist: How will you ... act? The ring is not in a safe place ... what will you ... do?

Lisa: (frowning) I don't know. I'm thinking about it. It's difficult to find a really safe place; somewhere where no one will find it ... maybe ... under the lounge. No one would look there, I don't know ... (a long pause)

Therapist: Where is the ring now?

Lisa: Oh, I'm holding it. I have it in my hand. I'm thinking what to do. I just don't know where to put it; the cupboard in the spare room would be safe ... no one would ever look there. (pause)

Therapist: That is a safe place?

Lisa: Yes, I'll put it in the cupboard in the spare room.

Therapist: Do you ... put it there?

Lisa: Yes, I'm doing it now, I've opened the bottom door and I'm climbing up the shelves. Now I open the top door and put it right at the very back in the left hand corner ... there! Now I close the door and I'm climbing down. I close the bottom door.

Therapist: The ring is safe now?

Lisa: Yes (visibly relaxing).

Therapist: You feel at ease in your mind?

Lisa: (nods) ... yes.

Therapist:	What do you do now?
Lisa:	I have a drink of water and go to bed. I sleep.
Therapist:	Do you get up again during the night?
Lisa:	No.
Therapist:	Now you sleep . . . when you wake . . . what sort of day is it?
Lisa:	A nice day, sunny (her voice had taken on a lighter tone than before).
Therapist:	(touching the left hand to anchor the conscious state) What are you thinking about?
Lisa:	(frowns) My ring . . . thinking about my ring. I have a feeling it isn't in the box.
Therapist:	Is it there?
Lisa:	No, it's gone.
Therapist:	Do you know where it is?
Lisa:	No . . . but I wonder . . . I might have given it to Dad to put in the safe. I'll ask him later . . . . It couldn't have been stolen, not just that . . . money is still there.
Therapist:	Relax now. I'm going to touch your right hand. As I do so . . . you will return . . . to that part of yourself . . . which acts when you sleep . . . (touching right hand) . . . now where is the ring?
Lisa:	In the cupboard in the spare room. (deeper tone of voice).
Therapist:	Fine . . . now relax . . . and as I touch your left hand . . . as I do so . . . you will be aware of yourself as you are when awake . . . (left hand touched) . . . . Where is the ring?
Lisa:	I don't know . . . (the lighter tone had returned to her voice) . . . . I think I may have put it somewhere safe, I don't know where.

(The process was repeated once more to anchor the separate states of awareness and to ensure that dissociation was complete. It only remained to collapse the anchors — to integrate or blend the parts.)

Therapist:	Now let's put both parts together . . . to make a whole . . . (right and left hands touched simultaneously).
Lisa:	Oh! (laughs).
Therapist:	Where is the ring?
Lisa:	I put it in the cupboard in the spare room (laughs), in the top at the back that's what I did with it.
Therapist:	Good, now . . . relax . . . deeper . . . into those relaxed feelings . . . .

Suggestion then followed with the aim of improving concentration and therefore memory, and of encouraging her to be, ". . . more aware . . . of yourself . . . your whole self . . . and things around you . . . more aware of your actions . . . your desires, your needs . . . more motivated . . . to do . . . to attend to . . . those things you think . . . ought to be done . . . to be attended to . . . in everyday life . . . more at ease with yourself . . . more in contact with yourself both in . . . inner and outer worlds . . ."

On waking, Lisa reported feeling, "Great. Very relaxed and relieved." She had total recall of the therapy session and of her activities during the somnambulistic state. Later that day, Lisa telephoned from home and confirmed that the ring was indeed in the spare room cupboard.

DISCUSSION

It may be that the somnambulistic trance is an expression of feelings and thoughts which are of great significance to the person, either consciously or subconsciously: this young woman, an habitual procrastinator, had for a full week intended to put a ring into a safe place; in the somnambulistic state she merely carried out that intention.

There has been no further follow-up on this client and it is not known whether the integrative technique and subsequent suggestive therapy was generalized in preventing the recurrence of somnambulistic trance activity, i.e., whether future-pacing was successful. However, the procedure achieved the immediate purpose of bringing to full consciousness the entire sequence of events in this particular episode of somnambulism, giving the client the power of recollection, which was, after all, all that was asked for and expected by her.

Case 4

Dental phobia is not only unpleasant but can be a potentially dangerous situation of emotional helplessness in that it may prevent necessary work being carried out on infected teeth and gums. In the following case NLP techniques of anchoring and future-pacing were used in conjunction with the relaxed hypnotic state and paradoxical suggestion to enable a client to attend the dentist for urgent dental work.

The client was a thirty-one-year-old married woman with one child. She had not seen a dentist in ten years, and was unable to accompany her son to the dentist as the smell associated with the office caused an uncontrollable urge to "run away screaming."

She found it difficult to bring herself to enter a building which housed a dentist, and she had an aversion to thoughts of being touched inside the mouth, especially on the teeth. Dental treatment had now become a matter of urgency because of the formation of abscesses in two of her teeth, plus numerous cavities. Several weeks before, her husband had made an appointment for her to see his dentist, who had sent her tranquilizers to take prior to the visit. She had taken the medication as directed but had nevertheless been not only unable to face the appointment, but could not bring herself to walk outside the door of her home on the morning of the scheduled visit and had canceled the appointment five minutes before it was due.

The client presented as nervous and agitated. She had an unhappy childhood, she said, and didn't wish to discuss it. She remembered being forcibly held down in a dentist's chair as a youngster, and she requested that age regression not be used as she did not, "ever wish to look at the past again." In the past few years she had undergone several minor operations, and reported feelings of deep sadness and fits of crying immediately after recovery from the anesthetic. She was at present taking no drugs except the occasional aspirin for toothache.

During the first consultation the client was taught a meditation type exercise, and given a cassette tape on which the exercise was recorded, to practice at home. A very light and guarded trance state was achieved via arm levitation, and general ego-strengthening suggestions were given emphasizing confidence and independence. It was noted that she particularly enjoyed water imagery, especially being at the beach, and felt totally relaxed gazing at the water. The second consultation took place one week later and the client was much more at ease, readily entering the hypnotic state on suggestion. The therapy was in two stages. Firstly, she was asked to recall the relaxing freedom of being at the beach . . . smell the salt air . . . feel the sand . . . hear the waves . . . see the water . . . the sky . . . On her confirmation of involvement with this imagery, a touch to the right shoulder served as an anchor. In the midst, then, of this pleasant reverie, she was informed, "You are in a dentist's chair . . ." She reacted with trembling, increased respiration and obvious agitation.

She was then immediately informed, "You are at the beach again (the shoulder anchor applied simultaneously) . . . the smell of the sea . . . the feel of the sand . . . the sound of the waves . . . birds in the distance . . . blue sky . . ." And, as she visibly relaxed . . . "and you are . . . just thinking of . . . just thinking of . . . just dreamily thinking of . . . being in a dentist's chair."

As she again abreacted, she was told to, "smell the anesthetic . . . hear the clink of the instruments . . . feel the CHAIR . . . under you . . . " and at the word 'chair,' her shoulder was touched and the beach imagery immediately re-introduced as above. The above procedure was repeated several times before relaxation "in the dentist's CHAIR" was achieved; and in this way the good feeling of being at the beach was anchored to the relaxation "in the chair" (the reclining chair where she was in hypnosis), which in turn was to trigger a relaxation response in association with the dentist's chair and dental treatment.

The second stage of this session involved a more authoritative technique where she was asked to extend her right arm and told, "Your arm is very stiff . . . very stiff and straight . . . if you should try to bend the arm, it will become . . . even more stiff . . . and the more you TRY to bend it the stiffer it becomes . . . in noticing this, you will be also aware . . . of the properties of power . . . and strength . . . in your mind . . . that you never before knew you had . . . TRY now and bend the arm . . . TRY." (She tried without success) "You see how powerful your mind is . . . much more powerful than mere muscle . . . your mind prevents you from bending the arm . . . no matter how hard . . . you try . . ."

She was then told to relax as the shoulder anchor was applied and the beach imagery re-introduced . . . "You are now in the chair . . ." (shoulder

touched again) . . . "the dentist's chair . . . the dentist is there with you
. . . soon he will ask you to open your mouth and you will do so . . .
you will do it because . . . you know . . . the more you TRY . . . to
keep the mouth closed, the wider it will open. You will be aware of that
. . . strength . . . that power . . . of your mind . . . once again. Now,
open your mouth." The client opened her mouth slowly, and with no
signs of distress kept it open as her teeth were gently tapped with a pen,
which was then pressed more firmly on several teeth, and finally pressure
was applied to her tongue. She remained passive throughout.

During the third consultation, the above procedure was checked to ensure constancy of the anchoring, then while still in hypnosis she was told,
"although you are relaxed . . . at ease and comfortable . . . and this feeling
. . . will stay with you . . . you will notice a vague anxiety . . . a restlessness
. . . a discomfort . . . perhaps later today . . . or even tomorrow . . . this
discomfort . . . this restlessness . . . will remind you . . . of something
you have to do . . . to attend to . . . something pressing . . . even urgent
. . . and you will recall . . . that you must ring and make an appointment
. . . with the dentist . . . as soon as you recall . . . this fact . . . you will
immediately make that appointment . . . and as soon as you do so . . .
as soon as that appointment is made, you will feel completely calm"
(touched on the shoulder) "relaxed . . . confident . . . just as you do right
now." The "stiff arm" technique was then repeated with the following
variation of association: "no matter how hard you TRY to feel . . . fear
of the dentist . . . no matter how hard you TRY to be afraid . . . the
calmer you will feel, the more . . . relaxed . . .you will even be more
aware of that . . . strength . . . that power . . . of your mind . . . once again."

Finally, general confidence building suggestions were given and in addition a suggestion was given to ring the therapist on the morning of
the dental appointment and, "as soon as you hear my voice . . . on the
telephone . . . you will feel a sense of calmness, well-being, strength, and
you will easily be able to enter a deep state of relaxation at the count
of five."

Another appointment was not made for this client and she was told
she should contact the dentist and make her appointment as soon as possible. She left in a resourceful physiology.

The client rang a week later to say her dental appointment was for
10 that morning. She had been quite calm until the morning dawned,
but was now very nervous. Hypnosis was induced as suggested previously
— with the added instruction to hold the phone securely resting on her
right shoulder and remain seated comfortably — and a brief collapse of
the beach scene on the events leading up to the dental treatment was carried out: "You are now walking into the dental surgery . . . feeling so
calm, relaxed, as if . . . on the beach . . . the waves . . . the smell of the
sea . . . the sand . . . and now in the dentist's chair . . . in the chair
. . . leaning back, restful . . . as if . . . sitting on the beach . . . or relaxing

in the chair . . . your back to a tree, gazing out to sea . . . aware of that strength, the power . . . of your mind as you hear the dentist ask you to open your mouth . . . aware of it opening easily . . . you are looking forward to feeling that power again . . . so much so . . . that . . . the closer you get to the dentist . . . the more confident you will feel . . . more relaxed . . . looking forward to experiencing the power. . . of your mind." She was then awakened. The entire sequence took little more than five minutes.

Two weeks later, the client telephoned for a further booster as her next appointment was due with her dentist at 9:30 a.m. that day. She said her first visit had been "great." She'd wanted to feel scared, but couldn't. While driving to the surgery, the closer she got the better she'd felt. In the chair and during treatment, she'd felt "marvelous." The dentist was a "beaut" and told her there was a lot of work to be done on her teeth.

However, she was just a little tense this morning and felt she needed some reassurance. A procedure similar to before was followed, this time accessing the good feelings from the first appointment. Emphasis was put on the idea of independence and the ability to "rely on your own strength, your own abilities."

One month later, this client rang to report that all was going well and she had no further worries regarding the dentist, nor any recurrence of the phobia. Not only had her own teeth been attended to, but she had taken her son to his dentist and remained with him while dental treatment was carried out — just, she added, "like a real mother should."

DISCUSSION

The effectiveness of this technique lies in the simultaneous resolution of tension and substitution of relaxation response to instill a feeling of 'power' rather than emotional helplessness.

Abreaction was induced to release emotional tension associated with the dentist and at the same time relaxing stimuli (the 'chair' as a constant, for instance) were introduced as not only an escape from tension but an association with pleasantness (the beach) to become an anchor to trigger good feelings in the face of dental treatment.

With a good hypnotic subject, I find this method much quicker than that of a systematic desensitization technique, and, in my experience, more permanent. Future-pacing is achieved as "power of the mind" is perceived by resolving the fear. Because it seemed important in this case that encouragement and support be at hand at the crunch — the support she never had in her childhood — the conditioning for hypnosis via a telephone call on the day of the dental appointment was implemented. Without this extra boost available should she need it (and as it happened she did) fear may well have overwhelmed her. If she had canceled that dental appointment, the chance to "prove" the post-hypnotic suggestion of power would have lapsed and perhaps made it harder for future suggestion and association of that type to be accepted by her.

Cases 5 and 6

The two final cases here presented deal with young clients involved in long-term psychotherapy with the author. Brief histories are given in context, and the session, or series of sessions in the final case, became the turning point, the realization of personal power over long-standing psychological helplessness, in the therapeutic process and the focus of future-pacing.

Case 5

Mary, a twenty-three-year-old part-time teacher, had been in psychotherapy for some months in relation to a long-standing anxiety-depression with elements of a narcissistic personality problem. Therapy included exploration, cognitive and behavior modification, and a great deal of supportive counseling in conjunction with hypnotherapy. Work was also being done on the accessing of resources, without much result since she felt she had none.

The particular consultation with which this presentation is concerned was two days prior to a job interview about which Mary was anxious, depressed, and negative. She desperately wanted the job as the insecurity of part-time work was getting her down. Applications for full time positions in her college were invited every six months or so; and this was her third such interview, and she felt, although it was not necessarily so, her final chance. She described her previous interviews as "disasters" that exacerbated her innate feelings of self-doubt and worthlessness to the point of nervous prostration, perceiving herself to be without power, completely helpless in the face of the coming interview as she asked, "What will become of me?"

In the hypnotic state she was asked to, "access that part of your self which stops you feeling confident — which makes sure you don't get disappointed." Mary identified this part as saying, "You must be prepared for the worst, you can't trust what you feel. You can't win so don't expect to." It was clearly her mother's voice and it was triggered whenever she began to feel good about herself or to hope. The gut feeling associated with the dialogue was *fear* producing a sense of *cowering* as if being *physically beaten*, *a pain* in the chest, a feeling of being *pinned down*, and a knot *blocking* her throat. When asked to color this part of herself, she saw it as brown. She was then asked to visualize and experience this part in its totality — to identify with it which she easily did. It was then anchored by pressure to the right shoulder.

She then volunteered the information that a second voice, quite distinct from the other, seemed to be in the background saying, "I don't want to know any of this. Don't tell me about it." She identified the voice as that of her father and it elicited a feeling of *extreme tension and anger*. It was triggered by the feelings of despair and confusion engendered by the 'brown' part. It was also associated with the chest pain . . . "the pain," she remarked, "of keeping a grip on myself." She was asked to color this second part and saw it as white. She was then instructed to visualize and experience this part in its totality, to become the part, which she did and which was then anchored by pressure to the left shoulder.

The anchors were checked and proved secure as she changed from 'brown' to 'white' on cue, i.e., as pressure was applied to each shoulder in turn she accessed the appropriate part or ego state. She was then told to relax, "to concentrate on your breathing . . . only the breathing . . . to relax more with each breath . . . deeper and deeper." When relaxation seemed complete, she was asked to envisage what it would be like if the interview were over, "and you have been successful . . . you are selected for the job . . . your future assured . . . a good feeling . . . relief. . . success." This feeling was described by Mary as one of strength and achievement, and the color was 'rosy'. This state was anchored by pressure to BOTH hands which lay close together in her lap; and she was again directed to her breathing and allowed to relax.

The next stage involved accessing each feeling, one at a time, ensuring that she 'became' the part as an anchor was triggered, and relinquished it during the relaxation period between, i.e., "just breathing easily . . . only the breathing . . . the relaxation . . . ," in order to differentiate the states before the next part accessed as it, in turn, was triggered. The sequence was repeated several times with the relaxation period becoming shorter and shorter and finally not used at all. With each part clearly defined and accessed instantly when triggered, she remarked as the 'rosy' part was accessed, "I'm standing straight. I feel strong and quite happy." With this confirmation, the final steps were implemented: pressure was applied to both shoulders simultaneously and suddenly, collapsing the anchors, immediately followed by the application of pressure to both hands. Next, the right shoulder and both hands were touched simultaneously, and the hand trigger tested for 'rosiness;' then the left shoulder and both hands were touched simultaneously, and the hand trigger again tested and found 'rosy.'

This was followed in quick succession by firm pressure on the hands and a quick sudden sharp tap to the shoulders and again firm pressure to both hands. The session was terminated after three or four minutes of quiet as Mary was invited to, ". . . go into the quietness of your mind . . . and rest there."

On waking, Mary reported the following: A sense of blankness and confusion when the shoulder anchors were collapsed; a sudden surge of energy from the solar plexus when the hand anchor was triggered; a further strengthening of energy as each shoulder was touched together with the hands. This was followed by a sudden "clearing" shock when the shoulders were sharply tapped, and with the grasping of the hands she had a sense of standing upright, of being herself as she had never experienced before while the 'rosy' color glowed and shimmered all about her. She commented that the experience was "magical" and that she felt quite philosophical about the coming interview — that she had as much chance as anyone else and more than some. In fact, Mary got the job.

DISCUSSION

This application of NLP technology in dispersing and realigning energy was unplanned. The author was unaware of the 'white' part until told of it by the client in hypnosis. The rationale therefore developed in logical sequence and is as follows: in defining each 'part' so thoroughly, in all modes — visual, auditory, kinesthetic, aesthetic — the part and its total energy was accessed by its anchor. The combining of both hands for the positive or 'rosy' anchor was done to increase the energy and to contain it; and also as both shoulders were triggering negative energy, positive conversion was available in both hands when anchors were collapsed. Collapsing the anchors of both 'brown' and 'white' had the effect of 'blanking out' or short-circuiting the associated energies, so by instantly triggering the 'rosy' anchor, gave a focus on which to grasp (as occurs in a confusional hypnotic induction technique). This naturally increased the positive or 'rosy' energy as it was the only *totally defined part* now available.

The collapsing of shoulder and hand anchors in turn served to 'blot' out any remaining 'brown' and 'white' energy by overwhelming it with the now powerful 'rosy' energy. The final sharp tap to the shoulders was a shock measure to disperse and direct any remaining remnants of energy into the 'rosy' area as the hands were finally and firmly grasped to access it. The short meditation period before waking was seen as essential in order for Mary to experience the new self in the quietness of her mind.

As Mary commented, this is a magical procedure, and luckily combined with the actual attainment of the full-time job she wanted. Her perception of personal power is greatly enhanced. Having experienced this power, it becomes a resource which can be called upon again and again by Mary in many and varied situations, and so future pacing is achieved.

Case 6

Cathy is a twenty-four-year-old married woman with a three-year-old daughter. This defensive, cynical, provocative, and likeable young woman was at the time of this study entering her third year of psychotherapy with the author. Her diagnosis is that of personality disorder, probably borderline, with cyclic reactive psychoses.

Her background was a dreadful one — abandonment by her parents at 12 months of age, followed by many unsatisfactory institutional and foster placements where she was abused both physically and emotionally. Cathy had a history of prescription drug overdoses and self-mutilating behavior on and off since the age of twelve. She first received psychiatric treatment at the age of four at which time she had an imaginary companion; at about 10 she underwent some form of 'exorcism' by a priest to remove the 'devils' in her and recalls this as a terrifying experience. She received episodic ongoing psychiatric treatment until fifteen years of age. She coped satisfactorily for a while by working in a child care clinic and getting some vicarious parenting from this. Cathy underwent two legal abortions prior to the birth of her daughter. During the pregnancy, she attempted suicide twice, and afterwards postpartum depression plagued her for six months. She has been involved in psychiatric treatment as an outpatient as well as an inpatient in the public system, and also on and off with various private psychotherapists.

Cathy married at the age of twenty-three, while involved in the current therapy, after living with her boyfriend of some two years. Cathy talks of 'voices' in her head and defines two other personalities which seem to embody respectively the 'bad' and 'good' parts of her psychological makeup. These seem to have manifested since the birth of her child. She wanted, she said, to be a good mother, one who her little girl would respect and admire. At no time had Cathy mistreated her daughter, and in fact had handed the child into short-term care at those times when she had felt absolutely unable to cope. There was, then, a measure of control, a responsibility probably introduced by way of the apparent 'personality split' at the child's birth. This measure of rationality and control would form the basis from which to overcome the emotional helplessness in the face of disordered thought and psychosis.

The first twenty months of therapy were somewhat turbulent and erratic. Cathy was treated four times for overdosing on various tranquilizers and sedatives, once after arriving for her appointment and collapsing at the door. She acted out by smashing her hand against a brick wall, slashed her arms and legs-with razors, hit herself to produce marked bruising, and on one memorable occasion covered the walls of the consulting room toilets with graffiti. Once the author arranged admittance to a psychiatric center, where she remained for two weeks while psychotherapy was continued twice a week.

Throughout this period psychotherapy involved exploration, analysis, supportive counseling, active and confrontational counseling, and imagery techniques to elicit feelings such as fear, anger, hate, love, the goal being that of teaching her to experience a feeling rather than act it out. Resistance was encountered in all stages, as Cathy tested the therapeutic relationship continually and exhaustively; and progression was slow but nevertheless encouraging. Suggestive therapy in hypnosis not unexpectedly triggered strong defensive responses, so hypnosis was used only to enhance imagery and as a relaxation technique. Cathy expressed her emotions in poetry, painting, and drawing. Against the author's recommendations, she continued to see many different medical practitioners in order to get supplies of tranquilizers.

Soon after her marriage, her husband received a transfer in his job and they moved to the country. During the time she was away she corresponded several times by letter. Problems within the relationship precipitated another overdose and subsequent admission to a local psychiatric ward from which she discharged herself after three days. Shortly after this episode she left her husband and brought her daughter back to the city and back to therapy. For the first time, Cathy found herself alone, trapped with herself, her thought disorder, her responsibility and love for her child, and her commitment through strong transference to the author, who now was able to use her own 'personal power' in the powerful security of the therapeutic relationship to bring about change in this client. The next six weeks heralded the turning point for Cathy and are set out below:

1. Cathy presented in a depressed, paranoid state, having the day before deliberately kicked her toe against a brick wall, cracking the bone. Feelings which precipitated this self-destructive action were elicited as 'trapped,' 'no way out,' and 'stifled.' Her uncommunicative and hostile attitude was mirrored by the therapist. Cathy got no more than she gave.

2. Two hours following the above consultation a suicide note was delivered by courier to the reception desk addressed to the author. In response to this, a phone call was made to the client and she was told to present herself at the consulting rooms within the hour or the police would be notified, arrangements would be made for her daughter to be taken into care, and Cathy would be scheduled into a psychiatric ward. She presented herself as instructed, in obvious and genuine distress.

   The suicide had been held up due to the illness of the friend with whom she had arranged to leave her daughter; otherwise she said she would have been long gone before my phone call. We contracted that she would attend daily therapy, the alternative being admission. She also undertook as part of the contract not to obtain drugs without first consulting the author.

3. The next day she was anchored into the 'trapped' feeling by the author closing in on her physically until in an effort to escape she cowered in a comer of the room and covered her head with her arms, sobbing. This was the first time she had ever cried in therapy. Following this catharsis she produced this associated memory fantasy:

   She had been naughty. Mum (her foster mother) had belted her, tied her up and put her into the hall closet where she remained for three days and nights. Her foster father discovered her there when he went to investigate the smell coming from the closet. He carried her out, untied her and cleaned her up. He then put her to bed, making her promise never to tell anyone what had happened.

4. At the next consultation Cathy presented angrily, was rejecting and uncooperative. She said, "You have no right to bring back those awful memories — they should be left alone . . . they should never be touched." Signs of internal dialogue prompted the question, "What are the voices saying?"

   "Death . . . Bloodbath! liar! liar! liar!"

   The same words were thrown back at her in a mirror of her own attitude until she suddenly said, "Don't tell or I'll kill you," and shuddered violently.

With the regressed state resolved she was able to take part in rational discussion and became open to exploration of her feelings.

5. The following day, Cathy's manner was self-deprecating and hostile. She discussed the actual memory released by the fantasy of two days ago: her 'rescuer,' the foster father, had sexually abused her, then accused her of trying to seduce him when discovered by his wife. Cathy felt no compassion for her child-self. She had 'deserved it all,' there was something 'evil' in her or these things wouldn't have happened, she insisted.

   In the relaxed state, the 'good' part of her personality was called forth and she was asked to recall the love and closeness she felt for her little daughter; this resource was anchored by a touch to the hand, then extended back to the past — to her child-self — by association: i.e., she was asked to go back and look at the child she had been and the anchor of love triggered. The procedure was repeated with the 'bad' part of her personality. She left the therapy session in a much lighter and easier frame of mind.

6. Two days later: The previous evening Cathy had applied a lighted cigarette to her arm and had scored LIAR in ink into the skin of her forearm. She was withdrawn and obviously engaged in intense internal dialogue as she paced agitatedly up and down the consulting room. Her attitude was mirrored closely by the therapist until finally Cathy's thinking cleared enough to volunteer that the conviction that she was a liar pervaded her mind and frightened her. This was the first time in therapy that this client admitted her fear.

   This conviction was anchored by pressure to the shoulder and attention to the corresponding internal dialogue: "Liar!"

   She was then easily able to identify the accusing voices as those from the past, and experienced the very real fear associated with the old threats of 'death' if she told the truth about the way she was treated. The conviction of being a liar was in this way anchored where it belonged — in the past — then collapsed by recall and resolved in the experiencing. This was the last time she experienced the *irrational* belief that she was a liar.

   On conclusion of this session, she was quite at ease. It was then casually suggested that she please not bring her flat-mates's child with her own little girl to the clinic on therapy days as baby-sitting facilities were not generally available. The noise made by the two children was causing concern to the author's partner and his clients, not to mention some despair to the receptionist. Cathy seemed to accept this limit-setting philosophically at the time. However, the following morning:

7. A letter from Cathy was dropped into the mailbox. She terminated therapy because of her 'obsessive love' for the therapist which she could no longer handle. She stated, "I am ruining your life and must step out before things get worse." An immediate reply was prepared and posted to Cathy in anticipation of her adverse reaction to her own

vulnerability on exposing these feelings. The following points were made:
   a. Her honesty was appreciated.
   b. Honest feelings should not be fought or denied, nor should they be a source of embarrassment.
   c. Agreement that her "degree of caring" is "not o.k." (using her own written expression), but only because she was afraid of it — i.e., that it would overwhelm her, and "I cannot guarantee anymore than you can, that at times it may *seem* to do so." Love should not be made her enemy by fearing it.
   d. It is sometimes necessary to work through the need of a mother's love by experiencing that need, and by handling the limitations which must be set in such a relationship.
   e. And finally, whatever decision she made in regard to therapy would be respected, however, the writer would be available if and when she decided to continue.

8. Cathy's defensive reaction to her written confession began with an abusive phone call early the next day. She rudely demanded a referral to a medical doctor for medication. She was politely refused a telephone referral but was invited to come to the office and collect a written one. She subsequently arrived, noticeably distraught, pale, and preoccupied, and snatched the referral letter from the receptionist's hand. The author, who was present at the time of her arrival, remarked that she should read the reply to her letter, which she would receive in today's post, carefully. Cathy reacted momentarily with surprise and then left. As previously agreed with him per telephone, the referral doctor gave Cathy, not a prescription, but a single dose of I.M. largactil.

9. Cathy kept her appointment the following day. She was shy but communicative. The events of yesterday were discussed in the light of her feelings of vulnerability in revealing her emotions, and her projective reaction. Points in the author's letter of reply were clarified and confirmed. In addition, it was noted that she had adhered to her contract and did not attempt to obtain drugs without permission of the author, even in the face of such intense feelings. Warm approval and appreciation was expressed for her strength and control.

10. Work on a cognitive level had continued for two sessions, and then Cathy presented herself in a distressed state, very confused and asking that her child be taken from her. Apparently she had woken in the night with an overwhelming desire to strangle her daughter — the urge was associated with a feeling of finality and "giving up the fight." She had her hands about the little girl's neck when the child woke and asked, "What are you doing, mummy?" which broke the regressed state but left her with such fear of what she might have done and of what she might yet do that she sat up till morning smoking cigarettes, afraid to let herself sleep.

In therapy she was asked to recall the feeling of the dream the night before. Sensations of choking, along with voices screaming, "Blood, blood!," were elicited. Without warning these feelings were abruptly anchored as the therapist placed her own hands around Cathy's throat. Immediately, a severe abreaction ensued, after which the following memory/fantasy was related:

Cathy had been hit by her foster mother and her nose was bleeding. She wanted to go outside and show everyone the blood, so they'd know and take her away. She tried to escape but the woman had chased her, hysterically caught her and thrown her onto the bed. Cathy was screaming, "They've got to see the blood, then they'll believe me . . . the blood, the blood . . ." The woman grabbed her around the neck with both hands telling her to "shut up!" After initially struggling, Cathy became aware of a languorous feeling as she began to lose consciousness — and, a pleasant floating sensation of release as she sank into oblivion. She came to, to the sound of shouting voices as her brother (the foster mother's eldest son) confronted his mother. Cathy recalled her feeling of bitter disappointment at finding herself still alive. The young man had sat with her for a while, telling her there was "nothing he could do to help her" when she pleaded with him to get her away from his mother.

Through the experience of accessing this emotional memory, Cathy gained some insight into part of the pattern of her overdosing behavior — a kind of re-enactment to gain the pleasure of an oblivion which could never be permanent.

11. Several sessions were now spent in reality orientation. On one occasion, she said that extreme anger was triggered in her when a friend who had confided in her asked her "not to tell anyone." She instantly recognized the reaction as anger about her past, i.e., "don't tell or I'll kill you." This present anger was reframed as strength, a healthy rejection of old internal messages once anchored by fear.

12. Three days later, Cathy arrived with a bandaged hand and her head shorn. At 2 a.m. that morning she had slashed her hand to the bone and hacked off her hair with a razor after surfacing from a fearful nightmare. She had received six stitches to the hand, telling the local doctor she had had an accident, and had been to the hairdressers for a repair job. She was most embarrassed about the whole thing. After explaining all this, her attitude became defiant, abrupt and off hand. She demanded hypnosis, accusing the therapist of not using the very thing which would cure her. She seemed quite paranoid, although there appeared to be no evidence of internal dialogue.

Mirroring her offhanded attitude, the author invited Cathy to sit in the 'hypnosis chair', which she did. Suggestions relating to the gaining of insight, strength, courage and confidence to face up to responsibilities and overcome fear and anxiety were given. On being told to wake Cathy jumped up, and with the angry accusation that, "you are putting it all back on me!," walked out, slamming the door behind her.

13. At 5 that same evening, a phone call was received from Cathy who stated that she was calling from a nearby coffee shop, adding bluntly, "I've taken an overdose and what are you going to do about it?" After ascertaining the name of the drug (a mild tranquilizer) the therapist ordered her, just as bluntly, to go home and vomit. She was, in addition, to phone the author at 6 p.m. and confirm she had done as instructed and if the call was not received by 6:15, she was warned, the police would be contacted immediately. After a short silence, the receiver at the other end of the line was slammed down.

Her expected call was received at 6:20 p.m.. She sounded coldly furious as she said, "Don't you EVER back me into a comer like that again. You don't own me! You have NO RIGHT to interfere with my life."

This was countered with a reply in similar tone, "Then don't you ever put me in a position again where I have to, my dear. YOU involved ME, you know, by telling me what you'd done."

There was a short silence, then she replied in a thoughtful and reasonable tone, "That's true isn't it? I really don't think I'll do that again. Well, see you tomorrow," and rang off.

14. The previous day's events were discussed and interpreted as a bid to perpetuate the old attention-seeking behavior triggered by the hair-cutting and hand-slashing incident.

Cathy then recalled that the evening preceding the slashing, she and her flat-mate had been fooling around in front of the mirror trying out new hairstyles when suddenly an uncomfortable thought, "vanity is wrong," had crossed her mind, and all the pleasure in the game was lost. As she related this incident, her increasing preoccupation was noted, and she was asked to verbalize the internal dialogue. She replied, "Bloodbath . . . death . . . evil . . . Cathy is evil, no good . . . Cathy is a whore . . . a slut . . . vanity is sin."

She was anchored further into the dialogue by mirrored repetition of it, then suddenly her hair was grasped and pulled. A tearful abreaction resulted after which Cathy related her nightmare:

. . . I am 12 and growing my hair, looking into the bathroom mirror and admiring its length. I noticed my body was beginning to get a bit of shape and wondered if I was pretty. Mum came into the room and saw me. She began to scream at me, accusing me of being a slut and a whore and said, "vanity is a sin . . . a sin!" So I start to yell back, to tell her to get out, and then she grabbed the mirror from the wall, broke it over my head, and then rushed from the room. I was picking up the broken pieces of mirror and saw my bleeding face reflected and noticed blood on my hands from the glass. Suddenly mum raced back into the room with a pair of scissors and grabbed my hair, cutting it off in great hunks. We struggled and fought in

silence as the hair was hacked off. Then I was on the floor, crying, picking up bits of hair from among the broken pieces of
glass. Blood was spattered about the room, on my face and hands,
and in the bath . . .

With the relating of this symbolic association, the core of Cathy's
psychosis was broached as Cathy came to realize that the 'nightmare,'
obsessional, and masochistic quality was of her thinking in relation to
her memories and perceptions the basis of her cyclic psychosis and
thought disorder.

Since that time other feelings have been dealt with by association and
accessing rational memories, for instance, a feeling of suspicion and
'paranoia' brought the memory of a sudden change in foster homes at
the age of about four. She recalled being smacked by her 'mum' for refus-
ing to kiss her good-bye when she was handed over to the next 'mum.'
The child had simply forgotten that this woman, with whom she had
lived seemingly forever, and called mum, was not her real mother and
was confused by what was going on.

Work on relationships, behavior modification, and the 're-alignment'
of memories continued for two months. Cathy now lives interstate with
her daughter, has coped well with various crises without resorting to
psychosis, and in her last letter stated that she is studying drama, involved
in the mothers' club at her daughter's pre-school, and is learning to drive.
She comments, "I came to you locked in a prison I had built . . .
I found the keys to set myself free . . ." She says she is still learning
. . . and making progress in accepting herself and others, and life as it is o.k.

DISCUSSION

The sessions involving the unraveling of the complexities of this client's
personality problems and related psychosis took place over about six
weeks. However, it seems obvious that this could not have occurred
without long months of preparation, for without the combination of the
trust and personal commitment of the client to the therapist in the strange-
ly binding ambivalence of the transference, *and* the innate strength and
power evident in her deep responsibility and love for her child, her
motivation to continue with what must have seemed a destructive process, involving as it did the breaking down of all her defenses, would
have collapsed. These essential elements in combination with her "alone
and trapped" situation made acting out to the triggered ghosts of the
past inappropriate for her without the protection and support of the context of the therapy.

The anchors to the past were in part the 'voices' whose symbolic ut-
terances strove to protect her from the 'death' she thought would surely
ensue if she remembered; and yet she had to remember and break the
barriers of symbolism in order to live in the present and handle her
responsibilities. By using NLP techniques to anchor *into* the related feeling rather than *reacting* to it, the wall of fear was systematically broken

down to release real memories through the emotional intensity of her symptoms. In the reframing process anchors from the past were collapsed and the triggering mechanism defused. The therapist, in mirroring the client's attitudes and mood states, forced this client to see herself objectively, to respond to herself, and to reframe.

It was seen as important for the therapist to remain as objective as possible, to care enough, but not too much. In the face of the client's declared love it was made clear that there was no problem with this, that in fact it was quite acceptable, but there would be no involvement beyond the context of therapy.

This was a lesson learned through personal knowledge that two of this client's previous psychotherapists, to preserve themselves, no doubt, had become her 'pals', thereby rendering themselves ineffective as therapists. Remaining objective was not always easy, of course, and the author had occasion to stand back from time to time and to reframe, as all psychotherapists ought to, through discussion with a colleague. The limits set were continually tested by the client, at last being accepted in the final overdose incident (13) where she suddenly gained insight into her behavior and decided to take on the responsibility for her own actions.

Throughout the three years of therapy, Cathy's drawings, paintings, and poetry depicted the progress of her inner struggles. From themes of violence, confusion, blood and destruction, alternating with idealized love for her daughter, her art changed to reflect anger, desire for revenge on those who had ill-used her in the past, and then to self-questioning and soul-searching. Now there are glimpses of tranquility and peace, and the awareness of something different — the wonder of a quiet mind, never before experienced. Future-pacing is achieved as the energies previously locked in combat are released, and as the 'veil' is lifted Cathy looks out to see the world more objectively. Feelings of vulnerability in the wake of loss of the old defenses give way to growing confidence and the realization of personal power as her self-esteem increases and is reinforced by the knowledge of control and by her perception of positive, and at times negative, responses, without projection, from her environment.

CONCLUSION

In presenting these six case studies, I have sought to illustrate the application of NLP technology, in conjunction with hypnosis, in ways suited to the individual personality and particular problem to assist people to gain perception of their personal power in the world. Each case is different; degrees of complexity vary. But the object of therapy is the same: Change . . . to gain personal power over emotional helplessness.

REFERENCES

Berne, E. (1961) <u>Transactional Analysis In Psychotherapy</u>. N.Y: Grove Press.

Cameron-Bandler, L. (1978) <u>They Lived Happily Ever After</u>. CA: Meta Publications.

Grinder, J., DeLozier, J. & Bandler, R. (1977) <u>Patterns Of The Hypnotic Techniques Of Milton H. Erickson, MD</u>. CA: Meta Publications.

Haley, J. (1973) <u>Uncommon Therapy — The Psychiatric Techniques Of Milton H. Erickson MD</u>. Canada: Geo J. McLeod Ltd.

Matheson, G. & Graham, J. (1979) "A rapid induction technique" <u>The American Journal Of Clinical Hypnosis</u>. 2(4) 297-299

Mead, G.A. (1934) "Mind, self and society" in Kimmel, D.C. (1980) <u>Adulthood and Aging</u>. N.Y. John Wiley & sons.

Meares, A. (1979) <u>The Wealth Within Melbourne</u>. Hill of Content Publishing Co.

Sullivan, H.S. (1955) <u>Interpersonal Theory Of Psychiatry</u>. London: Tavistock.

Winnicott, D.W. (1978) <u>The Family And Individual Development</u>. London: Tavistock Publications Ltd.

Wolberg, L.R. (1945) <u>Hypnoanalysis</u>. New York: Grune & Stratton.

THE USE OF METAPHOR IN FAMILY THERAPY
by
Norma Barretta, Ph.D., Clinical Psychologist
Phillip Barretta, M.A., M.F.C.C., Psychotherapist
San Pedro, California

INTRODUCTION

The use of metaphor within the practice of clinical psychology provides the therapist with a non-threatening way to symbolically present the patient's situation, drawing out of the patient the responses and resources needed to resolve the metaphor and the patient's own problem. Metaphors provide patients with the opportunity to modify old or outdated belief systems while simultaneously offering a bridge to change. The combination of the metaphor model with hypnosis offers the therapist a particularly effective avenue for treatment, in the most economical time frame. While there are patient situations which require the use of metaphors, such as with resistive patients, the model can be used effectively in most patient situations. All metaphors follow the same five basic steps of construction; establish rapport with the patient, gather information about the situation, create the metaphor, make the metaphor well-formed, and deliver the metaphor. An effective metaphor is isomorphic: it needs one character for each actual participant, one story line for each actual event, sequencing within the story to parallel the real life situation sequencing, and a solution or the resources to resolve the story/problem. A general metaphor speaks in broad terms and can be utilized in virtually any situation with any patient. Specialized metaphors are formulated in response to specific patient problems or situations and are tailored to the individual patient. There can be an ending to the metaphors, or sometimes it is more beneficial to allow the patient to utilize his/her own resources in solving the problem and providing an ending to the metaphor.

Case 1

The Smith family was being treated for concurrent problems. A specialized metaphor was developed in response to the problems being experienced by the youngest family member, eight-year-old Ralph. Mr. Smith was an aerospace engineer who worked long hours, often seven days a week, and was away from the home a great deal. Mrs. Smith had just undergone successful surgery for a brain tumor; however the surgery left her permanently blind. Mrs. Smith had always been a homemaker, and was going to school to learn to handle her new blindness. This blindness has not harmed the relationship between Mr. and Mrs. Smith, in fact they are closer than ever before.

The children of the family were 20, 16, and eight. The 20-year-old daughter had been forced to assume the homemaking duties once fulfilled by Mrs. Smith. She was resentful at being forced to return to the family, just as she was ready to leave the nest. She had given up her part-time job outside the home to care for the family.

The 16-year-old son was in high school. He was getting good grades, but contributed to his brother's discipline problems. He was devoted to the game Dungeons and Dragons. He prodded his little brother into mischief, but was not a discipline problem himself.

The eight-year-old son, Ralph, was the center of the family's attention; his behavior was the "problem." Ralph was a bright child whose grades had fallen off since his mother was blinded. He resented his mother's blindness and the resultant increase in responsibility expected of him. He had moved the furniture, so that his mother would trip and fall. He was a severe discipline problem at school. He played Dungeons and Dragons with his brother, and was susceptible to suggestions of negative behavior from his brother.

METAPHOR

Metaphors fall into three broad categories: iconic, isomorphic, and homomorphic. Iconic metaphors are one word, one picture, or one line stories that tell the entire message in a single "aha!" Isomorphic metaphors present each person in the patient's situation as a single thing — a person, object, or animal — within the metaphor. Homomorphic metaphors present the many as one or the one as many. A single person might be represented by a herd of buffalo while a family might be represented by a single rock.

An effective homomorphic metaphor designed for Ralph and used with the Smith family involved a herd of wild horses that needed to be broken and trained to be good, steady, work horses.

Once upon a time, there was a herd of wild horses roaming the hills of Southern California, eating the scrub grass, and running through the valleys. (Ralph) This herd of horses had many beautiful, wild horses in it. None of these horses had ever been around human beings, and none had ever been broken to do work. None of the horses in the herd could be controlled by human beings. All of their lives they had roamed free.

In the valley below the mountains where the horses ran there was a town where many farmers lived and worked. As you know, farmers often have horses on their farms to help with the work and to give rides to the farmers and their families. When any of these farmers needed a good horse to help them with the farm work, they went to Bee Haven (read: Behaving) Ranch.

The Bee Haven Ranch was a famous ranch in that part of Southern California, for the rancher who owned the land was an excellent trainer of horses. In addition to training horses the ranch raised bees and made an excellent honey which was sold in the town. At the Bee Haven Ranch there were all kinds of horses and they all had jobs for which they were being trained. There was a strong and dependable work horse. This work horse (Father) was smart and knew just how to best help the rancher with the duties and responsibilities at the Ranch. Sometimes the strong work horse worked longer hours than even the rancher, making sure all the jobs on the ranch got finished. This horse was a steady worker. The rancher knew he could depend on this well-trained workhorse.

There was also a group of well-trained show horses at the Bee Haven Ranch. These were being trained for the circus. (Sister) This team of show horses consisted of four snow white horses who knew exactly what the world would expect of show horses. They had been trained for this job, and they were ready to join the circus. They were in the final stages of training, and the rancher was just about ready to send the snow white show horses to the circus. As they waited for the final days of their training, the show horses worked together and worked with other, not-so-well-trained horses to help the rancher in the horse training activities at the Ranch.

The Ranch also had a lovely horse named Lady who was the rancher's wife's horse. Lady had recently fallen and had hurt her knee. (Mother) Lady was being treated by the vet. Lady could not help the rancher with the training of other horses while she was sick, but she was still strong and would soon be able to help the rancher again. Lady would never be able to carry heavy loads again, the vet told the rancher, but she could help with some of the easier training jobs.

A team of brown horses that were supposed to go to the Budweiser stables was also at the ranch. These horses had been well-trained, at least as well as the snow white show horses, but did not like to remember their training. The brown horses did not like to work together and did not like to remember all the things they had been taught by the rancher and the steady work horse. These brown horses knew what to do, but they didn't like to do what was good, so they just played around all day and didn't learn their lessons and didn't help the rancher. (Brother)

As you can see, the brown horses would not make good work horses and would not make good show horses. It is very difficult to know what to do with such horses. The rancher at the Bee Haven Ranch is getting ready to catch the wild horses in the hills and train them to be good work horses.

When the rancher catches the wild horses he saves them from starvation (from over population) and provides warm, safe homes for them. Wild horses, when there are too many of them, can get into trouble. So, the rancher will catch some and make them into good, dependable work horses. It is important, too, that when the rancher starts to train the wild horses only the best horses on the ranch share in the training duties. It would not be a good idea for the wild horses to learn the brown show horses' bad habits. The training of the wild horses must follow the examples of the steady, dependable work horse, the snow-white show horses, the lovely horse Lady, and the rancher himself.

DISCUSSION

This metaphor presents the family members as various participants of a horse community. Ralph is presented as the herd of wild horses. Using the most important family member in the dominant role within the metaphor allows that patient's unconscious to receive a strong message about his importance within the setting. The father is presented as a steady, dependable work horse. The 20-year-old sister is a team of snow white horses who are well-trained and just about ready to go to the circus. The mother is presented as the injured horse, Lady, who will soon be able to help again although not in the same ways. The 16-year-old brother is presented as the team of unruly brown horses who will not learn their lessons.

The first requirement for the development of an effective metaphor is to establish rapport with the patient. This process was done over several counseling sessions with the Smith family and when this metaphor was presented Ralph was comfortable with and attentive to the therapist. It is important to join the patient where he or she is now; Ralph needed to understand which of the Smith family members were good influences and would help in his day-to-day growing up. The linguistic patterns within this story help to maintain rapport with the client; the metaphor is presented as a story for the eight-year-old.

Secondly, one must gather information. Determine where the client is now, and what other family members are involved in the current situation. Ralph was being unduly influenced by his older brother in the torment of his mother and his discomfort in his changed role within the family. The father's role as the work horse and mother's role as the injured horse must relate to Ralph's position. The characteristic events in the actual situation must relate to the events within the metaphor; the father is a work horse, the mother is sick, the sister is ready to go out into the world, and the brother is a negative influence. You must have all the pieces of the situation, and it might be desirable to work some specific action by Ralph into the behavior of the wild horses.

While gathering information it is important to determine what problem is to be addressed and what the desired state would be. In this metaphor, the problem is how to get the wild horses trained without the negative influence of the brown horses. The problems of the sister, mother, father, and brother are not addressed. The desired state would be the appropriate training of the wild horses. Ralph must understand which members of his family will help him in this training process.

In order to meet the desired state, which of the patient's belief systems need to be changed? Ralph must understand that the wild horses must be trained, and the mother cannot help in that training right now. The sister is able to help with this process and is willing to do so. Which of the patient's responses need to be changed in order to reach the desired state? Ralph must understand that to be a contributing member of the family he must change the way in which he relates to the other members of his family. Can the patient describe the desired solution? Can Ralph identify the horses in the story that are good influences and that can help the rancher in the training duties? Further, Ralph must understand the desirability of training the once-wild horses.

During the first two-thirds of the metaphor it is the responsibility of the therapist to pace the metaphor with Ralph. To follow his breathing patterns, to mirror his physical position, to change or amend the story based on the physical signs/responses being given by Ralph as the story is presented. The last third of the metaphor requires that the therapist change the presentation and lead the patient to the conclusion. The leading of a metaphor begins when the listener begins to participate in the move toward the end; in agreeing that the wild horses do need to be trained, that the brown horses are not good trainers. It is during the leading portion of the metaphor that the therapist is able to place the embedded commands for the patient. While the pacing portion of a metaphor may put the patient into trance, it is during the leading portion that the client may experience the most vivid response to the story; when the unconscious may be the most receptive to the message designed specifically for that patient.

The delivery of the metaphor can make or break the metaphor for the patient. Metaphors should be told at about one-third the normal speaking speed in order to allow for unconscious processing time. Ralph's reactions to this metaphor guided the speed with which it was delivered. Language is a powerful tool, and the effective use of language in the delivery of a metaphor allows for the placement of embedded commands. Tonality can dictate the effectiveness of a metaphor; how the therapist uses tonality will determine how deeply the patient goes into trance.

An effective tool in the delivery of a metaphor is the mis-spoken, mis-pronounced, or mis-delivered word or phrase. While the conscious mind is attempting to sort out the actual meaning of that "mis-speak," a message aimed at the unconscious can be put into the metaphor and reach the unconscious without interference from the conscious mind (which is still attempting to translate the mis-spoken word). In this metaphor for Ralph, the name of the ranch was the Bee Haven Ranch, a message to his unconscious.

CONCLUSION

A single client with a single problem could have all three kinds of metaphors developed to address his or her unique problem. The development of a metaphor for any single patient's situation is simply another tool the therapist can give to that patient. Metaphors provide the solutions or resources to the unconscious mind.

Ralph's situation within his family structure has changed. He is unhappy with his present role, but that unhappiness must be addressed and solved if the family is to continue smoothly. While the conscious mind continues to rebel at this change in assignment, Ralph's unconscious mind has been provided with the information necessary to ensure that he makes the transition to become a cooperative family member. It is now up to his unconscious mind to process the information and integrate it into Ralph's activities and into his conscious decisions about his new choices of behavior.

Case 2

Donna was referred to us by her family physician when she was informed by her oncologist that she had terminal cancer with about 6 weeks before "termination." The physician asked us to "help her die with dignity and in peace." The time was April, 1979.

She arrived on a beautiful sunny afternoon, depressed, distraught, and looking not at all ready to "die with dignity." This was a beautiful 60-year-old woman who had been a very "nice lady" for all of her life, and to quote her: "I was rewarded with cancer of the bone." We call it the "anger down under" disease.

Donna was being prepared for chemotherapy (despite the morbid prognosis) and we decided to use a metaphor to reframe that usually negative experience.

We told her about our home in Falls Church, Virginia, which stood on a third of an acre of ground — most of which was weeds when we bought it back in 1958. I was discouraged, but Phil said, "We'll use 'Weed-B-Gone'. It's a selective weed killer. It kills the weeds, and actually fertilizes and regenerates the good stuff."

I said, "Come on, Phil. You're making it up. How could such a thing be?"

At this point, Donna spoke up, "It's true. Kellogg makes it and it works! It kills all the weeds and saves the good grass and rebuilds its strength and makes it grow healthy again. I do a lot of gardening and use it all the time."

Donna had capped her own reframe. The chemotherapy went very well. She had minimal side effects, kept her hair and grew stronger. She was still doing well in October (four-and-a-half months past her oncologically predicted "termination date").

While bathing one day, she slipped, fell, and broke her collarbone. At the hospital, the oncologist met her in the E.R. and scolded, "It will NEVER heal." Donna came in immediately to our office from the hospital. In tears, she reported the doctor's doomsday message.

Phil said, "He lied to you in April. He told you that you'd be dead by June, and this is October." Donna smiled, "Yes, he did, didn't he — Well! We'll just see about that."

Donna had a beautiful, well-behaved German Shepherd who was her shadow at home. We asked if he'd ever been to obedience school. Donna said, "Of course! Where do you think he learned to heel properly? It's his best feature. With a dog that large, if he doesn't heel properly, you'd have a problem, and he is an excellent heeler." And once again she provided her own reframe.

The collarbone healed. The cancer was now oncologized as temporarily "in remission." Though she felt better, Donna remained inactive and housebound a great deal of the time. She disliked "being stuck" but no amount of encouragement seemed to help her become more active, until she heard about the frog.

Once upon a time there was a frog hopping down the road. While he was hopping, he happened to hear a familiar frog noise, "ribit, ribit." Although he looked around he couldn't see who was making the sound. So he hopped to the middle of the road and looked down into a very deep rut made by tire tracks and happened to see another frog at the bottom of this rut.

The frog at the bottom of the rut said, "Boy, am I glad to see you come along! Can you help me out of this hole?"

The first frog said, "Well, I'll do my best," and stuck his arm down for the frog to grab, but it was too short. Now everyone knows that a frog's legs are longer than its arms, so he extended his leg down into the hole, but the other frog still couldn't reach it, no matter how hard he tried.

The frog in the hole said, "Now look — why don't you jump down into the hole with me. I'm sure I can leap out of this rut with you to give me a boost."

But at that the frog on the road looked down into the very deep rut, backed away and said, "Look, I've tried everything I know to help you out, but I'm not willing to climb down there with you because I also might get stuck. So I wish you the best of luck, and I have to be on my way now." So the frog hopped on down the road.

About 15 minutes later, directly behind him, he heard, "Ribit, ribit, ribit." He turned around and saw the frog that had been in the hole grinning at him. The first frog said, "My goodness, the last time I saw you, you were stuck in that rut with no hope. How did you ever get out?"

The frog who had been in the rut shook his head, smiled and replied, "Well, there was a truck coming."

Donna bought an organ and began taking lessons; she redecorated her bedroom; she began to attend the theatre again; she earned Christmas "pin money" by wrapping in very fancy, beautiful fashion the packages her neighbors and friends brought to her to save themselves the trouble of Christmas gift wrapping. She joined the local Senior Citizens group. In November 1980, she attended a national convention which was held in Ohio as a delegate. She spent an extra 2 weeks and visited her mother in Iowa, her sister in Nebraska, and a brother in Colorado before she came home. She continued to tend her garden, and began to grow vegetables and strawberries.

She continued to come in to see us about once a month for what she called her "tuneup" and "tale-telling" time. Donna lived "with dignity" until December 1983 when she died quietly in her sleep following an evening at the theatre.

CHAPTER II

HEALING AND NLP

Preface to
HEALING AND NLP
by
John T. Grinder

In May 1985, I had the good fortune, as has happened on so many occasions in my life, to meet a remarkable individual, a touch healer, the seventh son of a seventh son of an Irishman — Finbarr Nolan. The context was a seminar in which I was to teach the fundamentals of the modeling process, the process that constitutes the express purpose of NLP, indeed, the process by which Bandler and I had coded the patterns of excellence which most people believe (mistakenly) to be the field of NLP. The sponsors of this workshop had selected the theme of ESP, and I was to apply the modeling technology to phenomena identified by our society as "Extra Sensory." I have always stumbled over this phrase: it seems to point nowhere. My perception is that:

(a) We as Westerners have such poorly developed competencies at the level of sensory acuity in the five commonly recognized senses that it would be at best premature to conclude that the source of certain classes of information must lie outside the five identified senses. It is typical that close scrutiny of an ESP experience reveals complex clusters of minimal cues surpassing our conscious ability to appreciate the configuration (usually called intuition) from which the information is derived. That is to say, we know more than we know we know. To flee pell-mell, rather like Chicken Little, into the dubious security of a new nominalization, Extra Sensory Perception, is very poor epistomology and is likely to retard our movement toward learning useful patterning.

(b) If the phrase, ESP, is intended to suggest that there are channels (circuitry) other than the five recognized sensory channels by which we obtain information, then by all means let us design and explore these channels with precision and specificity. The assignment of such experience to the phrase ESP advances this endeavor not at all. In fact, in another section of this casebook, Cecile Carson presents the initial work she has done on a sixth representational system, a deep and highly integrating sense — the vestibular system — thereby providing suggestions about how to approach such exploration.

At any rate, strange, amusing and somewhat wondrous things occurred there in Florida. These somewhat wondrous things happened at two different logical levels. First, people came there (both seminar participants and people local to that part of the Southeast who had afflictions) to heal, and heal they did. Healing was, of course, the reason Finbarr Nolan was there; and he did his job very well indeed.

I was there, however, with a different purpose. My challenge was to create a model of Mr. Nolan's behavior which would make possible the *transfer* of the ability (the relationship) to touch heal to participants in the seminar. Thus the event wherein Mr. Nolan entered the loop with a patient for healing purposes was simultaneously a healing experience for the patient (and possibly for Mr. Nolan) and an example of the process I was to create a model of. Finbarr Nolan's task was to heal people; my task was to enable people to heal others. I would say on the whole that Mr. Nolan was the more successful of the two of us. While there were a number of indications, at the time the seminar was in process, that many of the participants were succeeding in capturing significant parts of the model, I was reluctant to consider the transfer of the touch healing model (my personal criteria) successful until the process had been demonstrated by a participant both:

(a) outside the context of the seminar itself; and
(b) over some period of time after the seminar was completed (minimum 90 days).

The first two articles in this section are reports from two of the seminar participants whose ability to touch heal has been sustained to date (Spring, 1988). These women (Linda Schapiro and Stephanie Rachel Alt) are not universally effective in their touch healing endeavors (nor is their model, Finbarr Nolan: do you suppose they learned more than was useful?), yet they have entered a strange and wonderful arena. Their journey is an excellent example of how it is possible to learn astonishing things without being conscious of that which we are learning.

For anyone who has explored various forms of healing, it is axiomatic that healing is a simple word for a very complex and inherently cybernetic process. I am confident, for example, in asserting that Finbarr Nolan's touch when he touches someone who heals and when he touches someone who does not heal is, at least initially, the same quality of touch. The third article in this section, *The Doctor Within* by Hilda Cole Espy, suggests that given appropriate support an individual can come to occupy both positions in the healing loop: the healer and the healing one. While the article is inspirational, it raises many questions, perhaps well summarized by: How did these two women, Hilda and Marina, choreograph their successful dance of life?

The fourth article attempts not only to describe healing experiences but also to explain the specific mechanisms, maneuvers, and strategies for thinking and behaving effectively in the context of healing. Hejmadi and Lyall offer a rich representation of an approach to healing, an approach which an NLP-trained practitioner can draw upon to begin their own exploration into the complex field of healing. The detail, the recognizable patterns of NLP (e.g., enter the reality of the patient for pacing: use the personal metaphors of the patient in healing; well-formedness conditions) give a fine representation of an integrated sequence of patterning woven together into a pleasing fabric by two fine practitioners.

It is only appropriate in my capacity as the framer of this section to alert your unconscious processes to the opportunity these articles present in terms of personal applications. To understand these articles in any deep sense is to access or reaccess the circuitry within yourself homologous to what is being described. Thus, an invitation for your unconscious to linger and mull over the portions of these articles most directly relevant.

Responses To:
Florida NLP/ESPerience Conference
by
Linda Shapiro, M.S.

July 1985

To: JOHN GRINDER
From: LINDA SHAPIRO, M.S.
Re: 3 Month Up-date, FLORIDA NLP/ESPerience

Dear John:

My experience with you in Florida was a radical shift in gears. For the first time in a learning environment I was invited to trust my intuition, to dare, if you will, to put my rational, logical mind aside. In so doing, I created a powerful, persuasive myth of my own. I became a healer. A glorious feeling of coming HOME. A return to a natural, primal position where I become, with ease, an even more effective instrument of change.

During a healing, my mind — the one I've known and trusted for 44 years — is on hold. It's not a matter of losing my mind and coming to my senses but rather one in which the senses become mind in a new and miraculous way. From what I can only describe as a "gut level knowing," a multidimensional intelligence emerges which puts me "in touch" with the body/mind/soul of the other person. The feed-back loop is simple, direct, complete. The healing flows from my heart's center and swells to a place of integrated oneness with the patient. The entire process is one of FOCUS and INTENT.

I continue to question the HOW'S and the WHY'S, but the answers are incomplete. I know that I experience healing, but as yet there are unexplained elements. A fundamental question remains: If I am replicating Finbarr's touch, I feel as though I'm doing so from an experiential position, and I don't know whether such learning can be classified as scientific. What I do know is: I observed Finbarr. I observed the interaction between him and those whom he was attempting to heal. I internalized his process through observing it. I reproduced his external behavior (perhaps thereby experiencing similar internal states) and consequently I now participate in healing.

What do we call this? Will others be able to do what I am now doing? How will I be able to assist them? These are the questions which need to be addressed. Is such a phenomenological approach compatible with the basic laws of science? Can this method indeed be replicated? And, if so, what are the necessary conditions?

Florida Experience:

It started when I first entered the conference room. Within minutes, I felt myself vibrating, pulsating in a way that I've experienced only a few times in my life. I wasn't sure what was getting triggered that morning, but I certainly received a powerful signal.

After the first day with Finbarr, I awoke the next morning with swollen hands. I was unaware that blood rushes into Finbarr's hand and that it actually appears to swell as he is healing. I learned that the following morning during discussion time.

That's when you gave me feedback in the form of a question. You asked if I knew how to take what is useful and discard what isn't. Indeed! In watching Finbarr, I had internalized his movements. I felt a person's head, stomach, eyes, whatever Finbarr touched, as though I was touching it. So, at your suggestion, for I certainly agreed that I did not need swollen hands, I took myself to a quiet place and did a reframe. Within an hour, the swelling disappeared.

With regard to Titos, I felt self-conscious and was skeptical as to the relevance of his African drumming to our participation. I was nevertheless determined to give it a try.

As I entered the room, I felt drawn to the moonface beauty of an infant held in someone's arm. She reminded me of my daughters, now adolescents, and when I was asked if I cared to take her, I consented. I got the OK from her mother and scooped the baby into my arms. However, something strange happened. My hands seemed to utter the word SLEEP and moments later she was sleeping soundly. Her unknown yet familiar body comforted me, and as she nestled into my shoulder I moved to Titos's drumming for nearly two hours. All the while, she slept or at least was deeply relaxed, and I thrived, feeling at one with the music and the total environment. I mention this because it is not inconsequential.

Our actual dance was, in fact, what healing has been for me: a union, on some level, with another's rhythm and energy, a total centering for me while the other appears in trance and is comforted. This then was my beginning. Corny? Symbolic? Perhaps. But more than a mere symbol. For me, it was a breakthrough experience.

A few days later, Jean Blair asked me to heal her foot. She said she'd been watching me and was convinced that I "had" Finbarr. I was startled. I wondered about her evidence. After all, I'd taken no notes. She couldn't have seen me attempting to learn his strategies in that way, and I was not aware of imitating his gestures in a way that would have been noticeable to anyone watching me. Yet, I accepted her challenge because of what had occurred earlier that same evening.

A study group, led by Richard Clarke, was discussing how to build into one's personal history the piece that Finbarr already had — namely, that he was born a healer. I listened as they talked abstractly about NLP interventions that might work. When I could no longer contain myself, I chuckled aloud and said that they were making it much too complicated The first day when Finbarr had been introduced to us, I'd already done what they were contriving to do. Indeed, as Finbarr spoke, I heard a voice declare:

> One day. . . Manya Poretskaya will marry Mosheh Appleman. They will birth two children. The youngest will be a daughter. She will be called Linda, and she will be a healer.

Though I found it amusing, I had fully accepted the message as real from day one. I believed it. No doubt, you'd have to know what a rational, concrete thinker I am to appreciate first, my hearing such a message, and second, my believing it.

After sharing this with the group, I was asked to think about something else that I "believed," and after doing so to find out whether the submodalities were equally powerful. They weren't. I went inside myself and asked to be provided with a visual component for my otherwise loud message. Instantly, I saw before me a tribe, the tribe, in fact, that had previously proclaimed my birthright. The time was early evening. They (mainly women) were standing in a circle, deep in a valley, around a fire that was burning brightly. The chief spokesperson was an exotic beauty with long, dark, silky hair. She wore a white toga with golden threads woven throughout the fabric that seductively draped her body. She then proclaimed the exact words that I'd heard previously, thereby giving me my fully represented personal history.

Someone in the group said that when she had done personal change work where she'd added a piece of history, it took on a life of its own. She wondered how I'd prevent that from happening. That wasn't a problem. My ceremonial scene was in a still frame, as complete as was the circle in which the members of my tribe stood. It was incredible in its simplicity and clarity. It was complete. It could go nowhere else. What's more, I felt exhilarated.

It was soon after this affirmation that Jean approached, asking if I'd heal her. Feeling high with a sense of power, I agreed and took my belief in hand (pun intended). She said she wanted to dance with Titos but couldn't due to swelling in the heel of one foot and the joint behind the knee of her other leg. The healing lasted 4-5 minutes and took place in her hotel room with two other people present. My recollection is that as soon as I put my hand on her foot, my left upper lip began to quiver uncontrollably, as does Finbarr's. Everyone burst out laughing, me included. Yet, even as I laughed, the quivering continued and my focus remained on healing her. Result: Jean danced the next day and every day thereafter. She claims that even now, while swelling does occur from time to time, it's never as severe or as limiting to her movements. Did she believe in me? Yes. Was she motivated to change? Seemingly. Are both necessary for healing? I assume so, but I don't know.

The next day was Thursday, April 25, the day that Finbarr was asked to identify who among us had the healing touch. Prior to my group's going up, you gave us a fifteen minute break. I needed to clear my head, because the competitive part of me was already doing its number, screeching into my ear, "You'll be the one person he'll say can't heal." I not only needed to leave the room, I went upstairs and called home in order to feel grounded. When I re-entered, my dear friend Stephanie, who has always said that I have "hot hands," gestured to her heart and whispered across the room to me saying, "Let it come from your heart."

Then a new friend, you, John, said to the group (though I still maintain you were talking to me), "Remember, you're not up there to learn. Your only intention is to heal." With those words, I was set free. I entered a place I'd never been to before. It felt almost holy and definitely religious. I heard myself say to myself that it would be a privilege to heal someone who'd healed so many others. And, as I approached Finbarr from behind, I could feel myself focused only on his left shoulder. All of me seemed to exist in my hand, and as my right hand approached him and my left arm used his chair for support, again my left upper lip began to quiver. My focus remained intense throughout, so much so that when I return-ed to my place in line I did not know that Finbarr had given me the YES nod, identifying my touch as being healing. The same occurred moments later when I was again asked, as a further test, to approach him from behind.

Although in his feedback he said that what distinguished my touch was its heat, I don't sense a difference in my own body temperature although I am acutely aware of changes in the other person. When he graciously asked, "How many people have you healed?," I flashed back to my mother, a year before her death in 1984. One night, in the throes of a depressive episode and feeling agitated and unable to sleep, I offered to do a Reiki healing. I'd taken first degree Reiki some weeks before, and while I hadn't felt that I'd integrated any of it, my mother knew that I had taken the course and giving a name to something I was about to do did seem to offer it credibility. Eventually, she fell into a deep sleep. The following morning, she asked me what ointment I'd been given that produced such heat and acted as a tranquilizer. When I told her, "none," she said: "Don't make fun of me! You can't fool me!" I remembered that as Finbarr questioned me. I offer you here a word about my mother and our relationship. I believe it is relevant to who I am and what I do in the context of healing.

Throughout my life, and particularly until thirteen years ago when mother was widowed and came to live with us, I'd witnessed her numerous and recurrent depressions. There are no words to describe the antennae that one develops in such frightening situations. Nuances — a particular look in the eyes, a slight gesture of a hand, a simple change in speech — might be the sign that a dark cloud was descending. As a child, nobody talked to me about so-called "mental illness." I didn't know that I could ask, and I did not consciously confront her/my demons until I was nearly twenty. I believe I am still confronting them. Now I know that one does not have to suffer such experiences to become a "sensitive" adult. I do believe, though, that whatever extra-sensory ability I have today, whatever detectors seem to work for me, are either the same ones or connected to the ones I've known since birth . . . feelings, knowings, a non-verbal synchronization of rhythms that give me clear messages, prepare me, guide me. The stimuli can be miles away or nearby. I pick them up, tap into them in dreams or in reality. Their frequency, their vibrations are felt and acknowledged, if not always sorted through. I offer this for what it may be worth to you as you examine the larger picture and question other meanings.

Florida Experience Continued:

In Florida, when we broke into small groups, I joined Duncan Johnston who demonstrated Dolores Krieger's "therapeutic touch." We worked in pairs, attempting to recreate the body scanning that Duncan had shown us. I then worked, for the first time, with Britt Ewing. This encounter, too, was surprising. As I scanned his body, beginning at the top of his head and working down to his toes, I sensed enormous smoothness and health in all but two areas. In those two, there were vibrations of a different nature. Britt confirmed that he'd sustained injuries in both places (upper right shoulder area and behind the right calf, if memory serves me). The two of us later worked together in Lin David Martin's afternoon workshop. While Britt healed me, I felt extremely calm and relaxed, and as trite as this may sound, I felt a warm, universal love emanating from his soul through his hands. When I healed him, I felt filled with energy.

All of me was pulsating as both of my hands — I no longer limited my healing to the right hand — moved![1] They led me and talked to me again almost as though there was a direct line from my heart center to

---

1. Prior to that day, I had struggled to use only my right hand, as Finbarr does. The result was that I developed a huge black and blue swelling on my upper right arm. I innocently announced to you that it was as though I'd bumped into something very powerful, but I didn't remember doing so. Here again, the lesson for me was learning what to take in during the learning process and how to allow that which is mine to flow. That gut reaction, that heart-felt signal is one that I am still in the process of learning how to trust. You may recall also, that after lunch on the 25th when I was asked to heal Finbarr yet one more time, every part of me said, "No, don't perform on demand. You're not in that centered place!" And, indeed, he did not affirm my touch, thank God. Also, though I often lead with my right hand, I now use both hands to heal, and my lip hasn't quivered since Florida.

my hands to his body. As when healing Finbarr, I felt wrapped in a spiritual blanket which protected both of us. I felt and believe I was healing. When Lin asked for feedback, I remember saying that healing Britt felt, again, like a dance where my hands somehow knew how to lead and when to follow. In his wonderful Australian accent, Britt's remark about me was, "This lady's hands should be dipped in bronze." I am grateful for his confidence and support, and whenever I do feel any doubt I bring that memory into consciousness.

My Experiences With Finbarr:

I was in the first group that Finbarr attempted to heal. I offered him my toe because I thought a toe would or would not give easily verifiable proof of his ability. I had had an ingrown toenail that kept re-infecting itself, even after surgery, and more surgery had been recommended just before my trip to Florida.

After the first session with Finbarr, my toe became totally inflamed. After the second, it began to ooze and the skin around the nail began to peel. After the third, it truly appeared to be healing. Yet, Finbarr's actual touch was not impressive. It did not feel extraordinary in any sense other than perhaps its purpose. That is, it seemed to have short, precise movements that, like a surgeon's scalpel, knew what to do, where to go, and how long to stay. No heat emanated.

During the third session, I asked him to heal my head as well. I get migraine headaches and didn't dare ask for so much the first time around. Here, however, where my need was certainly greater and my own belief more in question, Finbarr's touch penetrated intensely. It felt as though he was working harder. His touch felt even more studied and there was considerable heat, even sweat, coming from his hand.

What is the relationship between a subject's need, intent, belief, and that of the healer's? These, still, are the questions we must ask. I did experience a real difference.

What follows includes brief descriptions of 15 healings I have performed since Florida and a discussion of the healing process as it has evolved.

Case 1

A sixty-two year old therapy patient who originally came to work on issues surrounding her husband's death "and was always open to NLP and hypnotic techniques" was suffering from a suspected case of diverticulitis prior to my leaving for Florida. She came to see me before her appointment with an internist. I did lay my hands on her then, but this was done out of sympathy for her pain, with no real belief that I had healing powers. I told her that I did not "sense" anything ominous. When

I returned to New York and we had another session, she said that whatever I'd done in our previous session was embarrassing to her because by the time she reached the doctor's office she had no pain. He found nothing wrong with her after x-raying her stomach. We laughed together, and I then shared some of my Florida stories with her.

Consequently, she asked me to heal eczema that she'd had on her neck for the past six or seven months. I placed my right hand on her neck for a minute or two, and we continued on with our session. Five days later, I received a note saying that the rash had totally disappeared. In a follow-up inquiry, it had not returned three months later.

Case 2

A tile contractor in his thirties with a very twisted back and crooked legs began talking about his physical pain and asked me to put my hands on him. I did so for a minute or two in my driveway, not exactly a private or professional environment. He said he felt my hands were burning and the heat offered enormous comfort. He has a complex family history with a father who has multiple sclerosis. Now that he knows what I do, he said that he'll be calling me in the fall. I suspect the work will include more than laying on hands.

Case 3

A forty-five year old woman came for treatment of severe bronchitis. During the first session, I sensed enormous congestion in the upper area of her back corresponding to the front portion of her lungs, and I treated that as well as the chest where she complained about having the most pain. After the first treatment, she reported discharging a great deal of mucous and feeling less congested. After the second treatment, the congestion eased even further and she never had to stay home from work, which had been a major concern. I should also note that during the second visit I felt extreme heat coming from the front of her head. The patient later told me, in a phone conversation, that a couple of hours after seeing me she developed a severe headache. I don't believe that my touch caused the headache, but I do think that I was picking up something that was brewing, because that has happened to me with other people. In any event, the bronchitis was gone in less than five days, and the patient experienced a comfort never before felt with such quick relief in so short a period of time.

Case 4

A fifty year old man who was due to have back surgery in June called in a panic. He'd been taken off all medication prior to surgery and was having a terribly painful episode. He did not, in fact, believe that he could get himself home, a half-hour drive from his office. I was nervous before he arrived, because he was the first person I worked on who was in real agony. The pain was even obvious in the muscles of his face, and his body was bent and pretzeled. However, in spite of my concern, I did feel centered and decided to first do a total body scan. I asked him not to tell me where the exact pain was, and as I began, I felt heat coming from and surrounding his head. It felt as though this was due to the tension/fear of the pain itself.

Also, I felt active vibratory fields on the entire right side of his body, mainly from the waist down to his toes. Oddly enough, I sensed nothing special in the area of his back and embarrassingly told him so, thinking that was a sign for me not to work with him. Instead, he responded by saying that he hadn't had pain in his back for over a week. All the pain was on his right side — the buttocks, the thigh, down the leg, and in the foot. I knew I was on target then and proceeded to work first on his facial muscles and head and then wherever he said he was in pain. We worked for an hour. For forty-five minutes I did healing work, the longest I've worked with anyone to date. For the remaining fifteen minutes we explored secondary gains followed by NLP interventions/negotiations and future-pacing. He was aware that without the actual pain he would abuse his body by doing carpentry, a real passion. And while consciously he seemed ready to divorce himself from the symptoms, his body language expressed ambivalence. I taught him imaging exercises that he could do at home, and he was very receptive. As we concluded the session, I was delighted to see that the tension in his face had disappeared. The muscles had become flat and smooth. What shocked me, though, was the degree to which he could also stand erect. He practically waltzed out of my office. Afterwards. he reported having absolutely no pain for 8 hours. Analgesics had offered relief for 4 hours. I consider him to be my real success story.

Case 5

My fifteen year old daughter felt extremely congested one night before bedtime, usually a sign that she's about to get an upper respiratory infection. I treated her nose, eyes, and head for three to four minutes. She fell into a deep sleep and awoke the following morning totally symptom-free. This was a dramatic breaking of a pattern, and she is now able to lay her hands on herself for healing. Equally encouraging is the ease with which she discussed this experience with her friends who, in turn, are beginning to consider alternative solutions to their common aches and pains.

My twelve year old has been healed of a sore throat, a bruised leg, and a stomach ache. She's at summer camp now and called home the other day to say that she's going into my "business." Apparently, after offering to heal a friend who had a sore throat and sinus infection ("I just closed my eyes and did what I remembered you did to me, Mom,") others began to ask for her assistance. One time, she decided she couldn't help the person because the girl's aura didn't feel right. When asked what an aura is, my daughter answered, "You know, the field of energy that's around you." The other girl became frightened and asked my daughter if that was bad. She replied, "Not for you. It's your energy. It's just not comfortable for me." Bless her. She already knows how to protect herself, and I've urged her to assist herself in practical ways such as washing her hands after touching infected areas. She was also concerned about the healing being temporary, and we agreed that often one healing is not sufficient. Does she believe in healing? Yes. Has she experienced its power? Yes. Has she always had an open channel? I think so. Will she ever abuse it? I don't believe that's possible. Some years ago, when she was five, we healed a strep throat using guided imagery. The experience was so powerful for both of us that we do have a special bond as a result. In fact, one of the most startling experiences since Florida happened one night when she said she felt feverish. After touching her forehead, I placed my hand on her chest and felt frightened by what felt like an extremely rapid heart beat. I immediately removed my hand, thought for a moment, and decided to heal it.

As I returned my hand to her chest, I could actually feel the heart beat slow down. The difference was shocking, and as soon as the beat slowed she fell into a deep sleep within seconds. Both my girls seem to go into deep trance states which lead to sleep if I work on them at bed-time.

Case 6

Soon after my return from Florida, my husband, who seldom gets headaches, complained of feeling headachy. I immediately placed my hand on his head for about three minutes. He said, "Is that all?" I explained that it wasn't a massage, and though he looked disappointed, the headache was gone within minutes. However, since then, he has been the one person with whom I am not always successful. Perhaps it's because I feel self-conscious as I attempt to do healing work with him. For now, I trust there's a reason why this is happening.

Case 7

A sixty year old psychotherapist/mentor who suffers from allergies, extreme upper respiratory congestion, and related upper back pain wanted me to focus my energy on her back. We drove to the beach and found a quiet space overlooking the ocean.

The healing began with her pointing to areas of pain. From the start, it was easy to work on her body. That is, my hands moved easily, connecting to her body, moving as it were inside the body itself. As I observed her, her eyes closed almost immediately.

She appeared extraordinarily relaxed afterwards, remarking on the unusual nature of my touch and the heat that she perceived as coming from my hands. In speaking with her the following day, she said that her back still felt much better. She had gotten instant relief after the healing but had foolishly lifted something heavy early that morning and it had ached again. What she then did was to put herself into trance, recall with clarity my particular touch, and in recreating it for herself, healed herself further. I now encourage everyone with whom I work to do that for themselves.

Case 8

For the second time since Florida, Jane St. Sauveur, Jean Blair, and Jane Monteleone returned to my house to network. This time they stayed for two days. We talked and talked, listened to African drumming, and danced, and talked some more. As during their previous visit, we offered each other healings. Yet, this time the experience was different for me. I did a body scan (as we'd been shown Dolores Krieger's method) before working on each of them. With both Janes I was aware that they were feeling more relaxed and I saw them go into trance as I began to touch each of them, but I did not feel I was healing. I didn't feel centered in the same way, and I lacked many of the now familiar vital signs. With Jean, though, the moment I placed my hand on her head, I could feel it penetrate deeply into what felt like her entire skull. As I worked my way down her body, I spent a significant amount of time on her right hand, and she claims that I said, "What's happening to that hand?" as I did so. I asked her afterwards to describe what she felt when my hands were on her head. She said she thought my hand was going to go right through her head and come out the other side. That is exactly how it felt to me.

The day after they left and returned to Massachusetts Jean called. "Witch, witch, witch," she screamed, before even saying hello. Then she went on to tell me that she woke up that morning with one of the fingers on her right hand swollen beyond recognition. Needless to say, I felt somewhat responsible to offer a healing, albeit over the phone. I told her that I was imaging her hand and asked her to place it first palm up and then palm down. I told her when I was healing each finger and as I moved to her wrist, using my actual hands as models of her own, I said that I felt the pain extending about three inches beyond the wrist towards the elbow. She said, "Exactly." We laughed, and I continued. When I moved back to the swollen finger, she began screaming again. This time she said that as I touched it, long distance, it became hot and beet-red. After a few minutes it cooled, and I was aware of the reduction on my end as well. I told her that I thought it would be fine by two o'clock the next day. Sure enough, when we spoke the following day, she said that it was much better by morning, almost fine by noon, and fine by two o'clock. Her wrist still ached a bit, and I healed it again, long distance, as we spoke. Do we have a special connection? I didn't even know Jean until Florida. Does her belief in me enable me to heal better? I don't know. Both Janes also have faith in my ability, yet my experience didn't feel authentic, although they seemed to have positive healings.

Case 9

Though while in Florida I had promised myself that I would only heal people who asked to be healed, this time was different. A ninety-two year old woman, who I was interviewing for an oral history project, began coughing and complaining of a dry throat.

I sent someone for water, then stood up, placed my right hand on her throat, and my left hand on her upper back for a minute or two. She never asked why I was touching her. I never volunteered an explanation. (She was very sharp and extremely coherent.) After returning to my chair, she continued to talk with ease for another twenty minutes, never even sipping the water that had been brought to her.

Case 10

One day while on vacation with my husband, I overheard someone complain about being in pain. I had a tremendous urge to lay my hands on her, but it was not appropriate and I was not going to break my vow. Moments later, my right hand became stiff and achy. I had to stretch each finger and comfort each one with my left hand before it began to feel normal again. It was as though the hand was denied its function and was suffering, as a result.

Surely it doesn't have a life of its own! Does it?

THE HEALING PROCESS

When I begin a healing, I immediately center myself with no real, discernible preparation. Sometimes I work as Finbarr does, going directly to the area that the patient says needs healing. More often, these days, I seem to prefer doing a total body scan to determine for myself where and how to proceed. Once I begin, I feel almost fixated on the person's body, seeing it, feeling it through my hands, focusing on each given part but without looking at it in the <u>ordinary</u> sense of looking. My eyes are often closed or down left. My hands lead, although I do have an accompanying auditory internal which says, "move on," or, "stay here longer."

When I truly feel connected to another person, it is a spiritual experience, a oneness with what feels like the other person's essence. My hand, while only touching the surface of any muscle, feels as though it's penetrating deeply. My whole body, in fact, feels as though it's swaying forward, leaning into the area of healing, although I'm told that I hardly move at all. Everyone, without exception, has gone into trance and has reported feeling relaxed during and after a healing. Interestingly, too, I also relate to my own body in a positive way. The energy flowing from the heart to the hands does cycle back at some point to the head where it, too, feels clear.

Obviously, John, the months since Florida have been explosive, and I hold us both responsible. Me for having the courage to attend the conference, and you for not only creating an atmosphere that enabled me to achieve excellence but also for giving me the push to continue.

However, my healing work has been primarily with family, friends, and colleagues, and I'm anxious for that to change. Basically, I feel frustrated and isolated. Please, if you plan to continue this work, include me in any way that we can be helpful to one another. All of me, not only my hand, is itching to do more.

Many thanks for everything,
Linda Shapiro

To: JOHN GRINDER
From: LINDA SHAPIRO, M.S.
Re: 2½ Year Up-date, FLORIDA NLP/ESPerience Up-date

Dear John:

It is now two-and-a-half years after our Florida meeting and, I'm happy to report, hundreds of healings later. I continue to feel challenged by this work, but I am no longer stunned by the impact of my touch. I can say with confidence that I am able to act as an effective agent of change in the healing process. I know that energy passes through my hands unmasking symptoms, unblocking and releasing areas of distress. The result is not, as skeptics might imagine, simply comforting.

I look upon this ability as a gift, and as an elderly Moroccan patient advised me, I now "thank God every morning and every evening for giving me the hands through which the medicine comes to heal the people." I don't speculate on whether or not I would have received the touch had I not modeled Finbarr. The fact is, he was the catalyst that made it all possible, and for that I am extremely grateful.

Whereas the seventh son of the seventh son tradition of healing that was passed on to Finbarr has clear parameters dictating the correct times of day that one should heal, the hand one should use, and the number of healings one should offer: such boundaries provide structure and protection, but in my model of the world they also limit one's role. My work is therefore different. It reflects my cultural and educational inheritance. As such, it has become more authentic to who I am.

I work with people holistically and treat the entire body, as I had already begun to do only three months after Florida. Before I touch anyone, I usually rub the palms of my hands together. Then I place my right hand on the person's forehead and my left hand behind the skull. As I make contact, the penetration feels deep. A retired judge who I treated called me his "minister of health," and said it felt as though I was "rearranging his brain." I no longer laugh at such a statement, for the description resonates with and verifies my own sensations.

Those initial moments of contact with the person's head are extremely important. It is as if the head serves as a repository for bodily pain, and I receive an imprint of this either as thought or visual image. Furthermore, at this point, I often sense other issues of deep concern to the patient. When touching additional parts of the body I "pick up" on surgical procedures or areas of stress that may no longer present a problem but nevertheless exist as part of the person's history and can be relevant to the treatment. For example, in working with a physician, my hand seemed to sink into an area of her lower abdomen, penetrating so easily that she described the sensation as feeling as though, "the molecules were dissolved."

In fact, it felt to me as though there was a gaping hole, a place from which something had been scooped out. After inquiring whether surgery had been performed there, the initial response was in the negative. Later in the session, she was reminded of previous abortions. This information, which may never have been revealed otherwise, profoundly influenced the remainder of the healing.

The following is a partial account of that session written jointly by myself and the physician/patient.

June 6, 1987

The healer began by placing her hands upon the patient's upper right side of the skull in the temporal occipital area. The patient was lying on a healing table, flat on her stomach, supported by pillows under the head and upper thighs. After laying hands on the patient's head, the healer's hands directed themselves to the patient's right arm. The healer heard (auditory internal) words: "Balance, heal, wholeness, and confidence," as her eyes remained closed and she asked for guidance, reminding herself that her only intention was to heal that which was appropriate for healing.

She did not share this information with the patient at the time, but the patient's experience was that of straightening out a bone that had felt curved. She experienced a reshaping of the upper arm into a straight line. The arm felt very malleable, almost like silly putty, as the healer continued to lay on hands. The arm, as reported by the patient later, was then aligned with the shoulder and the healer's hands then got directed to the patient's forearm. The patient then experienced, in *her* words, "a wholeness, a sense of continuity," as a Gestalt of the two parts (not experienced before), a feeling of the bones aligning and belonging. Then the healer was directed toward the spleen area where her hands felt as though they were sinking into an empty space, a hole, and she sensed the words: "Something has been taken out here, lost." She asked the patient, "Have you had any surgery here? An appendix removed or anything else taken out?" The patient said, "No." The healer then felt directed towards the patient's left leg, and as she got closer to the knee, vibrations were felt.

She mentioned this and the patient said she had twisted her knee that morning. "Great, now I have something specific to work on. The right leg doesn't call out to me anyway." Perhaps it should be mentioned here that the patient had witnessed the healer work successfully on someone else and had simply come for the experience, registering no specific complaints.

The patient at that point mentioned that "there is no pattern here." She was unable, at that time, to figure out any apparent structure or pattern to the healer's work. As the healer had her hand on the knee, however, the entire knee, en bloc, began to rotate. It rotated seventy degrees to the right. At the same time the patient experienced a rotation of the left hip bone, as well as the left sacroiliac joint opening up on the left side. The patient and healer then laughed, rather hysterically, for fear that the knee would not stop rotating. The healer then removed her hands and after a few moments her hands were directed to the patient's heart chakra, then to the right ribs, lifting and re-aligning them with the sternum.

According to the patient/physician, the right arm healing physiologically necessitated the left leg re-alignment as well as a re-alignment of the sternum and rib cage. This was anatomical information that the healer did not have.

The patient was then asked to lay on her stomach and the healer's hands were directed to the same ribs on the right side of the patient's chest. Then, going down from the shoulders to the toes, following the meridians which correspond to the kidneys, the healer lay her hand on each side, first the left and then the right. At this point, after sitting up, the patient gained an insight regarding past experiences of loss.

The insight came with kinesthetic chills, which was a signal that confirmed the experience for her, and re-accessed the loss of three babies. Major issues relating to those losses were then explored before the completion of the session. This patient was seen three times.

When I am centered and trusting, the contact made with patients is not made merely with the body but with the mind and soul as well. My intention is always to heal that which is meant to be healed. It is not to thwart the body's signals of distress which might call for medical attention.

As such, I've stimulated healing in people suffering from bronchitis, arthritis, dermatitis, ulcers, pneumonia, heart palpitations, headaches, sore throats, eye infections, kidney stones, night cramps, lower back and neck spasms, depression, and anxiety. The condition/disease can be new or chronic. Duration does not seem to be a factor in determining whether the touch can penetrate and move towards healing.

As for the role that belief plays in this process, I have participated successfully in healings where people came to me because they believed I would help them and in others where relief from pain was the desired outcome but where those suffering did not believe that my touch would in any way alter their condition. In the case of an infant, I assisted in lowering a high fever to nearly normal within minutes. This baby was seemingly unaware that I was doing anything but patting his head. One is tempted to conclude that his very innocence is what kept him open to the healing energy.

I did three sessions with a man in his mid-fifties who suffered from chronic hip/leg pain. He came to see me at a time when the medical community was insisting that only surgery would relieve his agony. Now, seven months later, he is still symptom-free.

When we are sick and we heal ourselves spiritually or physically, somehow we know what it is that our body needs. It's much the same with what I do. As information comes to me through my hands, kinesthetically and auditorily, I somehow know how and where to move in order to provide better health.

I don't know to what extent those who have been my patients will go on to heal others, but many have already begun to heal themselves, using my touch as their model. Thank you for sending Dr. Herb Lustig to study with me. He has certainly been turned on to the process, having studied with me and later with Finbarr. I know that he has already had success with some of his psychiatric patients.

I've recently begun to teach healing, and I now know that it is teachable. There are two prerequisites, however, for those who are interested: the desire and ability to be truly compassionate; and the ability to center, to feel whole and at peace with oneself. One's ego is put aside, because as healers we are not only using our own energy, we are tapping into a source of universal energy which enables us to facilitate and enhance the healing process.

Indeed, as a therapist, I find that healing is in progress on a larger scale as the "me" generation of the 70's and 80's is maturing into a "we" generation of the late 80's and perhaps 90's. Many, however, bear the imprint of a particular aloneness common to that earlier pseudo-independence. It is true for people who lead relatively full emotional lives as well as for those who are isolated. As a people we appear to be starved for even the superficial touch. Is it any wonder then that the therapeutic healing touch is so transforming? What is strikingly impressive about touch healing is the speed, intensity, and integrity of what feels like a more direct pathway to health, one that cuts through fluff and excesses.

Doing this work has not only expanded the realm of possibilities I see for myself and other healers, it has changed my world view. "Reality" no longer has the same boundaries. I respect the impressive technological accomplishments of rational minds, but I now believe that the body of evidence we call "scientific" is often as subjective, given the collective agreement of any society, as intuition is mind-full. I concur with modern physics. All form is created from energy. Nothing is solid. Nothing is fixed.

New possibilities then emerge when we extend this thinking into the social and political arenas. For if we are able to link the consciousness of people through healing, then why not the consciousness of nations? If nothing is fixed, then today's enemy can be tomorrow's ally, and political as well as personal cancers can find their cures. In short, it seems to me that when we cease to worship the rational/scientific mind, we will rediscover the channels to intuitive powers. Only then will a healthy balance be achieved, even in a global sense.

Cells, organs, and dis-eases can, of course, be scrutinized, isolated in the laboratory. Ultimately, though, they are a part of a whole, elements of a human eco-system which must include mind and soul as well as body. Treatment of one element which excludes the other two is not complete. Healing must work to unite and harmonize, not isolate and kill.

More often than not, we have within us all that we need in order to heal, for it is our own intuition that best reveals the secrets we search to uncover. Trusting the channels leading to that intuition is, perhaps, the greatest challenge of all.

My thanks to you, John, because that's what you've taught me to do. And thanks, too, for your continued encouragement. You have a special talent that enables others to succeed.

Best regards,
Linda Shapiro

SINGING IN THE SPIRIT
April 1985
by
Stephanie Rachel Alt, M.S.

Tommy is nine years old. He displays marked autistic behavior, for example, marginal eye contact, withdrawal or rigidity when touched, self-stimulated rocking, handflapping and head banging. He doesn't talk and hasn't been toilet trained.

Tommy has been living on the pediatric floor of our hospital for almost a year. He was found wandering Interstate Highway 195, and because of suspected environmental neglect, he has been housed here on a protective hold until he can be placed in either a residential school, or an appropriate foster home.

As director and sole staff person of the Therapeutic Recreation Program (Child Life Program), I see Tommy daily. Unfortunately, our hospital has been hit with budget and funding cut-backs and consequently, we suffer from a familiar staff shortage.

The pediatric ward is a forty-two bed unit, with children ranging from infancy through adolescence. I have organized two sessions, a morning session for infants and toddlers, and the afternoon session for the rest.

Because Tommy requires one-on-one supervision, the quantity of time I spend with him is limited. It is upsetting, because when he is not with me, he is left in his room inside a closed bar crib. I did try bringing him into the room during afternoon session. My sense was that the noise and activity level was too much stimulus for him. He ran around the outside of the room like a whirlwind, toppling anything in his path, and sweeping things off the table onto the floor. So I created a third session, Tommy's session. With a quieter, visually simple room, I hoped I might be able to engage him in an activity and help him come out a bit from his world into mine.

During our play sessions, I offered Tommy a variety of toys, one at a time, such as busy boxes, musical wind-ups, cars, and dolls. He showed no apparent preference for any of these, ritualistically rattling, flipping, shaking, and chewing any of the above. I introduced art materials, chunky crayons and easel paper, tempera paint, and obtained the same response. Often, he'd "lock into" one object timelessly, until I removed it and replaced it with another. I mimicked his chants and squeaks, trying to catch his attention. Sometimes I noted a fleeting glance, but, mostly his focus was glazed far beyond me. I worked side by side rather than face to face, to be unintrusive. I encouraged him to climb on my make-shift gross-motor equipment, the tables, covered sandbox, and chairs. About the only time Tommy would stay fixed in one spot was on a chair I'd set for him so he could look outside the window. There he'd let me pat his back as I talked to him about the things we could see outside.

Basically I followed his lead. I crawled under the table with him and lay on the floor with him, hoping somehow and some way, to see and feel as he did and find a way for us to connect. Needless to say my work with Tommy was challenging and frustrating. I remember the desperate feeling, the gnawing inside, telling me I was stuck. I felt myself pulling away from him. This was just before my vacation which I'd planned to spend attending a modeling seminar in Florida. I anticipated and welcomed the reprieve. Perhaps there I'd get some new ideas.

At the seminar, I had the pleasure of studying with a Congolese dancer/drummer, who taught us ceremonial dances as well as some African chants, which continue to resonate in, through, and beyond me. The experience of dancing touched me deeply, and moved me in ways words can't begin to describe.

When I returned to the hospital, I was reluctant to bring Tommy into the playroom. I still hadn't thought of a new plan of action and so when I gave him the same old toys, I wasn't surprised when he resumed his same old self-stimulating behavior. In spite of my own feeling of inadequacy, I felt less driven to get Tommy to respond. I sat down next to him and without thinking started singing one of the African chants to him. Tommy stopped what he was doing, LOOKED ME SQUARELY IN THE EYES, cocked his head in my direction, and smiled. Then TAKING MY HAND, he placed it on his thigh putting his HAND ON TOP OF MINE and BEGAN TO PAT OUT THE BEAT OF THE SONG AS I continued to sing!

NOW WE'RE TALKING!:
August 1985

It has been four months since I first wrote about Tommy. In the time that has passed, Tommy has attended a day program outside the hospital. He also went to Summer Camp for six weeks, which has now ended. The teachers have sent reports back to us saying Tommy is making great progress.

I've begun to bring Tommy into the playroom during afternoon session. In general, I am skeptical about the "great gains" the school had reported. The more pessimistic I've become, the louder another voice pipes in, and questions my expectations. What do I want Tommy to do to prove to me he's changed? Am I waiting for an arbitrary signal that will demonstrate our powerful exchange has shifted something dramatically inside of him? Am I really waiting for him to say something? And in my failure to see and hear what I want, what important shifts might I have missed?

I backtracked and began remembering Tommy three months ago, six months ago, a year past. And like a swift boot in the behind setting me straight, I realize there are many things he's doing differently!

For one, Tommy is in the playroom with other children, a good sized group of children. The room is filled with many activities and plenty of noise. When I set up a gross motor obstacle course using my chairs, free tables, and the covered sandbox, he moves independently, negotiating different levels and planes. Previously, I needed to supervise him closely so he wouldn't step off a table or chair in mid air! I used to mold his body to bend and sit and mechanically move his hands and feet so he'd know how to get up and down.

Without prompting, Tommy is sitting near or next to the other children. Before, he'd run around them, seeming oblivious, or avoid them, retreating under the tables and huddling in the corners. Now, he plants himself in the middle of something that is going on.

He has maintained his repertoire of self-stimulating behaviors, rattling, twirling, shaking, and chewing the things he picks up. He rocks himself as he sits on a chair or the floor. Sometimes I wonder if these behaviors act like the company of an old friend. They seem to happen less frequently. There are many times he just sits and intently watches the other children play. I continue to mimic his chants, his series of squeaks, squawks and grunts. Sometimes the children do too. When we do, Tommy looks a bit startled and confused. He's added new sounds and perhaps, like an infant, this is preliminary to his forming and uttering words. I sing all the African chants I can remember and other songs. I've demonstrated how to use the children's xylophone, tambourine and a collection of rattles and shakers. He handles them in the same way he handles the other toys.

I know he's present in body. Will I be able to find a way to bridge the gap between our worlds, find ways to teach him how to relate to us and utilize learning materials, so he can function in this system more effectively? The following happened one afternoon recently . . . Tommy climbed on a table and began to twirl round and round. As I came towards him, he reached down to hug me, placing his arms around my shoulders. The hug turned into hanging and then Tommy started to drape himself on me. I was beginning to feel like a human jungle gym. "No" I said emphatically, "you may not hang or climb on me!" He started stamping his feet, biting his hand, and hitting his head. I reached to stop him before he hurt himself, and again he placed his hands on my shoulders, starting to lean forward and hang. I put one hand on his chest and my other on his back and began singing "Ay BoBo," another African chant, patting out beats on his body. When I stopped, he paused, a frozen moment, and then reached over my shoulder and repeated the sequence, patting on my back what I'd just finished patting on his! IF THAT'S NOT TALKING . . . WHAT IS?!

Somehow he seemed pleased with himself. I was beside myself. Tommy climbed down and sat at a table where I'd set out some toys that

I hoped would attract him. One in particular is designed to teach cause and effect: as you pull, push, dial, slide, or turn the gadgets an animal figure pops up. Placing this toy near Tommy, I opened all the doors. Without hesitation, Tommy shut them. I opened and he shut for awhile. (If I wanted to be analytic the symbolism of this play was perfect). I reached over and took his hand encouraging him to switch jobs with me. He reached over and took my hand placing it on the toy. "You do it," I said. "Open it." He refused. Sliding the toy in front of him, I turned away. I caught Tommy quicker than a wink, hit the "push" button opening the first door. I commended him and asked him to go on to the next door. He refused. I picked up another toy and played with it by myself, making sure that he could see how I used it. He acted disinterested. So did I, as I slid this toy in front of him and proceeded to pretend to ignore him. He began to extend his hand towards the toy, and as I looked to see whether he would follow through, he withdrew his hand. We seemed to be having a cat and mouse game going here! I got up to help some other children. Shortly after, Tommy also left the table and went to stand on his chair by the window.

While we were playing, Tanya, a nine year old, had been watching. She asked me if she could work with Tommy. "Please do," I said, "children are often better teachers than adults." Tanya took the toy I had set aside and stood by Tommy as she played with it. I suggested that when she was ready she slide it in front of him and see what happened. And guess what? He played successfully with it over and over again!

AFTERNOTE:
August 1987

In hindsight, I can laugh lovingly at myself when I reflect and review how I kept missing the boat with Tommy. It is a clear demonstration to me of how we can get trapped in our own model of the world.

Recently, a dear older friend of mine, who has raised his autistic son primarily at home within the family said, "It is important to find their talent or gift, develop it first and then work into other areas." I believe this whole-heartedly and have set out over the years to expand the parameters of my mind to have more to offer to the children and adults I work with. Where my life experience falls short the systems I've yet to develop fully are the auditory tonal and the kinesthetic (full body).

Everything I offered Tommy was something to look at or touch with his hands and manipulate. My learning strategy, not his. And the only times I did get a response from him prior to the seminar were when I mimicked his chants (not easy . . . comparable to learning the African chants), and when I patted him on the back and spoke to him while he looked out the window. I remember using different tones of voice as I pointed to what we could see, like you often hear when an adult speaks to an infant with exaggerated intonation, saying, "See the car?!" . . . "oh, there's a bird in the tree!"

I believe that people walk into our lives to teach us what we need to learn. Tommy pushed me beyond my limits, thank goodness. Ta Titos sparked and rekindled a whole other area in me that was lying dormant. It set me on my way and subsequently led me to Tommy.

I left N.Y.C. in September 1985. In my reports, I recommended to our staff who worked with Tommy's teachers that a sure way to reach him was through rhythm and sound. Unfortunately, I haven't heard about Tommy since.

VARIATION OF A THEME:
EXTERNALIZING THE CONFLICT MANAGER:
June 1985

This experience happened the day after I'd returned from a Framework for Mastery workshop with Judith DeLozier. At the workshops, she offered another piece of what I'd learned as the standard reframe/negotiation of parts exercise, which was assigning an Internal Conflict Manager. Using the metaphor of King Arthur and the round table, we were instructed to invite all our parts to a meeting place of our choice, where once gathered all would take their appropriate places as a session of personal change work was about to begin. We were reminded that all parts were to be respectful and responsive to the others. At the onset, a truce was declared, once again being reminded that all parts whether in agreement or not were designed to serve the whole. John also related a story about a tribe (the name escapes me) who'd gather at the village meeting place whenever two tribe members were at odds. Each member would take turns telling his tale. The tribe applauded them on. The grander the presentation, the greater their cheer. This continued until it stopped and things naturally evened out. These two pieces fresh in my mind were integrated and transferred in the following experience. The playroom had been closed for five days. The children could barely contain themselves as I set up the playroom. They crowded at the door, knocking, as Naomi, a persistent three year old, incessantly chanted, "open da door I wan da doys peaz".

Moving methodically, as I often do on Mondays, I calmly and quietly reoriented and braced myself for an anticipated busy morning.

The doors opened and four children between the ages of two-and-a-half and four years FLEW into the room. After about thirty minutes of attempting to establish some semblance of order CHAOS prevailed. One child toppled an entire bucket of toys as another smeared red paint on his hands and then on the UNcovered easel. The third child systematically poured sand OUTSIDE the sand box onto the floor, while the fourth ran from corner to corner of the room like a pinball ricocheting off target points.

At this blessed moment my conscious mind surrendered. I stood up, walked into the closet, and re-emerged as the Conflict Manager, carrying every musical instrument I could find. The children had come to find me and I led the procession to our small Round Table. Each child was assigned a seat and as they did were permitted to choose an instrument. A brief moment of silence ensued and I perceived this as a truce declared. Each child took a turn playing his piece (speaking his peace). Ramon took the lead, banging a 4/4 beat double time. We all copied. At an opportune moment, I gestured for silence and then pointed to the child seated next to Ramon to begin. Circling round-robin, every child played while the rest of us listened, keeping respectfully still. Starting a new round, I invited all parts to join together and began to play Ramon's initial theme marking it this time with body posture, voice tone, tempo and volume, saying "LOUD, LOUD, LOUD, LOUD." Holding the same tempo I shifted my tone of voice, posture, and volume introducing, "soft, soft, soft, soft!" We practiced these modes. The Soft mode was a little more challenging for the musicians to maintain! Then I introduced a new tempo, half-time! Clearly disinterested, the children passed over this, and began their own improvisations. I stopped playing and gazed off. From the corner of my eye, I caught Ramon smirking as he picked up his instrument and then another, and began playing a half-time tempo alternating beats on these two instruments. I chuckled and nodded to him. After some deliberation, indeed, we'd finally reached an agreement! I most appreciated his conceding to me on this point.

At the close of the morning session, long after our jam had dispersed, Naomi and I found ourselves back at the round table. She picked up an instrument, assumed a familiar posture, and whispered "soft, soft, soft, soft" as she congruently played! I was left thinking about how many ways there are to give and receive.

ANCIENT VOICES:
June 1985

Kay is the oldest of three daughters. Shortly after the last child was born, Kay's mother became severely depressed and disassociated. She was hospitalized and over the course of some fifteen years has been under medical and psychiatric care and in and out of hospitals. As a result, Kay spent much of her life helping her dad around the house, taking care of her sisters, and being a support to him in whatever way she could. Kay moved away from home to go to college, returning home on weekends, until recently now it's once every few months.

There is a part of Kay that wants to be a "star" free to do the things she loves, like dancing, and acting. Another more prevailing part keeps her working in jobs where she finds herself taking charge, becoming responsible for the up-keep and maintenance of the office or agency that employs her. In her personal relationships with friends and her lover, she consistently takes the role of supporter, motivator, and organizer.

Kay and I have worked in sessions to transfer the abundant resources she supplies to others back to herself. In the time we've worked together, she has enrolled in action and dance classes and has started to audition.

She recently moved out of a living arrangement that "didn't feel like home" and now lives with her man-friend until she finds her own apartment.

Kay arrived this evening feeling frustrated because an apartment she thought she had fell through. She made a statement which acted as a spring board for the bulk of the rest of our session, saying, "I have to move out from Stan's because, I'll never prove to myself that I can take care of myself." I challenged her "have to, don't and never," and then had her create a picture to represent what she looked like living on her own with self-control. She checked it kinesthetically by stepping inside the picture and popped in and out, adjusting it visually, until it looked and felt right. Next, I asked her to see herself living with self-control in Stan's apartment, repeating the same process until it looked and felt right. She nodded and then shook her head, verbalizing the incongruency I was witnessing. "I can take control of myself wherever I am," she said. "I think I'm really afraid I'll become totally dependent on Stan like my mother became when she married my dad."

Something Kay said triggered a conversation I had with a teacher who gives classes in metaphysics and the ancient tools, Tarot, I Ching, and Runes. Joseph and I were talking about how some organized religions present the "way" to be virtuous versus be a sinner, often packaging and delivering it in a fear-and-guilt based frame. Children receiving this information without ample life experience to be able to filter it for themselves can misconstrue their thoughts or actions as "sinful" and embody the onus in the unconscious mind. I was curious to learn what Joseph thought about early programming and its effect on our ability to develop other powers of the mind such as telepathy, precognition, and clairvoyance. I also wondered to what extent this could influence the touch of a healer. (I'd successfully modeled a healer who does hands on healing and was searching for more answers).

I told Kay that this conversation with Joseph had "popped" into my mind, offering her some of his thoughts regarding blocking and unleashing one's "personal powers." I knew Kay had been raised as a Catholic and now identified herself as eclectic "spiritual" in her beliefs about God. She had also wondered out loud with me in another session about the possibility of past lives and afterlife.

I asked Kay whether the idea of being a sinner generated a past memory. She paused, looked up and remembered a scene when she was about ten years old. Her mother had come to pick up Kay and her friend after school. She didn't really like staying at home all the time and would often pack the kids in the car, driving around for hours going anywhere and nowhere. This day her mother pulled the same stunt, only her friend was in the car, and Kay felt humiliated and embarrassed. She remembered hating her mother and wishing she'd die and leave Kay in peace, free of her mother's craziness.

I invited Kay to close her eyes, shift her body into a comfortable position and let herself begin to relax. For no apparent reason other than a chance for a change, I decided to put some background music on to assist her in altering her state. I reached and pulled out the album "Common Ground" by Paul Winter and selected a song that features an African instrument I love, the thumb piano.

As Kay's state of relaxation deepened, I proceeded with instructions for arm levitation, further deepening her trance. I requested her arm return to her lap only as fast or slowly as it took for her to locate the first or most impactful time in which she felt she had sinned and as a result still harbored guilt. I then established a "yes/no" signal system and had Kay signal when a time and experience had been located. I decided to invite Kay to speak while maintaining her level of trance. When she began I could barely hear her and it seemed my ears were deceiving me!

I thought I heard her say, "I'm pregnant." She'd never disclosed a pregnancy or termination of one. So I misinterpreted and fed back "Your mother is pregnant with you." Kay started to struggle to voice herself. I said, "Raise to the next level, and take your time allowing the scenario to unfold, such that as it does your words will come out effortlessly. Describe what you are seeing." Her head raised slightly and she spoke again. "I am running towards a fence away from my husband. I am pregnant and I am escaping." The lights flashed and I registered PAST LIFE. I continued to elicit more information.

Prior to this, I'd been on my way to doing a reframe and proceeded now, utilizing the context of the past life. I instructed her to find the lessons that were relevant in that life which she can apply in this life. I guided her to raise to the highest level and offer the thought forms of sin and guilt to God in order that they be released and transformed into new creative energy. Kay's head lifted up and fell all the way back.

As she began lowering it again, I instructed her back to the present moment, time, place, and year. I rose and put another piece of music on to guide her home. When she opened her eyes she smiled and sighing, she said, "I didn't expect that to happen. That was interesting!" (She had my full agreement.)

Later in the evening I re-ran the session in my mind. Whether or not the notion of past life is viable was the least of my concerns. I was certain that the experience, perhaps through a powerful metaphor, had led her to some resolution, and that was the desired outcome. I reviewed the various choice points and backtracked to the beginning of the session when I reached for "Common Ground," which I'd selected merely because I enjoyed the instrumentals. I was perplexed. What process instruction had I given that accessed a so called "past life?!" As I read the blurb written on this piece called "Ancient Voices," I learned that it is based on a classical African composition by the Shona people of Zimbabwe for an instrument called the mbira. The instrument is used in a formal ceremony called the Bira in which the family gathers to call upon a common ancestor for support. The mbira is thought to have the power to project its sound into heaven and draw ancestral spirits down to earth!

To add to the unusual nature of this experience, my sound system has one speaker working and the volume was turned down very low. There are lyrics in this piece, however, given the technical shortcoming of my sound system and the way the words are woven into the instrumentals, it is virtually impossible to hear them clearly. I sat obsessed playing and re-playing the song, until I decoded these lyrics.

> Ancient voices sing forever. Guide me on my way.
> Carry me back from far away to dreams where I have been.
> Bring me back to where I left with eyes open again.
> I remember suns of morning promising the day.
> Turning, spinning, circle ending, life begins to play.
> Eagles fly beyond your back from places far away
> When this land is free again, you'll return to stay.
> Ancient voices sing forever. Guide me on my way.

AFTERNOTE
August 1987

Kay has written several times in the last two years, keeping me updated. She and Stan married in June of this year. They have formed a production company for aspiring playwriters and actors, promoting and producing off-Broadway shows. She is living her art, living her dream.

THE MARRIAGE OF THE CARETAKER
AND PRODUCTIVE PARTS
July 1985

Pam has had a series of relationships with men who are married. Hearing her time clock ticking, feeling the deep desire to be in a situation that would lead her towards marriage and having children, she came to me to help her untangle and sort this pattern of involving herself with unavailable men.

Pam is the youngest child in her family. She sensed she was her dad's favorite "little girl." Somehow, she had a way of making his eyes laugh, sparkle, and shine. When she was eleven she caught wind of her father's illness through bits and pieces of overheard conversation and all that was not said yet felt. A year later, after a brief hospitalization, Pam's father died.

We talked about her mixed feelings being the "special one" and what happened when the person she felt closest to, her hero, died. I proposed that in keeping herself single by dating married men, she might be able to protect herself from running the risk of loving so deeply and losing another loved one again. This statement seemed to hit home. She nodded as her eyes welled with tears. The death of her father was earthshattering. She had never fully mourned his loss. After the funeral, there was little mention of him and life just went on. Not wanting to further upset her mother, siblings, or relatives, Pam kept her fears, furies and fantasies about what happened to her dad silently buried inside of herself.

For years, Pam has concentrated on her career and is quite successful. Being totally consumed with work "she hasn't had the time to deal with her personal life." As a result of setting this aspect of her life aside her lovers seem to take the matter in their hands and run the show. Often Pam likens her social life to a serial soap opera.

In our last session I led Pam through a spatial reframe. She identified and became her two opposing parts, the Productive part who has been monopolizing her internal organization, and the Caretaker who'd resigned itself to acting as an office clerk much to its dismay.

Even before completing this process, an obvious shift was occurring. Pam was establishing an internal caretaker, a primary function she'd externalized and allocated to the men in her life. While in character the Productive part revealed that it had assumed its role shortly after Pam's dad had died. Its main emphasis was to keep Pam actively involved and accomplished so she'd feel proud of herself and successful. It also admitted that keeping her preoccupied with work prevented her from getting caught up in her emotions and becoming depressed from the pain of life's disappointments. The Caretaker, who'd also come on board in Pam's adolescence, was concerned about her overall health. The Productive part kept her driven and operating at a high stress level. It also wanted Pam to feel good about herself and be "successful," but not at the expense of all else. Pam took turns stepping in and out of these parts. With me acting as facilitator we worked until we all reached some agreements.

This week Pam waltzed into the session and announced that during the week her Caretaker and Productive parts had gotten married! She read out loud a list that was generated by the collective workings of these two and their new joint plan of action to keep Pam in good shape mentally, physically and spiritually. She was exuberant, feeling integrated, and in charge of herself.

Pam also disclosed a phone conversation she had with her current manfriend. She said she'd come to a resolution about this situation too. Gesturing with her hands, she began, "On the one hand, Jim wants to have a vasectomy; and on the other hand, I want children." (She uses each hand as she continues to weigh these sides out.) "Jim is often unavailable when I want to see him, and when he flies into town he expects that I will accommodate my schedule to his. I want him to be definite and he won't specify anything, and when I make a move to end the relationship he always makes a greater effort to prove to me he loves me and wants me in his life, promising me he will tell his wife he wants a divorce soon." As Pam continues now, the hand that has represented Jim drops into her lap. The other hand remains lifted and motioning. "The longer I continue to accept his calls and let him woo me, the longer I will deceive myself. I've decided to tell Jim to stop calling me and if he does not do so I'm going to refuse his calls until I feel ready to speak to him and can do so without getting caught up in the web of this affair." (The other hand returns to her lap).

I asked her how she'd know when she would be able to do this and she answered assuredly, clasping her hands together (collapsing the anchors), "I'll know, because it will feel right!" As she spoke she resumed the same posture, breathing, and voice that she had initially in our session when she'd described herself feeling "integrated" and "in charge of herself." She rose and walked down my hall to leave. I felt like throwing rice and confetti to mark this special moment, as she crossed over the threshold.

POSTSCRIPT
August 1987

It has been two years since the previous pieces were written. Re-reading and editing them now, it feels like two years is two life-times ago. It is like flipping through old photos almost in disbelief that the person in the picture is you, pulling an album from the collection and re-playing that particular song that was certainly written and sung especially for you. There is a beauty in having these markers that let you know where you were in reference to where you are.

I remember trembling as I raised my hand that first weekend of NLP training to answer John's question "What do you want to learn in your NLP training?" Most people responded by requesting information about the technology, anchoring, eye accessing, meta-model, eliciting strategies. I thought all of that was fine, and what I wanted to learn was how to build a bridge from my unconscious to conscious mind, knowing more specifically how I know what I feel I know. Now I can say that I truly wanted to learn to trust, rely, and depend on my unconscious mind.

I can still hear John saying that we should learn the technology, apply it, create variations, and then forget it all, traveling on into new unexplored territories.

When I wrote in 1985, two years after completing the master track and hypnosis training, I was at the point of creating variations. As is evident in *The Marriage of the Caretaker and Productive Parts, A Variation of a Theme,* and *Ancient Voices,* I played most with reframing.

I was still being surprised, startled, and delighted when "without thinking" I'd make an intervention which made "the difference that makes the difference."

My experience at the modeling seminar with Finbarr Nolan and Ta Titos Sompa set me on route back across the bridge to "home" (conscious mind to unconscious mind). In the almost two years since, after jumping into the abyss relocating to Monterey, Ca. from New York City because "I knew" I had to, I am now in the process of exploring those new territories.

In my private practice, as an Educational Consultant, I find myself far less strategic and technical. I am comfortable working from a vantage point somewhere between the two realms of consciousness. I am fascinated with the class of experiences that occur while I'm in or at "second attention" and how I know what I know without being told.

There are many unusual or "out of ordinary" events in my life including most recently the hands-on healing work I've done. And as I memorize my internal state in each of these contexts I can readily re-access them. The information I'm privy to is channeled consistently and fluently.

And just as I am fascinated with how I know what I "know," I feel more challenged by learning what I don't know, for it keeps "me" and "life" and "reality" an ongoing process rather than a fixed thing.

4060 Franklin Ave.
New Orleans, La. 70122

November 12, 1985

Dear John,

Enclosed is an article that was to have been published by WOMAN'S DAY magazine. Hilda, the writer, healed herself of cancer. I saw her as a client only twice. My outcome for this lady was to activate her internal processes into complete recovery. I tailored everything I did or said in accordance with the information I elicited. "Staring into a dog's face," isn't what I would have asked someone else to do. I asked her to use her painting ability, go inside, and reproduce something representative of healthy lungs, a healthy pink. Part of the therapy was for her to learn how to communicate with her unconscious, which she did quite nicely. Of course, she was an excellent candidate since she already believed she could heal herself and was moving in that direction.

I was told by some at WOMEN'S DAY that the story had been killed because the doctors said they must have made a mistake in their diagnosis. They couldn't accept that what Hilda said she did could possibly have healed her. When Hilda saw me two years ago, she was seventy years of age.

Kindest regards to you and Judith.

Sincerely,
Marina Kerkhoff

November 6, 1985

Dear Marina,

Since returning to Delaware Water Gap after I saw you, I have continued to have daily contact with my inner center, and feel that I'm usually using resources that I hadn't been in touch with before. I think this is a way of life, not just recovering from an illness.

Have been dividing my time between writing and painting and have been doing some volunteer work here and there.

Recently have been somewhat hassled by a root canal job on my teeth and am not feeling as well as usual.

Let's stay in touch. When I'm back in shape I'll write a better letter. Best to you and let me know how this worked out.

Hilda

THE DOCTOR WITHIN
by
Hilda Cole Espy

"It's supposed to be a professional secret,
but I'll tell you anyway. We doctors . . .
only help and encourage the doctor within."
                              Albert Schweitzer

My small yellow cottage is perched on the massive shoulder of Mt. Minsi, which rises from the Delaware River to form the Pennsylvania side of the Delaware Water Gap. Steeply up from me is the southbound Appalachian Trail. If you step into the woods and keep going you'll ultimately find yourself in Georgia. The sighting of bears is not uncommon in Delaware Water Gap. In recent history a bear climbed a tree on Main St. The scenery here is literally breath-taking and I began to notice that, particularly last summer, walking to the post office, I would gasp and have to stop to catch my breath.

During September, I developed a persistent bronchitis. I had pneumonia before Christmas and two relapses afterwards. When my chest problems lingered into February, despite three different antibiotics, my doctor in Stroudsburg ordered an X-ray and discovered a white spot on the right lung. I can still picture it on the illuminated film in his office. He suspected lung cancer and sent me to a specialist in thoracic medicine at the Geisinger Clinic, ninety miles west at Danville, Pa., advising me to prepare to stay for two weeks in the probable event of surgery. I hadn't seen the 1984 Facts and Figures of the American Cancer Society in which symptoms of lung cancer were described as, "recurring attacks of pneumonia or bronchitis." So I wondered why my doctor gave me such a comforting pat. I hurried home to arrange for care of my dog, Lollipop, and the watering of house plants.

I was due to fly to New Orleans early in March to visit my daughter, Mona, and her family. I decided not to cancel the trip until I had seen the surgeon. I could call it off from the hospital.

I drove to Geisinger on February 28, 1984, in an American Cancer Society car with a volunteer at the wheel. We left at 6:30 a.m. in a sleet storm. Trees on either side of route 80 through the Poconos were drooping with heavy accumulations of frozen rain. We passed trucks that had jack-knifed and broken guard rails where some vehicle had crashed through and down an embankment. I sat in back with a packed suitcase, a shopping bag full of books, and a huge brown envelope containing X-rays on which my doctor had scrawled, "once a heavy smoker." I didn't think much about what would happen at Geisinger, I just hoped we'd get there.

Dr. Albertini saw me immediately, examined me and the material I had brought, and sent me to the pulmonary lab and the X-ray department before we met again. He looked at the front and side exposures on the new X-rays, read the report from the pulmonary lab, and sat down to talk to me.

"The tumor is real but I cannot operate because you probably would not survive a lung operation. If you did you'd be a permanently bedridden invalid. You have emphysema and your lungs are operating at fifty percent of their capacity." I was startled. Five years earlier, when I stopped smoking, there hadn't been any breathing impairment. I hadn't lost my breath in those days. I remembered walking briskly to work in New York during the transit strike, an hour and a half each way. Nor had emphysema been mentioned during subsequent check ups. Dr. Albertini said we could not be sure of the nature of the tumor without further tests but that, considering my history as a heavy smoker, it was almost certainly malignant. He asked me to return early on April 3rd for new X-rays and a bronchoscopy, a diagnostic exploration of the bronchial area under a local anesthetic. He had me sign a permission form and gave me some literature to read about the procedure. Then he prescribed medication to help my breathing. He said we might begin radiation treatments in March.

Riding home through silvery ice-glazed mountains, I realized that I might just as easily have been in a hospital nightgown being visited by needle-stickers and authority figures who made me repeat, for the hapless edification of my roommates, how many packages of cigarettes I had smoked a day. I can remember when it was considered innovative and merciful to tell a cancer person the truth. Now a doctor's diagnosis tends to be scrupulously lacking in what some call false hope, and we have the placebo effect in reverse. Tell a patient that a pill is a new and peerless cure for what ails him and he tends to get better. Tell him that he has an incurable disease and that he has four months to live and he'll probably die on schedule. There is one ameliorating side effect to being at a possibly terminal stage: having nothing to lose can stimulate your sense of adventure and change your life. As Stephanie Mathews Simonton has said, "A diagnosis of cancer has a transforming effect."

Back in Delaware Water Gap, I was glad I hadn't called off my visit to Mona, but I realized that six weeks would elapse before my return to Geisinger and perhaps radiation treatments. Meantime, the tumor might grow, metastasize. What could I do to help myself? I was making a cup of coffee when something told me, the words appeared in my stream of consciousness and were heard as if spoken, to remember a book I had read about Dr. Elmer Green and his wife, Alyce, and their adventures pioneering in biofeedback at the Menninger Foundation in Topeka, Kansas.

The suggestion, coming out of the blue, was reminiscent of experiences I had had with inspiration when I was writing short stories. I might be exasperatingly hung up over how to end a story, encountering such a stubborn writer's block that I would give up and go do something else. Later, when the story was the last thing on my mind, the ending, complete with dialogue, would come to me like a homing pigeon. I'd rush to the typewriter and try to catch it, word for word. The suggestion to turn to a book I had read ages ago and whose title I could not remember, came to me as clearly as if I had received it on a Teletype machine.

In the mid-sixties, Dr. Green was convinced that if the mind could create illness, as psychosomatic medicine had established, it could also heal. He was determined to discover how it was possible to reach and deliberately influence the autonomic nervous system, hitherto thought to be beyond conscious control, impervious to willpower. You can raise your arm through a conscious command but you cannot raise its temperature by the King Chanute approach. An early, thrilling experiment of the Greens found that volunteers, relaxed in lab chairs, could actually warm their hands by imagining that they were warm. They might visualize themselves lying on the beach and feeling the sun sink in, or thrusting their hands into warm water. Up would go the thermometer taped to their fingers. This was their feedback, confirming that what they had imagined had actually happened. A skeptical observer could watch the mercury climbing. Make believe, the very stuff of day-dreams, could be as medically viable as penicillin! The Greens called it visual imagery.

I am an old hand at make-believe, although it was culturally discouraged when I was growing up as a rather reckless and time-squandering escape from the real world. When I was a small girl I had spent an entire summer under a mulberry tree in North Carolina, holding a stick to draw lines on the earth. I created the rooms of an imaginary house, upstairs and downstairs, on the bare ground underneath the branches. I invented the people who lived there; their sumptuous furniture, the delicious food they ate, their exotic pets. I was part of their lives day after day, and if I ever go back to that make-believe house it will be old home week for me.

Now I wondered what sort of thing to visualize to obliquely urge healing action. Somehow, I must stimulate my immune system, a secret part of me that had protected me from illness all my life, long before I was aware of being alive. But how does one persuade lymphocytes to go all out? Dr. Green was recently quoted in an article from Smithsonian Magazine, December, 1979, in which he precisely expressed my predicament, ". . . our bodies tend to do what they are told if we know how to tell them."

Then it occurred to me that writing and painting had provided a sort of bridge to this new experience. Thinking of the right words to create emotions that might affect my physical being was a sort of invention. I had once attended a conference in New York, assigned by Women's Day to write an article about how to encourage creativity in children. During the workshops, Elizabeth Drews (College of Education, Michigan State University) said that inventive persons, "don't know that some things are impossible." Dr. E. Paul Torrence (Director of Educational Research at the University of Minnesota) defined creativity as, "a successful step into the unknown." Lorraine Love Ort (Professor of Education at Bowling Green University, Ohio) suggested that creativity was stimulated by, "courageous adventures," and asked, "What is life but the release of imprisoned glory?"

On the morning of February 29, the day after my trip to the Geisinger Clinic, I sat in my favorite chair, closed my eyes, relaxed as completely as I knew how, subdued mental distractions, and brought some elating memories back, picturing them in color and with sound.

I smelled clean winter air and heard a bluejay call as I rested at the top of a ski slope. I watched a snowflake melting on a green woolen glove and marvelled that every snowflake in every blizzard in the world has an entirely different exquisite design. And that every human face is different, though having only eyes, nose and mouth to suggest an infinity of differences. Nobody was ever, even if always, only a statistic.

Back to two o'clock on an early Spring morning in Manhattan, the year that Franklin D. Roosevelt became president in January. I was walking home from a party at an hour when even the city is silent. Then shuffle, shuffle and there appeared the huge forms of elephants, going downtown in the dark, each one clasping the tail of the elephant in front. They were on their way to Madison Square Garden and the acrobats who would ride on their jeweled heads on the opening night of the circus. Their tiptoeing through Manhattan was so delightfully incongruous that it lifted my spirits. Weariness disappeared.

Memory then whisked me to Guatemala in the early seventies. I was standing on a sunny little plateau on the edge of a rainforest, opposite the scorched crater of the volcano Pacaya. "Boom!" went this living mountain. And out boiled a towering black cloud of volcanic ash, propelled by a white cloud of steam. Over the clouds soared myriads of rocks that were black in the bright sunlight. In a moment, I could hear them pattering like hail. Some, the size of large boulders, rolled down between the plateau and the crater. I felt again the awesomeness of Pacaya's presence. I was trembling.

As my body responded to the excitement I felt, I began to visualize, to imagine, the boundless vitality in nature meeting the energy inside my skin in a surging tide of well-being. I imagined this tide reaching every cell with a cosmic, transforming power. I actually felt an inner vibrance. I pictured the white blood cells of my immune system overwhelming cancer cells. I visualized the spot on my right lung as I clearly remembered seeing it on the X-ray film and I saw it shrinking. I imagined my lungs expanding more fully. I saw myself walking to the post office, swinging along with no need to stop and catch my breath time and again on the way.

"That's it," I thought. I was about to open my eyes when I realized I had become disconnected from my usual routine. I had had a world-shaking adventure in getting inside myself and how could I possibly snap my fingers and get with it in my usual comfortable way. So I instinctively did the right thing to find my way back. I visualized myself going about the things I had planned to do with a feeling of refreshed energy and confidence, and when I opened my eyes, I was all the way back. The worlds inside and outside my skin had a bridge.

During the week before I left for New Orleans, I held ten or fifteen minute healing sessions three times a day. Meantime, Dale Dealtrey, our pastor at the Church of the Mountain, brought me a book called GET-TING WELL AGAIN, by Dr. Carl O. Simonton, Stephanie Mathews-Simonton, and James L. Creighton, which describes the use of visual imagery at the Cancer Counselling and Research Center in Fort Worth, Texas. "We believe that emotional and mental states play a significant role in susceptibility to disease, including cancer, and in recovery from all disease," I read. "If the total integrated system of mind, body, and emotions, which constitutes the whole person, is not working in the direction of health, then purely physical interventions may not succeed."

Such support was very welcome because I had misgivings from time to time. Who can forget Murphy's Law or refrain from wishing he had never mentioned it? Sometimes, I felt that I might be kidding myself with my visions of wellness. I had a few bad dreams. In one, I was in a hospital bed and a young doctor was sort of hanging around in his white jacket with a stethoscope stuffed in his pocket. My conversational gambits had dried up and I was beginning to wish he'd leave. His presence was becoming a little heavy. Just to be saying something I asked, "when do you think I'll be going home?" He turned to me. "I was waiting for you to ask that," he said. "You won't be going home." And I woke up with a reverberation in my solar plexus as if somebody had clashed cymbals.

"Mental imagery is not a method of self deception," wrote Simonton, "It is a method for self-direction." It is another way of setting goals, where you are forced to be explicit. Visualizing, day-dreaming, fantasizing, if you will, not only leads you in a direction, it can ultimately take you there. It can sometimes catalyze a history-making idea.

Albert Einstein was imagining himself riding on a sunbeam, and he was a big boy at the time, when he got the basic idea for the theory of relativity. The late Ansel Adams, when he was asked how he took his famous photograph of Half Dome replied, "It came out just like I visualized and called the shot."

I hoped that I would be able to visualize and call the shot too. Meantime, something told me that there might be another ingredient to add to the recipe for cancer-ousting, and I decided to explore that in New Orleans.

There in the yellow house on State Street, Mona, Gene, and the four children provided an ideal ambience for communion with the positive. The weather, too, was buoyant. Azaleas were beginning to bloom in lovely colors in all the front yards. We walked on the levee, rode on the Charles Street trolley, and boarded the Memphis, a paddle wheeler, to go out on Old Man River. We watched a couple of otters play in a stream at the zoo. The food was wonderful. If joie de vivre was therapeutic, my family helped me experience it every waking hour.

I did manage to spook Joanna, eight, and her older brother, Jeremy. Once when I was engrossed in a healing revery, I became aware that Joanna was peeking at me with a solemnly appraising expression. Mona told me that she had come down to the kitchen and said that I, "looked funny." Later that day I asked Joanna and Jeremy if they were interested in what I was doing. They said yes, and so I told them to close their eyes, and I took them on an imaginary trip to the beach. We ran through the icy cold lace the waves left on the sand, listened to the gulls mew as they wheeled over the breakers. We built a sand castle and were bowled over by a wave. They loved it. "If you're ever sad and you want to feel as happy as you were at the beach, close your eyes and go back there," I suggested.

I wish somebody had taught me how to take a quick trip and change my mood when I was their age. When I was growing up I got the impression that when you were depressed it inexorably happened to you. To this day, it's culturally acceptable to talk about the cancer victim, a word that suggests no hope, no alternative to helplessness. Some doctors believe that people often see themselves as victims years or months before they succumb to cancer.

Soon after I arrived in New Orleans, Mona put me in touch with Dr. Arthur Samuels, a specialist in biofeedback in New Orleans and professor at the medical school of Louisiana State University. I asked him if he could find time to see me. "Maybe you can suggest something more then I'm doing." He had to go out of town and would not return before I had to leave but offered, "I think you should be working on more than one level. You should learn self-hypnosis. You probably are using it already to some extent."

He suggested a teacher, Marina Kerkhoff, a psychologist whose field was Neuro-Linguistics. I had never heard of it. Four days after my arrival in New Orleans, I was sitting in a deep easy chair opposite Marina in her office.

"I'd like to control the cancer," I said.

"Control? Don't you want to be fully healed?"

I nodded.

"Then you must tell your unconscious mind exactly that."

Marina asked me to think of something I liked to look at and to listen to. Saying, "Close your eyes!," she deftly steered me into a trance, very like my own healing sessions. "You are looking into a dog's face and listening to the rain and all the time you are relaxing more and more deeply, and ever more deeply . . ."

This wasn't my idea of what being hypnotized would be like. I was aware and awake with my eyes shut and at home in that easy chair. Marina prompted me to tell my unconscious mind that I wanted to be fully cured. I saw my lungs "healthy pink," Marina's phrase. I told myself that with every breath my lungs were improving. She then suggested, "Now ask your unconscious mind, 'Are you still with me?' " I did so. After a moment, Marina demanded, "Did you feel anything?" I replied, awestruck, "Yes, a big vibration in my solar plexus."

"That was your feedback," Marina said. "Now thank your unconscious mind and ask it to watch over your healing so that it will continue even when you are busy or asleep. Now open your eyes."

We smiled at each other.

"All there is to hypnotizing yourself is to stare at something until your eyes are tired. Stare at my fingers."

She held them up in a V for victory sign. "When your eyes are tired, close them and go through everything you have just done."

So I went alone through the sequence we had practiced. When I asked my unconscious mind if it were still with me, I got a tremendous affirmative vibration. I told Marina that appealing to my unconscious had been like praying. She nodded. I felt as triumphant as the little boy in a story my mother used to tell. He asked where God was and was told, "Everywhere." He demanded, "Is he in this room, near this table? Is he in this glass?"

"Yes."

The child put his hand over the top of the glass and yelled, " I've got him!"

Being in touch with my unconscious mind boosted my healing efforts. I was confidant that I had an ally. I knew now that the hitherto inaccessible part of my mind had always been the source of, "something told me," or of answers to problems that appeared in my stream of consciousness. Actually, it was inaccurate to call it my unconscious mind. It was my conscious mind that didn't work when I was asleep or anesthetized. My so called unconscious mind had been awake since minute one of my life, and had lived, in terms of hours, more than twice as long as my conscious mind had.

I have since learned that many people who visualize when meditating often repeatedly see a figure whom they call their Inner Guide. Dr. Bernard Siegel, a surgeon and a professor at the Yale Medical School, has an Inner Guide he calls George. Dr. Art Ulene, who often appears on television to interpret developments in medicine, asks a rabbit for advice.

Willis W. Harmon, Professor of Engineering Economics at Stanford University, addressing the August, 1979 annual meeting of the

Transpersonal Psychology Association, asserted, "Each of us has access to a supraconscious, creative, integrative, self-organizing intuitive mind whose capabilities are apparently unlimited." Knowing I could reach this part of me any time helped me feel more secure. I began to develop a better structure for my healing sessions, learned how to get into them better.

It is not possible to deeply relax until you have dismissed upcoming duties or unresolved anxieties from your mind for the duration of the session. There are visual ways. You can blow your worries off in an imaginary balloon and watch it rise over the treetops and disappear. I learned to make my troubles wait outside somewhere, and sometimes I forgot to let them in again. I began to value the state of pure beingness, like a wildflower, a thistle seed in the air, or a pebble on the beach. It was a revelation to get beyond the old, "What shall I do now?" habit my zealously industrious and active culture and I had created.

Visualization was helpful in getting into deep relaxation. I might imagine myself in a bathing suit, sitting on a raft on a July morning, dangling my legs in the tingly salt water, and feeling the sun's sedative presence warming my shoulders. In my mind's eye, I gazed into the green bay where shafts of light showed tiny saber fish zipping around my feet in schools.

Between healing sessions, I noticed a greater awareness of what went on in my consciousness as I was cooking, washing dishes, making beds, or whatever. This resulted in some dismaying, if educational, revelations of a theme prominent in certain fantasies. Getting even, sweet revenge, was something I relished more than I would have liked to think. Somewhere out in my head was a me inventing scenes where I was the star of the withering riposte, designed to smash to smithereens the self esteem of somebody who had hurt me. What I said to them in wicked glee was aimed to make them feel inferior, repentant, respectful, or whatnot. I knew that I had to learn to relinquish, not relish, this sort of grudge-hoarding. What lowers the immune system, I had read, was often hidden anger or resentment. Any unhappy or depressing event is itself a trouble maker. I began to realize that you have to deliberately choose to be happy, over and over again, because staying upset is downright dangerous. Research is establishing that if it is true that being unhappy can help you get sick, being happy can help keep you well.

My attitude toward the benefits of good nutrition became more respectful, as did the need for daily exercise, especially if I was too tired, and didn't feel like it. I began to believe that exercise did indeed make me feel more energetic. And energy was something I needed to help me overcome my problem.

When I returned to the Geisinger Clinic on March 7, it was a clear cold day, and the red barns of the valley farms were vivid against thawing patches of snow and gentle blue sky. Somewhere out there, a choir of peepers was probably singing.

New X-rays were taken before I saw Dr. Albertini and I spent two hours in the pulmonary lab, having my lung power exhaustively tested by mysterious machines that blinked red and green and wrote figures on big report sheets without any help from humble humans. When ordered to prolong an exhaled breath, the technicians would urge me on like cheerleaders, "Go on, go on, go on . . . you can make it . . . more, more, MORE!"

In the Department of Thoracic Medicine, I watched Dr. Albertini as he studied the new X-rays. "I should be on pins and needles," I marvelled, "but . . ." And suddenly I was on pins and needles, as if I'd never really been away from them. His repeated reviews of the old and new X-rays began to seem ominous.

Finally, he turned to me and said, "Your tumor is so small that I can't see it."

I was stunned. I had hoped that it would be smaller but that it was invisible left me pole-axed. "Your breathing has improved to almost normal" he went on. "Now you could have an operation if you needed one. Let's hope you never do."

Suppose I had claimed, "I got rid of the tumor and the emphysema by imagining I didn't have them." What would his reaction have been? It is medically acceptable to refer to such recoveries as, "spontaneous remissions," but for some lady from Delaware Water Gap to declare that she had been pep-talking her T-cells would have been a little overbearing, I thought. So, I didn't say anything except thank you and goodbye. I went home, "blissed out," as a musician I know describes such elation.

But the most momentous aspect of my experience wasn't over. If you find out that there is more to you than you had thought. if there is a veritable Minerva accessible to you, you don't part with this gift. It was wonderful to know that favorable changes of all kinds can be initiated and realized. I had always had a phobic terror of thunderstorms and soon it would be getting hot and those towering clouds would be rising up behind the mountains. So, not long after I got home, I made a beeline for my favorite chair, leaned back, and closed my eyes.

P.S. That was a year ago and I've been reading continuously with the help of the Monroe County Library Bookmobile and the librarian at the Pocono Hospital Medical Library, expanding my reading list from bibliography to bibliography, finding out what I could about the mind/body connection.

In this country, a thousand years ago, the Hopi Indians used visual imagery. A present-day Hopi, studying to be a doctor, told William Least Heat Moon that his people prayed for rain, "by sitting and thinking about rain . . . we picture wet things like streams and clouds. It's sitting in pictures."

Twenty-six years ago, Eugene Pendergrass, then President of the American Cancer Society, remarked, "There is solid evidence that the course of disease in general is affected by emotion. Thus we as doctors may begin to emphasize treatment of the patient as a whole as well as the disease from which the patient is suffering."

His prediction is coming true, but more slowly than he had perhaps anticipated.

Dr. Herbert Benson in a May 1984, interview (American Health) said, "Psychosomatic medicine emphasized how the mind affects the body in negative ways. We in medicine have difficulty accepting that the mind can affect the body in a helpful way."

Dr. Brugh Joy, who teaches self discovery and self healing at his Skytop Ranch in California writes, "any human being who by now doesn't recognize mind over matter as valid parts of reality is living in the dark ages of unenlightened science."

At this time however, there are relatively few doctors who believe that a patient can play an affective role in his treatment or surpass statistical expectations of how long he will live.

Dr. Bernard Siegel, one who teaches survival thinking, tells about a patient whose original doctor told her that her cancer was widespread and that recovery was unlikely. When she asked, "What can I do?" he replied, "You only have a hope and prayer." She asked, "How do I hope and pray?" He said, "I don't know. That's not my line." Siegel says he sees no reason to 'ell a patient, "There's nothing more that I can do for you." He made an investment of time and heart finding out how and writes, "Science teaches us to see in order to believe and the spirit says believe and you will see. I know the latter to be true."

He founded the Exceptional Cancer Patient's Association, a group therapy, self-help organization that has been a very effective resource in New Haven, Connecticut.

While the American Cancer Society at this date sees merit in the morale boosting achieved by mind over matter advocates, it is still doubtful of its effectiveness in assisting the body's recovery from cancer. In its June 29, 1984, statement on the Effects of Emotions on Cancer, it concluded, "The effort to find links between behavior and the immune systems have become increasingly more complex and psychoneuroimmunology has developed."

William J. Broad in a New York Times report of January 1, 1985, describes research, "that today is exploring the brain's powerful influences over immune defenses."

Dr. Andrew Weil mentioned the bonus of patient participation in cancer alleviation and recovery in which a number of Americans have been successfully involved. He writes (Mademoiselle, April 1984), "When the immune system does spring into action, it can eliminate even large tumor masses quickly, and interestingly enough, such remissions often go together with dramatic changes in the patient's outlook on life."

AUTOGENIC METAPHOR RESOLUTION: METHOD AND CASE EXAMPLES
October 1987
by
Arun V. Hejmadi, Ph. D., M. S. W.
and Patricia J. Lyall, B. S., R. P. T.

INTRODUCTION

For centuries, the human organism has struggled for survival against enemies which have ranged from the saber-toothed tiger, to microscopic bacteria and viruses, to the Internal Revenue Service. In this century, medical technology has made quantum advances in the prevention and treatment of infectious diseases. We are no longer in danger of succumbing to a large majority of those which have threatened our existence for centuries. A challenge which remains is the prevention and treatment of functional or stress-related illnesses, those in which no specific microorganism has been identified as the source of physiological breakdown. This category of dysfunction includes such major catastrophic health problems as cardiovascular disease, some forms of cancer, and the so-called auto-immune diseases, as well as some which are less catastrophic, such as gastric ulcer, many allergic conditions, myofacial pain syndromes, migraine, and PMS (premenstrual syndrome). It is estimated that 50 to 80 per cent of all physical illnesses requiring medical attention are stress-related or functional in nature (Pelletier, 1977).

Many stress researchers have demonstrated that interactions between body, mind, and environment can have a powerful effect on the existence and progress of many functional illnesses. In one model for tracking the response of an individual to a stressful event (Dohrenwend & Dohrenwend, 1980), the outcome is determined not only by the stressful event

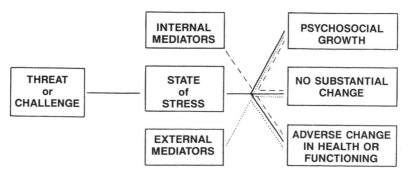

but by two sets of resources or mediators (see Figure 1). External mediators consist of resources such as social status, financial conditions, employment, and family structure. Internal mediators are resources such as physiological systems, coping strategies, learned behavioral responses, perceptions, beliefs, and values.

Any of these mediators can be a source of sustenance to an individual, a source of additional stress, or both. For example, the style of living identified as Type A behavior represents an internal mediator which can be a serious liability to cardiovascular well-being (Rosenmann, Brand, Sholtz, & Friedman, 1976), although it may be an asset in a corporate or professional context (Mettlin, 1976). The importance of mediators has been confirmed by several other investigators (Mason, 1971; Elliot & Eisdorfer, 1982), including Lazarus who asserts that choice and perception play an important role in defining what is or is not stressful for an individual (Lazarus, 1966, 1971; Lazarus Cohen, Folkman, Kanner, & Schaefer, 1980).

Elliot and Eisdorfer, in a study by the National Institute of Medicine and National Academy of Sciences (Elliot & Eisdorfer, 1982), reaffirmed that, "mediators play a crucial role in determining how individuals react to stressors, and what health consequences these reactions produce." They conclude, along with many other researchers, that, "Investigators need to study different types of mediators and to identify the systems they affect." In this paper, we present an approach to functional or adaptive illness which addresses this critical research need. Our work to date has been phenomenological with similarities being noted at an intra-individual level, since our focus has been on helping individuals with their illnesses. Through this work we have developed a pattern of intervention which allows an individual to identify mediators or groups of mediators which affect their physiological systems and, if appropriate, to alter those mediators so that homeostasis is restored.

Our interest in stress research began when we personally experienced functional physiological difficulties, allergies, back pain, a gastric ulcer, and were seeking direction in a struggle to regain our health. The conclusions, and especially the questions raised by this vast and complex field of research, laid the foundation for our success in resolving our symptoms.

In the more difficult task of articulating and integrating our approach and conclusions, we confronted a problem that has plagued pain researchers for decades. Pain, sickness, and healing are subjective phenomena. They do not lend themselves to quantitative measurement, and there are countless variables which cannot be identified, much less controlled. We encountered extraordinary difficulty when we attempted to frame our work in terms of objectivity and the scientific method.

The missing links came from two sources. Neuro-Linguistic Programming (NLP) provided a technology which models the structure of subjective experience and describes patterns which can alter individual subjective experience (Bandler & Grinder, 1975b). In addition, the model of hypnotherapy developed by Milton Erickson, M.D., which is part of the provenance of NLP, gave us a basis for our approach (Erickson, 1980).

The pattern of intervention that we call Autogenic Metaphor Resolution (AMR) addresses two areas of need that are articulated in the stress research literature. First, it is important for individuals under stress to maintain good health by mobilizing their physiological and psychological resources.

Second, if functional or adaptive illnesses occur, individuals may need to develop additional internal mediators in order to restore well being. Obviously, the patterns presented here work even more effectively in combination with the techniques and procedures already developed and presented in the literature on stress research and management.

AMR extends and integrates the techniques that are used in physical therapy, psychotherapy, NLP, and Ericksonian Hypnotherapy. AMR is a pattern of intervention which works directly with the interface between cognition and physiological function in order to affect the course of functional illnesses.

It has been applied successfully in cases of myofacial pain syndromes, migraines, endometriosis, colitis, rheumatoid arthritis, and multiple sclerosis, among others. AMR has been used with several presurgical patients with the purpose of optimizing the individual's response to procedures and minimizing postoperative discomfort. While numbers are too small to make generalizations, our surgical patients have reported a minimum need for pain medication and significant reduction in the length of their postoperative hospitalizations, (30 to 70 percent less than predicted).

Aspects of the overall AMR approach have been presented elsewhere (Hejmadi & Lyall, 1986, 1987a, 1987b). A clinical perspective on AMR was described in a paper which won the 1986 Annual Halos Award (Hejmadi & Lyall, 1986). We have found AMR to be most effective when clients have a cognitive framework within which it can be understood and integrated into their everyday lives. This framework has been described in a two-part paper (Hejmadi & Lyall, 1987a, 1987b).

In this paper, we present a brief review of material which forms the basis of AMR, describe some general considerations in applying this work, and present case examples of its application in cases of rheumatoid arthritis and myofacial pain. The case examples are described in the kind of detail which makes the AMR process available to the practicing clinician and the lay person.

BACKGROUND

The knowledge base for AMR includes information about the structure and function of the human body, the structure of subjective experience, stress research, theories of emotion, and theories of psychological functioning. The material in this section begins with the stress model for health.

The response of the human autonomic nervous system (ANS) to stress was first described by Cannon in the early 1900's and summarized later in his book (Cannon, 1963). The ANS, which sustains and regulates all automatic physiological functions, has two polar response patterns: the sympathetic, fight or flight response; and the parasympathetic, relaxation response. When an individual perceives a danger or threat, the sympathetic response is evoked to mobilize the individual's resources for survival. The relaxation response can occur after the perceived danger has been resolved or overcome.

Stress researchers have shown that everyday stresses are cumulative and evoke the sympathetic response. If these stresses are not resolved, or if the parasympathetic response is not evoked, an individual may continue in a state of sympathetic arousal, resulting eventually in organic exhaustion and damage. Thus, a chronic state of tension or stress significantly increases an individual's vulnerability to physical illnesses. This concept was first introduced by Selye who called it the General Adaptation Syndrome (Selye, 1936, 1946).

The sympathetic response, was very useful to primitive people when facing life threatening dangers. Modern day people face far fewer such dangers, and most common stressors are psychological in nature. Mason has shown that even direct physical stressors such as heat, cold, and exercise, are mediated by psychological factors (Mason, 1971, 1975; Mason, Maher, Hartley, Mougey, Perlow, & Jones, 1976). Indeed, Burchfield has defined stress as, "anything that causes an alteration of psychological homeostasis," (Burchfield, 1979).

Stress management programs teach participants to recognize the presence of the sympathetic response, and to evoke the relaxation response. The individual is encouraged to evoke the parasympathetic response using various techniques which are performed consciously on a daily basis, or whenever the physiological signs of stress are perceived.

It is generally left to the individual to identify the stressors that evoke the sympathetic responses and to find ways to avoid or change them. This is possible when stressors can be subjectively observed and are accessible to the individual's cognitive processes, for example, stressful life events such as those enumerated by Holmes and Rahe (1967).

Unfortunately a threat or stress need not be perceived at a conscious level in order to evoke or maintain a full blown sympathetic physiological response. On the contrary, it has been observed that there are stressors which are responsible for adverse physiological change which are experienced only at an unconscious level and are therefore inaccessible to the individual's conscious resources for self protection and change. The term unconscious processes, as used here, refers to mental and physiological processes that are out of conscious awareness.

For example, it has been demonstrated that individuals who generate Type A behavior are at risk for cardiovascular damage. Type A behavior is a, "relatively chronic and excessive struggle to obtain a usually unlimited number of things from (the) environment in the shortest period of time" (Rosenmann & Friedman, 1983). Indeed, we have seen individuals who, upon discovering that they manifest this pattern of behavior, treat it as yet another imperfection and experience intense time pressure to "fix" it. Harold, who suffered from nausea and hypertension, reported that prior to learning a relaxation technique, he could only relax after sixteen hours of hard work. He was very excited about the technique, which allowed him to accomplish a degree of relaxation in twenty minutes that had formerly taken sixteen hours; and he was sure that if he really worked at it he could learn to relax EVEN FASTER! He was completely unaware that, in his attempts to modify his Type A behavior, he was generating more Type A behavior, reinforcing the very pattern that, at a cognitive level, he desperately wanted to change. He was even less aware of the underlying belief structure which formed the basis of this compulsive behavioral response.

In order to identify and change the source of his stress and hypertension Harold needed to access the content of his automatic, unconscious processes, internal mediators which were not ordinarily a part of his conscious awareness. By using AMR, he was able to do so, relieve his nausea, and substantially reduce his need for anti-hypertensive medication.

The impact of attitudes and beliefs on the progress of cancer has been explored by Achterberg, Matthews-Simonton, and Simonton (1976). They have shown that working with attitudes and beliefs can have a beneficial effect on the prognosis for cancer patients.

Thus, it is clear that the psychological makeup of the person, that is, both the conscious and unconscious components of personality, especially unconscious processes, have a strong effect on the way in which a stressor impacts on the individual. It then becomes apparent that, in order to work with physical illnesses which are stress-related, one needs a working model which addresses the functioning of unconscious processes and how they impact on human physiology.

There are many theories, ranging from magical to scientific, which attempt to describe the structure and function of unconscious processes. There is reasonable consensus that unconscious processes express their content metaphorically (Sandler, Holder, & Dare, 1973), and this concept is well accepted and documented in western psychiatric practice. The importance given to the interpretation of dreams and behavior as metaphorical representations of an unconscious process is common among psychotherapists, regardless of their preferred technologies. For example, for over a century, psychoanalytically oriented therapists have used dreams, behavior, and the techniques of free association as a "window" to the unconscious.

In this century the work of Dr. Milton Erickson has opened that window further, by recognizing and MAKING FULL USE of metaphor including dreams and behavior, and also symptoms and creative and imaginative processes as the language of unconscious processes, a language which is both expressive and receptive. Erickson differed from many of his predecessors in the field of medical hypnotherapy in that he viewed unconscious processes with profound respect and trust. He considered them to be powerful resources for learning, change, and survival, with intelligence and wisdom equal to or surpassing that of conscious processes. Using metaphors which were verbal, behavioral, and experiential, Erickson interacted directly with unconscious processes in their own language and often in ways that were not understood or even recognized at the conscious level. His use of metaphorical communication to affect change in behavior and even to affect physiological processes has been well documented and speaks for itself (Bandler & Grinder, 1975a; Erickson, 1980; Grinder & Bandler, 1981; Haley, 1973; Lankton & Lankton, 1983).

We present AMR to clients in a cognitive model which we have presented elsewhere (Hejmadi & Lyall, 1987a, 1987b). This model is based on: the work of Paul D. MacLean, M. D., Ph. D., and his concept of the Triune Brain (1969, 1978, 1985); Brown's structural theory of cognition (1977); and the principles of the logic of the unconscious processes, articulated as, "magical laws," by Ahsen (Sheikh, 1978, p.204).

This frame is presented to clients in individual therapy sessions and in a self-help class. The self-help class includes information on AMR, NLP, and information from the stress research literature. We have observed that the class itself is a therapeutic modality, which has been confirmed by outcome data taken over a year for those who took the class (Hejmadi & Lyall, 1986).

Our work is based on the material that has been presented in this section and extends it into a pattern of intervention that we call Autogenic Metaphor Resolution. Using a symptom as a focal point, one can generate metaphors which are perceived as pictures, like a dream, or thoughts, perhaps as a series of words. These metaphors can then be explored interactively, and have proven to be rich and accurate sources of information regarding the specific conflict(s) underlying the symptoms. Some general considerations will be presented next and then the process will be detailed.

GENERAL CONDITIONS

The material that is presented in this section provides a clinical framework for the approach that we use. We believe that the generalizations and assumptions are of sufficient importance to explain them before detailing the process. Some of the principles stated here have been articulated by clinicians elsewhere and we will describe how we apply them.

When working with a physical illness, it is essential to respect the part that the symptom or illness plays in the "ecological system" or the "world" of the client. As has been noted by many other clinicians, the individual who is "cured" of back pain only to develop a gastric ulcer is an example of one whose ecological integrity needs more attention.

Thus, it is essential to elicit appropriate information regarding the client's general life-style in terms of internal and external mediators, any important events or changes which occurred within twelve to twenty-four months prior to the onset of symptoms and sometimes, early developmental history.

We developed AMR as a way to proceed with work in small chunks, often completely conscious level, with built-in protection for the ecological system. We suggest that when a client generates a metaphor FROM THE SYMPTOM ITSELF, the metaphor will be a perfectly isomorphic representation of the situation generating the symptom and will be at a level of ambiguity that preserves the intent of the symptom as well as the integrity of the conscious mind. It has been our consistent observation that when such a metaphor is processed successfully to closure or resolution the client experiences dramatic and immediate symptomatic relief. Clients who work through an autogenic metaphor to closure generally maintain their post-treatment level of comfort and often experience increasing levels of comfort over the 24–72 hours following treatment. It is common for cases of acute cervical myositis to require only one or two AMR treatments to achieve complete resolution, whereas four to eight weeks of treatment are needed using traditional physical and medical modalities.

In addition, symptomatic relief is often accompanied by a parallel change in the client's unconsciously generated behavior; for example, clients report changes such as, "I really seem to react differently to my children," or, "I just realized that I haven't been worried for almost a week," or, more dramatically, "I noticed that I stopped and looked both ways before crossing the street. Usually before, someone always put an arm out to stop me." These changes are frequently reported with surprise that change could occur without conscious effort. Occasionally, changes have also been reported in posture, voice pitch, tonality, and even visual acuity.

We have observed that these changes in unconsciously generated behavior (including symptom relief) frequently occur in the absence of cognitive understanding of the content of the work. Indeed this has been so common in our experience that we have concluded that conscious, cognitive understanding is often irrelevant to certain outcomes of treatment. This is especially true in the initial stages of treatment, or when an individual is treated just once or twice. If a client does not understand the content of the work, there can be no discounting or arguing with the outcome; instead, clients develop a sense of curiosity and respect with regard to their unconscious processes. Therefore we generally invite a degree of amnesia or mystification and have frequently observed clients who have no conscious memory of a piece of work just completed. They simply realize suddenly that 45 minutes have passed and their pain is gone. Of course in later stages of treatment it is often essential for the client to gain the degree of understanding necessary to adjust his/her life style so that illness does not have to be part of it.

We insist on making no attempts to explain or interpret the work, beyond reassuring the client that it is all right to be mystified or not to remember or understand at the conscious level, and that this serves an immediate purpose in working toward an ultimate, more complete understanding. In addition to maintaining the ecological frame constructed by the client's unconscious process, this rule also helps the therapist to overcome the temptation to impose his or her meaning of the work, which might not fit with the intent of the metaphor.

Clients under treatment for physical illness must be under the primary care of a physician, and the starting point of our work is to review the medical history/findings. In addition we assume, when a symptom is accessible and responsive to work at a "psychological" level, that the possibility of structural, physiological, or metabolic damage is nevertheless a real one.

We view all symptoms as indications or expressions of a situation in need of resolution. We have observed that the structural, psychological, and physiological/metabolic components of these situations coexist in physical illness and often interact in extremely subtle and powerful ways, demonstrated by the following two examples:

1. A young woman had intractable back pain several years after her third spinal operation, a vertebral fusion. She was understandably depressed. Her physicians did not want to risk another, possibly unnecessary, surgical procedure, and hinted that the pain might be psychogenic. X-ray findings were inconclusive. Her pain was relieved to a tolerable level by massage and metaphor work. However, her metaphors did not resolve completely, and they consistently expressed content such as, "I need to be fixed;" "You are playing with fire;" and "I am in danger." Based on this information she continued to seek surgical interventions, and finally located a surgeon who agreed to do exploratory surgery. Surgery revealed that her vertebral fusion had broken in three places.

2. A woman, nearly seven months pregnant, was grieving the sudden death of her oldest daughter. Shortly after this traumatic event she experienced a, "strange feeling of movement" in her uterus, and a fear that the baby was in danger. The autogenic metaphor technique accessed a poignant auditory metaphor: "What is the use of bringing a child into such a dangerous world, where I can invest eleven years of love and energy and she can be gone in the wink of an eyelash? It would be so much easier just to withdraw support right now." The part of her that made this communication was offered empathy and comfort, and the suggestion was made that each life deserves its own chance to make it in the world. It was also suggested that, "withdrawing support right now," would mean that she would have to grieve the loss of two children instead of one.

There was a visible physiological shift in response to these suggestions, including changes in muscle tone, skin temperature and color, lacrimation, and increased depth or respiration. The client reported that her anxiety was relieved and that, "the danger seems to have receded." Three weeks later, this client developed sudden eclampsia with convulsions, and the baby, five weeks premature, was delivered by emergency Caesarean section. A blood clot the size of an orange was found under the placenta: withdrawal of support had begun to take place but had not progressed to completion. The baby was born strong and healthy and has to date shown no sign of damage from her prenatal stress.

During the work of recovery from a long-standing physical illness, some clients achieve an awareness of a profound conflict which is related to survival. Even with the ecological safeguards inherent in the process of autogenic metaphor work, this awareness may precipitate a crisis or a time of undeniable danger during which protection and the immediate support and availability of the therapist are essential. We have seen such crises expressed in acute anxiety or depression, suicidal or prepsychotic ideation, and, in one case, a brief psychotic episode. The severity of these crises has been related to three factors:

1. duration of the symptom or illness prior to treatment;
2. severity of the illness or symptom in terms of life threat or pain; and
3. instability of lifestyle in terms of structure, support, and nurturance.

Thus, severity of a crisis can often be anticipated and a foundation laid for its successful resolution early in treatment, or a choice may be made against proceeding with treatment on this basis. In some cases, we have chosen not to work with clients who could not or would not structure their daily lifestyle to include stability, support, and physical nurturance.

Crisis itself must be welcomed as a time of choice for the client, i.e., a time when he or she can choose either to resolve the newly identified conflict and achieve a new and healthier balance, or to return to the old balance which was provided by the symptom. It must be emphasized that the client's AWARENESS is the only thing that is new; conflict has been present all along but expressed in a different way. It is awareness which provides the client with choice as to outcome. Any choice made by the client, including the choice to sacrifice awareness, must by respected as valid. The following examples illustrate different outcomes of these interesting choice points:

1. Kate was a 60-year-old woman with multiple sclerosis who had been stable and wheelchair-dependent for ten years. She was experiencing severe neuritis in both lower legs, requiring large doses of pain medication which left her so "dopey" that she could not concentrate to read. Most of her time was spent sleeping off medications. At the point in her treatment when she subjectively reported being pain-free, she began to experience acute anxiety, suicidal thoughts, confusion, and feared that she was losing her mind.

We presented options in terms of the positive intent of her physical pain, which may have been to protect her from experiencing this level of emotional pain and despair. Given the option of working through this crisis to resolution, Kate decided that the physical pain was easier to deal with and chose to keep it. Her pain did indeed return, at a diminished level, but with a very great difference: she now recognized the pain in her legs as an ally, the protector of her sanity. She no longer cared to fight it with drugs. She tapered off medication, and resumed an active social life, attending church, and enrolling in classes at the local community college.

2. Lil was a twenty-five-year-old college student with intractable back and leg pain which radiated to her foot. Her pain had begun when she left home at the age of eighteen. She learned skills which allowed her to be pain-free, then began to experience feelings of depersonalization, intense anxiety, inability to concentrate, and a brief period of semicatatonia. We presented options to her in terms of inviting the pain to return, hospitalization, or intensive outpatient work to resolve the crisis. She chose the latter, and was able to successfully work through this episode over the next three to four weeks. During this time we insisted that she contact us by phone several times daily to assure her safety, and see us on alternate days. She was able to complete her college semester without dropping out and graduated shortly after this episode. One year later she remained pain-free and has had no recurrence of psychotic symptoms. She has been self-supporting and reports that she is both content and excited with her life and future.

These two clients made dramatically different choices when faced with a crisis, and the outcome for each was favorable. We believe that no one has enough information to make such a choice except the conscious and unconscious parts of the individual involved. Should we experience disappointment with a client's decision, our firm rule has been not to interfere. If a client NOTICES our disappointment, we explain it in terms such as, "Well, I have this arrogant part of me who thinks she knows what's best for people better than they do." A final word of caution: before using the methods described in this paper with clients it is essential that an individual first learn to apply them successfully with his or her own physiological processes. This is a precaution that is recommended by teachers of many therapeutic modalities so that the methods can be used safely and effectively. For example psychoanalysts are required to undergo the process before using it. With the above principles and considerations firmly in mind, we proceed to a description of the method used with clients whose cases are discussed later in this document.

DESCRIPTION OF METHOD

Metaphors may be accessed either through verbal suggestions or a combination of touch and verbal suggestion. We found the latter to be the easiest accessing technique for symptoms which are accessible to touch, such as myofacial or joint pain, extremity pain, and headache pain. Generating metaphors without touch, using only verbal suggestions, is useful with deep visceral symptoms which are not superficially accessible, such as symptoms of colitis, endometriosis, or angina. This method is more subject to the client's conscious defenses, and is therefore more challenging to the skill and patience of a therapist attempting to facilitate a successful resolution. A step-by-step description of accessing and working with metaphors using touch and verbal suggestions follows:

1. Establishing rapport at the conscious level.
2. Induce a relaxed or altered state of awareness.
3. Locate a trigger point (Travell and Simons, 1983), or a point of increased sensitivity to pressure, with gentle massage/palpation.
4. We then watch for some palpable or observable physiological change to occur in the area, which indicates rapport with the client at an unconscious, physiological level. Changes in muscle tone, skin temperature or color, involuntary muscle twitches, peristaltic sounds, "gooseflesh," lacrimation, and breathing are some of the possible indications of rapport at this level. This step is essential to any further progress, and is sometimes difficult to achieve. We have found Ericksonian Hypnotherapy and NLP to be extremely powerful allies in this process.
5. Once physiological rapport has been established, we suggest that with the next breath the client access a metaphor (pictures, words, or feeling) that will give more information about this part of the body and its needs. Whatever is accessed is assumed to be a direct communication from the part in charge of the symptom. Admittedly, this is a grandiose assumption, not subject to proof, and may be a lie. After several years of work based on this hypothesis, however, our observations of empirical data and outcomes tend to support it. Whether objectively "true" or not, the process works as if this were the case.
6. Process the metaphor. There is obviously no set formula for processing, and one must be guided by the experience of the client. We have used NLP technology extensively, particularly reframing (Bandler & Grinder, 1982; Dilts, Grinder, Bandler, Bandler and DeLozier, 1980), the trauma/phobia procedure (Bandler, 1984), and collapsing anchors (Cameron-Bandler, 1985; Bandler & Grinder, 1982; Dilts, et. al., 1980). The minimum processing requirements are to greet the metaphor in a friendly and respectful way, to determine its need or intent, and to satisfy it WITHIN THE CONTEXT OF THE METAPHOR. For example, if the accessed picture is of a dry, wilting plant, we suggest that the client water it. Then we would set up a way for the plant to receive a continuous supply of nourishment automatically, such as an automatic sprinkler system, transplanting it to a richer environment, or finding a special caretaker who will agree to take responsibility for meeting the plant's needs. It is

sometimes useful to establish a yes/no signal with the metaphor in order to know how to proceed. For example, if a picture of a turtle is accessed visually, we will first ask if it can speak. If it cannot, a yes/no signal could be established with head-nods, tail movements, or withdrawal to its shell.

Occasionally a client will not be able to identify a metaphor immediately, stating that they see "nothing" or "blackness." In such cases, we greet the "nothing" and elicit information about its size, color, texture, weight, density. When we have ascertained that it is a huge, blue, quiet, opaque, soft, solid, pliable nothing, we might ask questions such as, "what will this nothing look like when it is completely satisfied?" This information can then provide feedback for further processing.

Since this process relies on imaginative and creative processes, literally anything may be generated, and content may be manipulated in infinitely variable ways until feedback from the client indicates that the work is complete. Our direction and emphasis is always toward respect and appreciation, meeting needs, and identifying and serving the positive intent of information which is accessed. Feedback from the client, both verbal and non-verbal, will generally make it clear when a metaphor has been satisfactorily resolved or that enough processing has taken place at a given session. It is not unusual to continue processing the same metaphor over a series of therapy sessions before resolution is complete. Occasionally a client will be unable to generate a metaphor or the metaphor resists resolution. In our experience, this has been indicative of three possibilities:

1. Our rapport with the client at a conscious or unconscious level needs to be improved;
2. There is structural or metabolic damage which needs repair; or
3. This step is not appropriate for the client in his/her world at that time, or secondary gain is an issue that must first be addressed. For example, a woman with severe neck pain could not generate a metaphor. Questioning revealed that her husband was planning to divorce her as soon as she was well and no longer needed his medical insurance. She was not ready to let go of the marriage and did not have the resources to replace those provided in her marriage.

The preceding is a general description of the structure of AMR work and some of the precautions necessary in its application.

The following section includes discussions and some transcripts of three cases in which AMR was used successfully to reduce or eliminate chronic pain from various sources. In these case studies, the metaphors were accessed through touch and verbal suggestion. Cases are presented of rheumatoid arthritis and of myofacial pain.

EXAMPLES OF RHEUMATOID ARTHRITIS:
Clinical Data

The client is a woman in her fifties, who, when first seen, had suffered from rheumatoid arthritis for about 17 years. She also had other serious medical problems. She was in constant, fairly severe pain. She was living alone in her own home, barely able to walk with a specially adapted walker, and at times unable to get out of a chair. She stated that she was "going downhill" rapidly and was afraid of having to enter a nursing home if her deterioration continued. She had experienced a number of tragic losses but maintained a cheerful outlook and said that she had, "peace of mind." She is a strong, intelligent, creative woman with an active, inquiring mind and an adventurous spirit. These qualities were extremely important in therapy, allowing her to persevere where others might have quit, or never begun.

She worked with us once a week for about a year and a half. After the first weeks she was able to remain fairly comfortable and began to regain her physical strength. At the time her treatment was terminated she was able to walk confidently with her walker, drive her car, work part-time, and get up from her chair on the first try.

The following three transcripts are typical examples of the process of Autogenic Metaphor Resolution, which we used consistently with this client. They have been moderately condensed to avoid repetition.

Case 1—Shoulder Pain

After induction of a relaxed state, the client was instructed to "breathe into" a localized tender area in her shoulder which had been located by massage. She could barely tolerate even slight pressure over this area. It was then suggested that, as she breathed the next time, she could "let a picture or thought float up into your mind's eye that will give us more information about this spot in your shoulder." Continuous, gentle massage contact with the tender area was maintained throughout the work. The following is a reconstruction of what followed:

Client: Oh, I see a stump. It's a stump of a very old tree, and it's rotten in the middle.
Therapist: Greet the stump and see how it responds.
Client: Hello stump . . . it didn't do anything.
Therapist: How close are you to the stump?
Client: Across the room.
Therapist: Move closer if you can . . . walk right up to it.
Client: OK, I am right next to it now . . . Oh! Gosh! It's all full of worms! Oh! Yech!
Therapist: Worms . . . are they alive?
Client: Yes . . . They are all squirming around inside the stump . . . Blechh! Ugh!
Therapist: You don't find them beautiful?
Client: Beautiful?! No! They are ugly!! Ugh! Worms!
Therapist: Look at them again. My prejudice tells me that every living thing has its own unique beauty. See if you can find the worm's beauty.
Client: They're just a bunch of worms. Ugh!
Therapist: Focus your eyes a little differently.

Client:	They just look repulsive and horrible.
Therapist:	Well, let's take just one of them. The one that's closest to the edge of the stump. Look closely at him. Does he think he is ugly?
Client:	Well . . . no, he says he knows he is beautiful and it doesn't matter what anyone else thinks. He's just doing his thing here with his brothers, chewing up this old stump . . .
Therapist:	So he is doing an important job?
Client:	They are like . . . They are eating up the old stump . . . grinding it up . . . there is a real sense of purpose and importance.
Therapist:	As they chew up the stump, and grind it up, are they recycling it so that it becomes part of the earth again . . . maybe a bed for new trees?
Client:	Yes, that's it . . . and the worm says he needs to get to work. He really loves his work
Therapist:	Tell him thank you for taking the time to talk with us.
Client:	Thank you, worm . . . Oh! he kind of shrugged himself. Now he's back chewing again.
Therapist:	There is wonderful diligence and order in these worms and their work (she is nodding), a real . . .
Client:	A real beauty . . . there really is . . . I couldn't see it before.
Therapist:	Take a few minutes now to fully appreciate the beauty of these worms and what they are doing for us . . . preparing the ground for new growth . . . taking a dead stump and making it a cradle for new life . . . Appreciate the beauty of this process . . . and of the worms who are making it possible . . . (client sighed deeply at this point) . . . that's right . . . and let this appreciation reach the worms, as they continue to do their work . . . and when all the worms know that they are appreciated . . .
Client:	My shoulder . . . it doesn't hurt anymore . . .

At this juncture, the tender area on her shoulder was again palpated with firm pressure, which had caused severe pain prior to the work. The client reported that it did not hurt at all.

Case 2—Leg Pain

The client was experiencing severe pain in her knee and upper calf. Again, after an altered state was induced, a tender area was located which was extremely sensitive to even very gentle pressure. Using the same suggestion as before the following metaphor was accessed:

Client:	It's just a lot of confusion . . .
Therapist:	What does the confusion look like?
Client:	I don't know, its just moving so fast.
Therapist:	Say hello to the confusion and thank it for revealing itself.

Client: Hello . . . it slowed down a little when I said hello. It's lots of little circles all spinning out of control.

Therapist: Thank them for slowing down so that you can see them.

Client: They slowed down a little more when I thanked them. I think they are surprised that I noticed them . . . they are so wild and confused.

Therapist: What do they need?

Client: They don't know where they belong. They are all racing around, trying to find a place . . .

Therapist: Poor things . . . I wonder . . . could you tell them that they are all welcome in your body, and that you have a special place for each one, and that you invite them to rest and be comfortable . . .

Client: (after a long silence during which a dramatic physiological shift occurred in her calf and knee, followed by a long sigh) They all slowed down and stopped, and then they just faded away into the background.

Therapist: Are they comfortable now?

Client: Oh, yes.

Therapist: And your leg? (I was pressing on the tender area with no response.)

Client: Why it feels GOOD! Isn't that just the funniest thing? I wonder what that was all about . . . What do you think it means?

Therapist: I don't know . . . it really doesn't matter. It's like one piece of a jig-saw puzzle that doesn't make much sense when you first see it all by itself, but later when you begin to see where it fits in with the rest of the pieces a pattern starts to take shape, and then each piece fits and its meaning is clear. The important thing right now is that your leg is comfortable. THAT tells us we're on the right track. If your leg is satisfied, I am too. It's OK not to know what it means.

Client: (Made a wry face, shook her head, then smiled) Well, OK . . . but I sure do wonder.

Therapist: That's OK too. It will keep you moving.

Case 3—Lower Back Pain

The client was experiencing pain in her lower back and left hip. After relaxation induction, a tender area was located. The most sensitive point was selected as a focus, and massage contact was maintained with the entire cluster during the metaphor work transcribed below.

Therapist: Breathe into this spot, and tell me what you see.

Client: I hear a fire . . . crackling . . .

Therapist: Do you see the fire?

Client: No . . . I feel the heat; I feel it burning . . . Oh, now

	I see it, too. It's a beautiful, roaring fire . . .
Therapist:	What kind of fire is it? Is it an angry fire?
Client:	No, I don't think so . . . No, it's more like . . . a party. It's having a good time, and there is music in it . . . there is singing.
Therapist:	What is the singing?
Client:	Hail, hail, the gang's all here.
Therapist:	Who is sitting around this fire with you?
Client:	It's . . . oh . . . oh . . . (She began to cry) . . . they're . . . all gone now . . . It's been so long . . .
Therapist:	That's right. Let your tears flow . . . gentle, healing tears . . . to quench the burning . . . to bring comfort . . .
Client:	The fire seems to be dying down now . . . there, it looks like it's out . . . just a little smoke . . . (She was breathing very deeply at this point, and was very relaxed. The tender area was no longer sensitive, and she did not react even to deep palpation in this area. Again, her pain was gone.)

COURSE OF TREATMENT

As treatment progressed we noticed that her metaphors seemed to converge on several different issues. Metaphors generated with low back pain were related to grief and loss; while those generated with shoulder and neck pain were related to the need to acknowledge her own beauty. Knee and calf pain consistently produced content related to permission to exist, particularly to exist comfortably. As the client worked toward resolution of these issues, she changed her responses to a number of painful situations in her daily life and her personal history.

She developed some interesting and complex on-going metaphors. One of these was a small bearded man who initially would not speak. He either stood with his arms akimbo, staring angrily at her (which meant "no" or "do something"), or he danced a jig (which meant "yes" or "right"). When he was satisfied that the piece of work was complete or resolved, he would dance off into the distance. This little man, or "the dwarf" as she called him, evolved into a wise and compassionate "guiding spirit" who insisted that she treat herself with nurturance and respect. He became a resource we could summon for help at an impasse or a difficult choice point in her therapy, literally her therapist within. He eventually did begin to speak, with great incisiveness and economy, always as an advocate for the client's growing sense of self assertion and entitlement. At one point he told her that she had to choose between comfort and "peace of mind," a concept which then meant discounting and suppressing deep, legitimate feelings, but which eventually came to mean acknowledging and resolving them.

SUMMARY

Three years after treatment was terminated, the client continues to be ambulatory, live in her own home, and do well, despite having sustained a complicated hip fracture in the interim. She has learned to apply some of these techniques independently, and can at times access information needed to resolve her physical symptoms. Structural damage from her disease process is no longer escalating. Damage from this process which occurred over many years is of course still present, yet she lives at a very high functional level despite it.

This case example illustrates the way in which AMR was used successfully to improve the condition of an individual suffering from rheumatoid arthritis. The next case examples illustrate how the same technique was applied in reducing myofacial pain where there was no apparent evidence of a disease process such as arthritis.

CASE EXAMPLES OF MYOFACIAL PAIN

Pain with Limitation of Movement Secondary to Traumatic Injury

The first case is that of a woman in her sixties who had been brutally attacked in her home by an intruder. She had been seriously injured in this attack, which had occurred two years prior to our work with her. She had moderate to severe pain in her left shoulder which radiated up into her neck and down into her arm, at times even affecting her hand. She had marked weakness of her arm and could not raise it past about 70 degrees. Her passive range of motion was limited to about 120 degrees of flexion, 90 degrees of abduction, 45 degrees of internal rotation and 10 degrees of external rotation. Normal range is 180 degrees for flexion and abduction and 90 degrees for internal and external rotation. She experienced severe pain at the limits of her range, and indeed her pain limited the amount of exercise she was able to tolerate. She had been receiving traditional physical therapy for several months and had made slow progress in improving her range of motion and strength; however, her pain had not responded to any of a number of treatment modalities which had been used with her.

Our first intervention was to induce a relaxed state during an ultrasound treatment. The client spontaneously began talking about the assault. After initially pacing the horror and pain she expressed, the context was gently shifted to the here-now time frame. A tonal anchor with the words "THAT time" was installed to refer to the assault. We then asked her to imagine herself a little older than she was, with her arm and shoulder again feeling whole and strong and comfortable. She was able to do this but said that she appeared to be about two years older than she was at the present time. The time period of two years was significant, since it had also been two years since the time of the assault. Metaphorically

speaking, time seemed to have "stopped" for her at the time she was attacked, and a part of her was still back there experiencing the pain of
that trauma.

We then asked her to "breathe into" her shoulder the information that
"THAT time" is over, the danger was past, and she survived it. Further,
we asked her to notice that she was now protecting herself in ways that
she had not known might be necessary at "THAT time." We then asked
her to breathe an awareness of safety and comfort into her shoulder, and
suggested that this would, "open up this shoulder on the inside, so that
all of your body's powers and resources for healing can be made available
to it in the best possible way." A profound physiological shift occurred
at this point. Our final intervention was to again ask her to picture herself
with her shoulder and arm again whole, strong, and well, and to notice
that each breath she took was bringing her closer and closer to that picture and farther and farther away from "THAT time." As "THAT time"
receded to a very tiny speck in the distance, she could come close enough
to her picture to reach out and touch it, and indeed to step right into
it and begin to experience those feelings of wholeness, strength, and
comfort.

The client emerged from this piece of work reporting dramatic, but
not complete relief of her pain. However, over the next few days her pain
continued to recede. At her next therapy appointment she said that her
arm and shoulder felt better than they had in years. She remained comfortable and was able to increase her exercise tolerance. Within three weeks
her range of motion had returned to normal and she was able to lift a
12 ounce weight over her head. She was discharged from therapy with
instructions for home exercises.

Myofacial Pain, Migraine

The second client was a woman in her thirties who was having severe
neck and shoulder pain with headaches, numbness in her face and scalp,
and loss of appetite. Her father, to whom she had been very close, had
died of cancer two years previously; and in the intervening years she had
experienced several stressful life changes. Her first symptoms of neck pain
had occurred within a few weeks of her father's diagnosis and had continued intermittently since then, dramatically escalating in intensity during the months just prior to her work with us.

Our first interventions with this client were aimed at establishing permission at the conscious level for processing her grief. She seemed open
to this, but had no idea how to proceed. We then worked directly with
her pain, using massage with autogenic metaphor work. With the pain
at the base of her skull she accessed only "blackness" which, as she greeted
it, became wood smoke. This client had ethical objections to burning
wood because it takes the life of the tree; she therefore initially refused
to greet the smoke, saying that the tree is dying and it has no choice.
She noticed that when she refused to greet the smoke, her neck became

tighter and her pain increased. She acknowledged feeling sad and angry that the wood was being burned and she was helpless to stop it. We then suggested that the smoke was the new form of the wood, whose life she had treasured.

Was it possible that she could still love it in its present state? She was then able to say hello to the wood and to express her sorrow at its being burned. As she tearfully told the smoke that she loved it, the smoke spontaneously enveloped her. She experienced it as being warm, soft, and comforting. We suggested that she fully experience the warmth and comfort that smoke held for her and allowed her several minutes of quiet processing time. When she emerged she was pain-free.

We suggested that, in the ensuing week, she allow herself time and space to cry if she needed to, and to "talk" to her father. When she returned the following week, she had had some recurrence of pain, but at a level which was much less than it had been. She had also been able to eat without forcing herself. The metaphors which she accessed through her pain at this session were entirely kinesthetic: "I can't see anything, but I am on a bicycle moving very fast. I can feel the wind on my face and feel the bumps in the road as I go over them." "Exploration" of the metaphor determined that she was safe in this somewhat surprising situation, because she was able to "feel" where she was going, and to perceive the terrain non-visually. She felt the presence of three pyramids off to her left. She had read about the "magical" energy attributed to pyramids, which made this a very powerful image for her. The pyramids agreed to be sources of energy, comfort, and nourishment, on which she could draw at any time. At the end of this session, she was again pain-free.

During the following week, she had a spontaneous metaphor experience while she was alone reading. She saw and felt herself rising through brilliant blue water laced with white bubbles, toward a circle of sunlight. As she approached the surface, she saw the sky, also brilliant blue; and as she broke the surface, she experienced something totally new for her: a joy that filled her entirely. She said, "I have felt comfortable, even peaceful, but never anything like this, so active and alive." She reported this at her next session with us, which proved to be her last. When we did a follow-up call six months later, she reported feeling better than she had at any time in her life. She reported no recurrence of her symptoms.

SUMMARY AND CONCLUSIONS

In this paper we present an approach for working with functional and stress-related illnesses. We begin by acknowledging the foundation laid by many researchers who have shown the connection between stress and physical illness. Their work also indicates that psychological stressors are of primary importance, and that if they are handled appropriately, the course of an illness can be influenced.

Stress management programs teach individuals to recognize the physiological signs of stress and to evoke the parasympathetic response, possible when stressors are within conscious awareness. The task is much more complicated if sources of stress are outside of awareness, such as unconscious beliefs, attitudes, and conflicts.

We have developed a way to identify and work with specific stressors, especially unconscious ones. Two approaches that profoundly influenced our work are Ericksonian Hypnotherapy and Neuro-Linguistic Programming. Use of metaphor is central to both approaches. We have developed a new way to utilize metaphors to impact human physiology. Our findings may be summarized as follows:

1. It is possible to access information about the unconscious content that is related to a symptom by working with the symptom itself. The information may be accessed by touch or through verbal interventions, but the latter process is more challenging.
2. This information is metaphorical and can be auditory, visual, kinesthetic, or, much less often, olfactory or gustatory in nature.
3. The metaphor is a perfect isomorphic representation of a situation that is related to the symptom, and is a more elegant and accurate representation of this situation than any conscious verbalization.
4. Resolution of the metaphor will lead toward resolution of the symptom.
5. It is important to pay attention to the part that the symptom or illness plays in the world of the individual, as has been noted in other therapeutic approaches.

Successful resolution of an individual's immediate physiological malfunction consistently occurs when the unconsciously generated beliefs, strategies, and behaviors which generate physiological stress are addressed and changed. However this does not mean that the client lives happily ever after. One always has the ability to generate symptoms and adverse physiological processes.

Our clients develop the ability to work with their symptoms to resolve the issues that generate them. Thus, a symptom may recur sometime after a course of AMR work, if stress occurs to reactivate it. However, the client will respond differently and more appropriately, frequently needing only minimal professional intervention. A typical comment, from a former sufferer with chronic neck pain: "I am so GRATEFUL to my neck for making sure that I dealt with all this!"

Our focus is on teaching individuals how to communicate with their bodies rather than on "cures." This is especially true in cases of medically recalcitrant conditions such as rheumatoid arthritis and multiple sclerosis. A major emphasis is on education, and we have developed a self-help class which incorporates our approach and information from the literature (Hejmadi, 1984).

We have applied this process in many cases of acute and chronic myofacial pain with excellent long-term outcomes. It has been used successfully with many stress-related illnesses including cases of allergies, colitis, endometriosis, migraine, and Raynaud's disease and even helped to stabilize cases of rheumatoid arthritis and multiple sclerosis. In all cases, we insist that our clients be under the primary care of a physician.

Our future work will focus on two areas. First, we will continue to develop AMR and incorporate any other method that will make the process more effective. Second, we will attempt to relate metaphors and their content to symptoms and illnesses.

For decades, Western medicine has observed the adverse effects of random environmental impact at the mind–body interface. We believe that AMR is a tool which can achieve specific and purposeful intervention at this level. If used appropriately, it is safe, non-invasive, and ecologically sound. In addition it has potential to be cost effective, since it is a skill which can be transmitted to most clients of normal intelligence, subsequently allowing the individual to access his or her unconscious processes independently, or with a minimal need for professional intervention. It also allows an individual to reliably determine when medical intervention is required, which facilitates the most efficient and economical use of the resources of the medical system. We do not consider AMR a substitute for or an alternative to good medical care. Instead we regard it as an additional tool which will render existing medical expertise and technology even more powerful in achieving and maintaining the physiological integrity of the human organism. As such, we believe that it has implications for Western systems of health care which are both obvious and profound.

ACKNOWLEDGEMENTS

We wish to acknowledge, in alphabetical order, the help given to us by the following:

Steve and Connirae Andreas for their teaching and support.

Charlotte Bretto, M. S., for her help in publishing this document.

Al Byers, Ph. D., for his support and his help in publishing this document.

Computing Services, University of Colorado, Colorado Springs, for providing computing/word processing services.

John Grinder, Ph. D., for his support and his help in publishing this document.

Janak Joshi, M.D., for his helpful comments.

Laura Smith, Ph. D., for her excellent constructive comments which helped clarify this presentation.

Gary Thrower, whose extensive help and advice with word processing made this document possible.

The authors appreciate:

My father, Vasudev Hejmadi, for his teachings, encouragement, and support, and to whose memory this publication is dedicated.

Support and encouragement from our families, Padma Perera, Sumana Chandavarkar, Rukma Hejmadi, and Virginia and Robert Lyall.

All of our friends for putting up with our obsessiveness while we wrote this document.

Our children, Ahalya and Shanta Hejmadi, and Charles Waller, for their support.

All of our clients for teaching us with their characteristic elegance.

REFERENCES

Achterberg, J., Simonton, O.C., & Mathews-Simonton, S. (1976). *Stress, Psychological Factors And Cancer.* Fort Worth, TX: New Medicine Press.

Bandler, R. (1984). *Magic In Action.* Cupertino, CA: Meta Publications.

Bandler, R., & Grinder, J. (1975a). *Patterns Of The Hypnotic Techniques Of Milton Erickson, M.D.* (Vol. 1). Cupertino, CA: Meta Publications.

Bandler, R. & Grinder, J. (1975b). *The Structure Of Magic* (Vols. 1-2). Palo Alto, CA: Science and Behavior Books.

Bandler, R. & Grinder, J. (1982). *Reframing,* S. Andreas & C. Andreas (Eds.) Moab, UT: Real People Press.

Brown, J. (1977). *Mind, Brain And Consciousness.* New York: Academic Press.

Burchield, S.R. (1979). *The Stress Response: A New Perspective. Psychosomatic Medicine,* 41, 661-672.

Cameron-Bandler, L. (1985). *Solutions.* San Rafael, CA. FuturePace, Inc.

Cannon, W.B. (1963). *The Wisdom Of The Body.* New York: W.W. Norton.

Dilts, R., Grinder, J., Bandler, R., Bandler, L.C., & Delozier, J. (1980). *Neuro-Linguistic Programming: The Structure Of Subjective Experience.* (Vol. 1). Cupertino, CA: Meta Publications.

Dohrenwend, B.N., & Dohrenwend, B.P. (1980). *What is a stressful life-event?* In H. Selye (Ed.), Selye's Guide To Stress Research (Vol. 1, pp.1-20). New York: Van Nostrand Reinhold.

Elliot, R.S., & Eisdorfer, C. (Eds). (1982). *Stress And Human Health: Analysis And Implications Of Research.* Study by the Institute of Medicine/National Academy of Sciences. New York: Springer.

Erickson, M.H. (1980). *The Collected Papers Of Milton H. Erickson On Hypnosis,* E.L. Rossi (Ed.). New York: Irvington.

Grinder, J., & Bandler, R. (1981). *Trance-formations: Neuro-Linguistic Programming And The Structure Of Hypnosis.* Moab, UT: Real People Press.

Haley, J. (1973). *Uncommon Therapy: The Psychiatric Techniques Of Milton Erickson, M.D.* New York: W.W. Norton.

Hejmadi, A.V., & Lyall, P.J. (1986). *Beyond stress management: Autogenic Metaphor Resolution.* Declared as the winner of the 1986 Annual Halos Award. In preparation for publication.

Hejmadi, A.V., & Lyall, P., (1987a, July/August). The mind-body reconnection. Part I—The Triune Brain: Implications for Holistic Practitioners. *Holistic Medicine,* p. 16.

Hejamdi, A.V., & Lyall, P.J. (1987b, August/September). The mind-body reconnection. Part II—Subcortical logic: In defense of magical thinking. *Holistic Medicine,* p. 8.

Holmes, T.H., & Rahe, R.H. (1967). The social readjustment rating scale. *Journal of Psychosomatic Research,* 11, 213-218.

Lankton, S.R., & Lankton, C. (1983). *The answer within: A clinical framework of Ericksonian Hypnotherapy.* New York: Brunner/Mazel.

Lazarus, R.S. (1966). *Psychological stress and the coping process.* New York: McGraw-Hill.

Lazarus, F.S. (1971). The concept of stress and disease. In L. Levi (Ed.), *Society, stress and disease: the psychosocial environment and psychosomatic diseases* (Vol. 1, pp. 53-58). London: Oxford Univ. Press.

Lazarus, R.S., Cohen, J.B., Folkman, S., Kanner, A. & Schaefer, C. (1980). Psychological stress and adaptation: some unresolved issues. In H. Selye (Ed.) *Selye's Guide to stress research* (Vol. 1, pp. 90-117). New York: Van Nostrand Reinhold.

MacLean, P.D. (1969). A triune concept of the brain and behavior. In T.J. Boag & D. Campbell (Eds.), *A triune concept of the brain and behavior.* Toronto, Ontario, Canada: University of Toronto Press.

MacLean, P.D. (1978). A mind of three minds: Educating the triune brain. *Seventy Seventh Yearbook of the National Society of Education,* 308-342 Chicago: University of Chicago.

MacLean, P.D. (1985). Brain evolution relating to family, play, and the separation call. *Archives of General Psychiatry,* 42, 405-417.

Mason, J.W. (1971). A reevaluation of the concept of non-specificity in stress theory. *Journal of Psychiatric Research,* 8, 323-333.

Mason, J.W. (1975). Emotion as reflected in patterns of endocrine regulation. In L. Levi (Ed.), *Emotions: their parameters and measurement.* (pp. 143-181). New York: Raven.

Mason, J.W., Maher, J.T., Hartley, L.H., Mougey, E., Perlow, M.J., & Jones, L.G. (1976). Selectivity of corticosteroid and catecholamine response to various natural stimuli. In G. Serban (Ed), *Psychopathology of human adaptation.* (pp. 1147-171). New York: Plenum.

Mettlin, C. (1976). Occupational careers and the prevention of coronary-prone behavior. *Social Science and Medicine,* 10, 376-372.

Pelletier, K.R. (1977). *Mind as healer, mind as slayer: A holistic approach to preventing stress disorders.* New York: Dell.

Rosenmann, R.H., Brand, R.J., Sholtz, R.I., & Friedman, M. (1976). Multi-variate prediction of coronary heart disease during 8.5 years follow-up in the Westem Collaborative Group Study. *American Journal of Cardiology,* 37, 903-910.

Rosenmann, R.H., & Friedman, M. (1983). Relationship of type A behavior pattern to coronary heart disease. In H. Selye (Ed.), *Selye's Guide to stress research* (Vol. 2, pp. 47-106). New York: Van Nostrand Reinhold.

Sandler, J., Dare, C., & Holder, A. (1973). *The patient and the analyst: The basis of the psychoanalytic process.* New York: International Universities Press.

Selye, H. (1936). A syndrome product by diverse nocuous agents. *Nature,* 138, 32.

Selye, H. (1946). The general adaptation syndrome and the diseases of adaptation. *Journal of Clinical Endocrinology,* 6, 117.

Sheikh; A.E. (1978). Eidetic Psychotherapy. In J.L. Singer & K.S. Pope (Eds.), The power of human imagination, (pp. 197-224). New York: Plenum Press.

Travell, J.G., & Simons, D.G. (1983). Myofacial pain and dysfunction: The trigger point manual. Baltimore. MD: Williams and Wilkins.

CHAPTER III

ARTISTRY AND NLP

Preface to
ARTISTRY AND NLP
by
Judith DeLozier

It is with pleasure that I write the framework for this section, Artistic Applications. It's a great freedom to be the one who sets up the looking glass through which to perceive these articles. The phrase, "artistic applications," in this case, has an interesting ambiguity. The context in which the NLP techniques were used, I believe to be artistic settings: a symphony, a choral rehearsal, and an author using an opening metaphor to capture the attention of his audience. I also believe the response of the authors to these various settings to be artistic. However this question of art in general is illusive to me, as it's easy to understand skill and the idea that with practice that skill may develop into craft; but when does the craft or set of skills develop into art? And what makes it artistic?

First, the idea of audience, as Malloy points out, certainly seems to be tightly tied to art. It's as if a craft or skill placed in a proper context becomes artistic (has artistic value relative to the perceiver that is). Thus the loop, remembering that artistic is a relational issue and not a characteristic applied to one side of a loop. So relationship is very strongly implied here with regard to what is artistic. Artistry cannot be evaluated without respect to context which always includes audience.

Secondly, as Gregory Bateson might say, for something to be truly artistic it must contain multi-representations or be multi-layered, a single surface structure but with many deep structures.

Thirdly, artists behave in such a fashion as to elicit a response of participation from their audience. Therefore, the painting, the dance, the novel, the music is the context in which we as witnesses are invited to join, to make a response, to choose one or more of these multi-representations.

There is another sense, perhaps more important, in which these particular applications are artistic and that is in each authors' ability to create a context by different means in which learning could occur, whether listening to a piece of music with a fuller sense of participation, upgrading the quality of a singing performance or developing strategies for writing by using your own internal, resources to your own best interest.

In all cases we are presented with the use of metaphor as a way of creating the context. In Diane Marshall's case she simply states the context, states the problem as she perceived it, and presents her response, a metaphor entitled "The Leap Frog Prince." As the reader, we may or may not perceive this story as artistic. However it's quite a different perspective as the reader of the metaphor and as the singer trying to prepare to give an optimal performance, so the metaphor is artistic relative to context. It worked in context. A higher level of performance quality was achieved.

In Michael Colgrass's case, we see the use of hypnotic principles applied in his "speaking" to the audience, and this monologue in conjunction with the different parts of the string quartet as a way of developing an understanding of the structure of the piece of music and the relationship of the piece to a historical context. Michael is bridging the gap between the musicians and the audience by literally instructing his audience in how to tune their neurology and train their attention in the art of listening, while covertly inducing states where they can actively participate in an artistic event and underlying this what is implied with respect to relationships, and the multi-layerng in representation that is achieved.

In Tom Malloy and Janus Daniel's case, we are presented with a final product of what the authors are trying to achieve in the development of a writing strategy. The product is "Mirror, Mirror," again a metaphor which sets a context for learning about certain internal processes which greatly enhance writing possibilities and some which may be critical to it. Malloy and Daniels develop the use of triple description and the use of second position in particular as important tools for writing.

What is extremely interesting in both the Colgrass and Malloy and Daniels cases is that we, the readers, are offered another level of learning as well. We are offered insights into the thinking processes by which the authors developed these learning contexts. Michael lets us know how he marked out various ideas with gestures, and used embedded commands on the concept of "the future pace" in developing the "deep listening" learning context. Malloy and Daniels not only offer a strategy for writing but give instruction and exercises on how the strategy can be applied and developed in the classroom. I found the qualities of artistry very apparent in these cases.

The ability to recognize, appreciate, and utilize relationship, with the understanding of enhancing learning in the artist audience loop and the ability to represent information in a multi-layered way so as to elicit active participation from the audience invites the audience to witness and participate in an artistic act. May you as well.

Reprinted with permission — Music Magazine Sept./Oct. 1982

Deep Listening

by Michael Colgrass

I have long been troubled by the lack of attentiveness of many listeners during concerts. Especially toward the beginning of a concert people tend to fidget and cough, rattle programs and even whisper to their partners. Although these mannerisms are irritating I realize that following a busy day many people have to overcome obstacles to get to a concert on time — finding a baby-sitter, rushing dinner, fighting traffic — and when they finally do get to their seats in the concert hall it may take them a while to settle down and concentrate. And I'm no different. More than once I've noticed at intermission that I'd been talking to myself for most of the first half of the concert instead of listening to the music!

So I asked myself if there might be a way to help listeners leave the cares and responsibilities of the world outside the concert hall and focus their attention on the music the moment the concert begins. My thoughts first turned to what people want from a concert. Some are music lovers, others like the social event, still others are curious and want to develop a new interest. The one thing common to all listeners in my experience is that they want to enter another world — one of fantasy and delight. Among the best compliments anyone can pay a performer or a piece of music is, "It was mesmerizing," or "I was transfixed." In short, listeners are seeking a form of altered state that will transport and rejuvenate them.

I have often talked to audiences prior to concerts, usually giving factual information about a work — pointing out themes, textures, orchestration, etc. — words that appeal to the conscious, logical mind. But the real power of music is beyond logic. What, then, if I attempted instead to invite listeners into my subconscious mind by describing what goes on when a composer is actually creating? In this state of mind a composer turns off the outside world and focuses his attention inward on his creative self — which I think may also be an ideal state for the listener to enjoy music.

A perfect opportunity to try this idea came my way last summer when Elyakim Taussig, Director of the Stratford Summer Music Festival, asked me to do something 'experimental' with the Orford String Quartet. These were informal morning concerts for small audiences and seemed perfect for this experiment. I planned a talk where I would actually go into a creative reverie on the spot, so to speak, for the listener to witness, with the hope that he would enter that netherland with me. To add the proper atmosphere we blackened the stage, elevated the Orford Quartet about three feet, covered the stage with black cloth to eliminate the visual reality of the stage floor, installed pin spotlights that would illuminate the hands and instruments of the players but only peripherally their faces, masked the windows so no sunlight could intrude and had the audience sitting at tables with candlelight. As the audience was filtering into the hall, the Ravel String Quartet in F Major — the only work on the program — was playing on a stereo unit extremely softly, almost like very quiet Muzak, intended to be unheard consciously.

The four players, wearing black, came onto the darkened stage one at a time (at approximately 1 minute intervals) while the audience was still arriving and settling down at the small tables. The effect of this one-by-one entrance of the musicians in half darkness onstage was that the audience gradually became quiet *before* the house lights were turned down and were already watching the stage in anticipation. Then the house lights went down and a spotlight came up on me, sitting casually on the steps leading to the stage. I introduced myself, welcomed the audience, and began talking informally about what it feels like to compose music — a kind of stream-of-consciousness report of a journey into a composer's mind. I invited the listeners to follow my subjective moods as I described them with the idea that they might thereby empathize with me and be able to "feel the way Ravel felt when he composed his String Quartet."

To ensure that the audience's attention was properly paced for the entire four movements of this 25-minute work, short sections of each movement were played very softly by the Orford while I talked about what each movement felt or looked like to me as a listener: the 1st movement was associated with the idea of "going inside oneself," the 2nd "becoming like a child again," the 3rd "being creative in an individual way," and the 4th "returning again to every day life." We had a special lighting for each of these movements — yellow for childhood, blue for creative, etc. — to make a visual association with my descriptions and the music. After we had sampled the four movements in brief, I invited the audience to "enjoy just sitting back and hearing and feeling the music the way Ravel did when writing it . . . just like a time when you created something that was really your own." The spot faded on me and the Quartet played the entire Ravel non-stop. This introduction lasted perhaps 14–15 minutes.

The audience was inordinately quiet and still during both our introduction and the performance and, at the end, applauded the Quartet enthusiastically (the idea had been built into the 4th movement that they "return again to everyday life"). From all the reports we heard, the reactions to this whole presentation were anything but neutral. Of the critics present at the five days of performances, three were very favorable and one hated it. Among audience members the senior citizens seemed especially pleased with this format and one man, who returned for several performances, said "I felt I didn't have to understand the music to enjoy it." On the other hand, a younger woman approached me angrily and claimed she came to concerts to *see* the musicians and was upset because their faces were unlit. I sympathized with her desire to enjoy the visual aspect of a concert and pointed out that at least their hands and instruments had been lit, and she said, "No they weren't, I couldn't see anything!" I was puzzled by this remark and mentioned to a friend that this was one listener with whom we'd failed. "On the contrary," he said, "she was obviously listening so deeply she'd blocked out the image of the musicians. Probably a first for her."

Many people have had no musical education whatsoever and yet are, I am convinced, wholly capable of enjoying music. And I have met scholars who sometimes became so involved in the analysis of music that they forget how to enjoy it. What is the best way to enjoy music? I have no ready answers, but one thing this 'deep listening' experience demonstrated was that listening — like composing — requires a special frame of mind, regardless of music education. What that frame of mind is and how to achieve it is the question. Arnold Schoenberg said that a composer's best music comes to him "as in a dream." If this experiment in Stratford was any indication, that state may also be the best one to be in when listening.

Notes On The
Deep Listening Script
by Michael Colgrass

Students of Neuro-Linguistic Programming will recognize that Ericksonian techniques were used in this audience induction. I first encountered these linguistic approaches to hypnosis from the book "Patterns of the Hypnotic Techniques of Milton H. Erickson, M.D.," by Bandler and Grinder, and later refined my understanding of them in workshops with John Grinder.

I'd like to point out one example from this induction that demonstrates the power of metaphor. As I mentioned in the *Deep Listening* article, since the Ravel *Quartet* has four movements and four distinct moods, I decided to establish a loop for those four sections at the unconscious level. The prime goal of course is to create in the listener's mind the idea of going into, and then out of, a deep listening state. I had researched the audience of Stratford music concerts and found that many were senior citizens. It occurred to me that they would remember the days when, as kids, they gathered after school at the local drugstore for an after-school snack. This is where I got the idea of the milkshake metaphor. Notice the line starting with "He'd put it together in his own special way. . .", and ending with "and he'd come back." These eight lines I read with a voice tone that suggested going into (voice going deeper), and coming out of (voice getting higher), an experience. I accompanied that verbal pacing on the visual level, leading the listener's representational systems with hand gestures (to my lower left for their kinesthetic, to my upper right for their recalled images). Important to me here was to associate Marek's ability to taste the milkshake by its *sound*, and to associate the word *sound* with the word *masterpiece.* Many listeners commented afterward how the memory of watching and listening to a milkshake being made took them back to their childhood, and the critic in *The London Free Press* commented, "Even if Mr. Marek and the drugstore with the thick milkshakes seem at first to be remote from the business at hand, it does create a mood."

Using a metaphor to reinforce a loop was only one of many techniques I used in this script, which also included myriad embedded commands (in italics); phonological ambiguities (hear for here and daze for days); and many word patterns and suggestions characteristic of what has come to be known in NLP as the Milton Model.

♩=63

and you

may re-call a time　　when you cre-

a-ted something　　that was

real-ly your own

may-be it was just　a little thing

but it was yours　　and it

feels　　good

does-n't it?

Sample in the composer's hand of the rhythmic notation used to read portions of the DEEP LISTENING script.

*DEEP LISTENING SCRIPT
by
Michael Colgrass

(COME ON STAGE WITH A COFFEE CUP, SIT DOWN ON
STOOL, PLACE CUP DOWN. TAKE OFF JACKET AND HANG
IT ON THE BACKREST OF THE STOOL, TAKE A LAST SIP
OF THE COFFEE, TAKE A BREATH AND LOOK AROUND
PLEASANTLY AT THE AUDIENCE, THEN SPEAK:)

It's really nice . . . to be able to
make yourself comfortable.
Good morning. I'm Michael Colgrass.
I'm a composer, and I like to meet *listeners* . . .
like you . . . and say a few things that might help you . . .
enjoy music in a new way . . . perhaps to . . .
listen the way a composer listens . . . because
when we listen . . . we
feel the music deep inside . . . imagine . . . you can
have that experience n o w . . .

And . . . I have a *special* reason for
wanting to do that with you . . .
hear today . . . in Stratford . . . because
Stratford is very much like Brookfield,
a small rural town outside Chicago, where
I was born and spent my . . .
childhood daze . . .
some of you are from small towns . . . others not . . . and
all of you . . . know the feeling . . . of going . . .
back home . . . so, talking to you is like
going back in time . . . and experiencing old friends.

A short while back, I visited Brookfield, and
I went downtown to Main Street . . .
which looks much like Downey Street here, where . . .
(pointing to the entrance)
you just entered the hall . . . and . . .
I went into Marek's drug store, a favorite hangout when
(conspiratorially) *we* were kids . . . and

*Copyright © 1981 by Michael Colgrass. Used by permission.

(with a sense of wonder) Mr. Marek was
s t i l l there . . . and
when I told him who I was, he said
(good-natured, gruff, midwestern voice) "Well,
Buddy Colgrass . . ." — that was *my* nickname when
I was a kid —
"I remember when you used to come in here
and ask for a milkshake . . . double thick . . .
so the straw would stand up in it . . . *remember?*"
And *I remembered.*
His milkshakes were . . . a *masterpiece.*
He'd put it together in his own special way,
and then place it in the mixer, push the button and
hum a tune.
And (low voice, downward circular gesture with left hand)
he was in another world . . .
when the tune was finished the shake was done
(voice rising, upward circular gesture with right hand)
and he'd come back!
Ya' know . . . I believe he could *taste* the milkshake . . .
by the *s o u n d* . . .

So we talked a while and he said,
"Ya' know, to me writing music is . . . (lower voice)
a *mystery* . . . (keeping voice down) How do you do it?
Do you hear a melody . . . or do you
(voice rising) *see* a sunset and (high voice)
get inspired!"

I had to stop and really (voice down)
go inside . . . and answer that question . . . and
I didn't know what to tell *him then* . . .
but I had a chance to . . .
think a lot about it . . . in the meantime . . . and
I can tell *you n o w* . . . I think the best way to
understand what tran-s p i r e s in a composer's mind
when he hears music . . . maybe for you to . . . (voice down)
go into that state yourself . . . imagine . . . if you could
feel now . . . the way Ravel felt . . .
back then . . . when he wrote his string quartet . . . and
be that creative right now . . .

(lighting down to 6)

I've watched composers, and when they're composing
they have many ways to . . .

go into that creative state of mind . . .
some sing out loud . . . others hum softly, or . . .
not at all . . . one might move, or talk while composing . . .
another might sit in a favorite chair, and . . .
be a b s o l u t e l y s t i l l . . .
sometimes . . . you compose with your eyes open . . . other times
you may wish to close your eyes . . .
the one secret . . . common to all composers . . .
or anybody, creating anything . . . is that you . . . (voice down)
go deep inside yourself . . . (child-like voice)
become like a child again . . . (voice going down) then . . .
capture those images and feelings that are really important . . .
and . . . when you're finished . . . (voice going up)
return to your every day life, renewed.
This journey into yourself may seem long . . . or,
it may happen in a few moments . . .

I wonder how . . .
many of you have already had this experience . . .
where you . . . *go into a daydream . . .* and
you might be with someone and they're talking . . .
and you don't hear a word . . .
you're a thousand miles away . . .
you might be out in public . . . but . . .
the creative you . . . is somewhere else . . .
even now . . . you know how to do it . . .
you've done it . . . over and over . . .

(lighting down to 5)

When I go into that state . . . I *sit back* . . . (inhale deeply)
take a deep breath . . . and . . . (exhale)
just look around . . . and notice . . . the colors . . . and
the shadows . . . the lighting . . . the changing
focus of your eyes . . . *as they fall* . . . on
certain objects around you . . . and people . . . and the
feeling of the chair . . . the *smell* of the *air* . . . and maybe
your eyes fix on something unimportant . . . for *no reason . . .*
just . . . to rest . . . and you . . . *go into a reverie . . .*
it's interesting . . . is it not . . . and you may . . .
notice your breathing . . . changing . . . and your pulse . . . and you
know no reason . . . (closing eyes) to do or say anything . . .
sitting in the chair . . . balanced and comfortable . . . and as you . . .
listen to my voice . . . and . . . *let the sounds-around you . . .*
your comfort can increase . . . and you can just . . .

(inhale and exhale) *let everything go* . . . and
know your creative part . . . is ready . . . to
listen . . . and enjoy . . . the feeling . . . comfort . . . and
you may . . . *recall a time* . . . where *you*
created something . . . that was
really your own . . .

(MUSIC CUE I: portion of Ravel Quartet, 1st movement:
5-6 seconds, then continue talking over music)

Maybe it was just a little thing . . . but it was yours . . . and
it feels good . . . doesn't it? (5-10 seconds music) And you
may be getting that feeling *now* . . . and you can wonder . . . when you
hear the sound . . . or *feel* the sound . . . I knew someone once who
could s e e sound. . .

(MUSIC FADES)

. . . and sometimes . . . music has a child-like quality . . . what a
treasure . . . to be able to . . . *go back* . . . and . . .
be a child again . . . whenever . . .
you really want to . . . so free . . . to *have fun* . . . and . . .
be any way you wish . . .

(MUSIC CUE II: portion second movement)

as a child . . . you *see and hear the world* . . . in a
new way . . . all the different ways . . . and you can . . .
bend over and look through your legs . . . and . . .
see a completely different view of the world
. . . and . . . you really e n j o y it . . .

(MUSIC FADES)

and you may *recall an incident* . . . later in your life . . .
that was important . . . to *you* . . . it may have been pleasant . . .
or otherwise . . . and you will always remember it . . . because you
learn something . . . that's *true* . . . for you . . .

(MUSIC CUE III: portion third movement)

and you really . . . *know for the first time* . . . how you
feel about . . . certain things . . . and people . . . and *you may*
hear . . . or *see* . . . those thoughts *in your mind right now* . . .
perhaps . . . in a *new* way . . . it can be your own personal
discovery . . . *a s e c r e t* . . . that you may . . . or may not
choose to share . . . it all belongs to you . . .

(MUSIC FADES)

. . . and . . . at a certain point . . . it will be time to return . . . and you'll be finished with that reverie . . . for awhile . . .
not too fast now . . . there's time . . . whenever you're ready . . .

(MUSIC CUE IV: portion fourth movement)

. . . and gradually . . . (voice rising) you can . . .
return to your everyday thoughts and feeling . . . completely
refreshed . . . and you . . . *see how easy it is*

. . . you *know* how to do it . . . you always have . . . and you each . . .
do it in your own unique way . . . and *e n j o y* it . . . and
whenever you wish . . . you can . . . *go back into that special state* . . .
and *know your creative part* . . . is ready to listen . . .
like that time . . . when you . . . *make something* . . . that is
r e a l l y your own . . .

(MUSIC FADES WITH LAST WORDS, LIGHTS DOWN, THEN UP AGAIN WITH FIRST MOVEMENT LIGHTING, AND COMPLETE PERFORMANCE OF RAVEL QUARTET BEGINS)

Reprinted with permission — The Toronto Star Syndicate — Aug. 27, 1981

Deep Listening Reaches Stratford

by William Littler

STRATFORD—If the movies have Deep Throat and the linguists deep structure, maybe it's time music involved deep listening.

But how do we listen deeply? By feeling the music deep inside ourselves, Michael Colgrass argued in City Hall Auditorium yesterday.

Colgrass, a Pulitzer Prize-winning American composer, now a resident of Toronto, had come to the Stratford Summer Music Festival to preside over an unusual kind of concert. He didn't play anything. He didn't compose anything for the occasion either. Rather, he sat on the steps leading up to the stage of the darkened auditorium and talked.

He talked about Brookfield, Ill., and double thick milkshakes, about how a composer feels music and how, if we are to understand him, we have to enter into his state of mind. He spoke very calmly and deliberately, almost like a psychiatrist dangling a pocketwatch, coaxing his patient into an hypnotic state. The words were soothing, encouraging, simple.

Snatches of Ravel

And as he made his points, snatches of music from Ravel's String Quartet insinuated themselves from the stage, where the Orford Quartet sat in near blackness. It was as if a bridge were being gradually built between sounds and feelings, as he spoke of becoming a child again, delving deep down inside ourselves to capture the really important feelings and images, and then returning to our every day thoughts refreshed.

In speaking this way he was obviously trying to make the process happen right there on the spot, or at any rate, to hint at the possibilities of the experience. Whether he succeeded en mass I can't say, but at very least an atmosphere of extreme quiet prevailed as his voice gradually trailed off, as the stage lights gradually came up a little, and as the Orford Quartet began to play Ravel's String Quartet straight through from beginning to end. Frankly, I can't remember having sat through a more concentrated audience experience of this music. Even if Colgrass may not have turned his audience into instant deep listeners, he had certainly calmed and focused their responses.

Acknowledges Emotional Basis

Call it auditory group therapy, gentle mass hypnosis or a little of both, he has come up with a listening technique that acknowledges the emotional basis of our musical responses. It is, I hasten to add, only a technique, a means rather than an end, and it in no way invalidates the case for literacy as prerequisite to musical understanding. But how often do even those of us with literacy fail to make visceral contact with the music only too well?

A work as sophisticated as the Ravel Quartet played as brilliantly as the Orford Quartet plays it, has so much to do with the processes of the intellect, that it is all too easy to let it go to our heads without passing through our hearts.

Colgrass, whose own music invited a complete journey, may not have come up with a foolproof map for the Ravel Quartet or any other piece. What he has done is demonstrated that as in the Chinese proverb, the journey begins by taking a single step. And the step to be taken is to regard listening as a profoundly active rather than a passive act.

A METAPHOR FOR
PERFORMANCE EXECLLENCE
by
Dr. Diane Marshall

In September of 1985 I participated in an Ericksonian hypnosis training in Charleston, South Carolina. "The Leap Frog Prince and the Magic Spectacles" is a metaphor written to complete my hypnosis training. It was later used to achieve performance excellence outcomes with a church choir I conducted and a private voice studio I taught.

It has been a distressing part of my musical career to see voice students or choir members who have attained high musical skill levels in rehearsal situations perform before live audiences with less than the level of excellence they are capable of. Some singers laugh or cry uncontrollably, some freeze and others exhibit shortness of breath, dry mouth, shaking knees, etc.

Over the years I have heard some interesting beliefs which result in some interesting perceptions that cause some rather unsatisfactory states. Singers rarely produce a convincing love duet if a perceptual Bengal tiger is in permanent residence on their stage. On the other hand a Bengal tiger is perfect for producing the physical response of fight or flight.

The "Leap Frog Prince" was written to challenge beliefs and perceptions so that singers might make the adjustments necessary at the unconscious level for artistic performance. A piece of music requires many small shifts of state throughout. For example, the familiar lyrics, "just remember in the winter far beneath the bitter snows, lies the seed that with the sun's love in the spring becomes the rose," ("The Rose" by Amanda McBroom) requires the state of the singer to change from dormancy to growth and into full bloom.

In my musical world, music is a performing art. We set the date for a concert, choose the music we wish to perform and build the skills needed to perform that music in front of an audience. If our skills have been mastered and our states are appropriate to the musical context there is apt to be a quantum leap. Live and onstage we have ourselves and what we have completed beforehand. Artistry seems to burst out of this condition of completing the prerequisites of consumate skill levels, possessing the integrity to adjust beliefs and perceptions and having the willingness to place ourselves in appropriate performance situations.

THE LEAP FROG PRINCE AND THE MAGIC SPECTACLES

The Leap Frog Prince, all green and sweaty, was trudging down a narrow forest road. The competition had been rough and the Prince had not jumped his all time best. His devoted companion, the Flower Backed

Turtle, walked by his side. Nothing ever bothered the Flower Backed Turtle — absolutely nothing. As a matter of fact, the turtle was walking and listening, allowing the gentle forest murmurs and sighs to soothe him. He liked to feel the soft forest floor giving beneath his little feet . . . propelling him forward in its affectionate way. Deeper and deeper into the forest . . . floating . . . safe with the sounds . . . one foot following the other . . . nothing to fear here.

Soon the Leap Frog Prince began to follow the strange reverie of the turtle . . . moving . . . gliding effortlessly . . . deeper and deeper into the green and brown woods. Little by little the Prince was growing more and more relaxed . . . each sound and each step . . . soothed him . . . more than the last. Finally he sat down on the spongy ground . . . laid his head on the trunk of a trusty tree and fell into a deep sleep.

As the Leap Frog Prince slept soundly, dream voices began to whisper in his ears . . . you don't have to dream this dream if you don't want to . . . you don't have to listen to a single word I say . . . edit this dream in a way that is right for you . . . take only what you need . . . in the time that is appropriate for you . . . in the way that is yours.

Something in the Leap Frog Prince decided to dream on in vivid and varying colors and textures. The sounds of the dream were as clear as crystal clinking on crystal. The frog body of the prince was vibrant with the subtle movements of the dream.

Suddenly the Flower Backed Turtle appeared in the vision, standing just on the edge of a deep serene pool. With a delicate motion of his turtle head he beckoned the Prince to join him at the edge of the pool. Then down they both dove . . . eyes open and peering into the motionless depths. The Flower Backed Turtle swam towards a strange underwater grotto and the Prince, readying his courage, folllowed him through the opening and inside the thick walls. All at once the grotto opened into a cool cavern where there was air to breathe and a soft cushiony ledge to sit on. "This is the waiting place," said the Flower Backed Turtle. "Here you must prepare to meet the Siren Below the Pond. She will help you with the leapfrog competition. You can trust the Siren Below the Pond."

After those words, the Flower Backed Turtle dove once again into the deeper clear water . . . diving deeper . . . effortlessly. The prince obediently followed, summoning his courage as he dove. All at once a large wooden door appeared off to the right. As they swam closer, the door opened and the changing underwater pressures gently sucked them in. The Leap Frog Prince and the Flower Backed Turtle found themselves unhurt and only slightly uncomfortable on a wet marble floor. Obviously, this was where the Siren Below the Pond lived.

Suddenly footsteps echoed from a distance . . . now getting closer . . . little by little . . . now the eerie swish of gauzy clothing and the Siren Below the Pond shimmered before the Leap Frog Prince and Flower Backed Turtle. She said not a word. There was only a brief flash of recognition and acceptance across her fragile face. She extended her hand to the Leap Frog Prince and led him down a long quiet hall.

Soon a black foreboding gate blocked the way, but the Siren Below the Pond sang one silvery note and the gate opened with a mournful creak. Once across the threshold the three were surrounded by a room filled with treasures — ornate music boxes, ancient instruments inlaid with jewels and thousands of beautiful leather bags — their contents hidden from view.

With a commanding and articulate voice the Siren Below the Pond spoke to the Leap Frog Prince: "Inside any one of these leather bags is the secret of the competition. This bag is for you. It is divided into three tiers and inside each tier is a pair of spectacles. Return to your land and join the touring Master Leap Competition. There are three events to occur over the next month. Wear the spectacles I offer you in succession — top to bottom. I will appear to you when you have finished this task."

The Leap Frog Prince gasped, for the Master Leap Competition seemed way over his head. The Flower Backed Turtle shot him a meaningful look that said, "Just try it, it will be fine." So the Leap Frog Prince sighed a sigh of resignation and with tentative movements made his way out of the room . . . to the waiting place . . . out of the pond . . . to the trunk of the trusty tree.

When the Leap Frog Prince awoke from the dream he was in a most agitated state. He screamed at the Flower Backed Turtle and stomped on the ground. Absolutely nothing bothered the Flower Backed Turtle. He just looked at the Leap Frog Prince and with a little smirk of disgust handed him the leather bag. "The Siren Below the Pond has spoken," he said.

Now it was the day of the first Master Leap Competition. The sky was blue and the air was clear. The Leap Frog Prince began to prepare himself in the usual way, stretching his long leg muscles and his delicately curved back. About fifteen minutes before his round of leaping he cautiously drew the first pair of spectacles out of the leather bag. The rims were gold and the lenses were green. As soon as the Leap Frog Prince put them on everything seemed different. The competition suddenly looked scrawny, barely able to jump at all. The judges appeared to be definitely in favor of the Leap Frog Prince. The crowd seemed to cheer only for him. The Leap Frog Prince scanned his body and quickly concluded that he felt like Hercules. The Flower Backed Turtle was calm and watched quietly as the Leap Frog Prince began his round of jumping. He came in last place, but he didn't believe it until he saw his score sheet.

By the time the second competition came around the Leap Frog Prince had some curiosity about the upcoming day. He prepared as always and then took the second pair of spectacles out of the leather bag. This time the spectacles were silver and gray. As soon as the Prince put them on his perception began to shift drastically. The day was hot, airless and muggy. The other frog competitors looked like fierce leaping Gods. The Leap Frog Prince wanted to sabotage them all for a while, but then he ended up sitting on the track and feeling helpless. He wanted to quit and go home. The judges seemed to be in a terrible snit about something and they were writing angrily. The crowd was petulant and sneering. Even the Flower Backed Turtle seemed strange. The Prince thought he was bored and impatient. He tried to loosen up, but he couldn't catch his breath and his body was racked with tension. The Leap Frog Prince jumped his all time worst.

When the day came for the third competition the Leap Frog Prince was not very excited and his previous curiosity had waned. He did not bother to prepare himself before the event, but he did reach into the leather bag at the last minute to retrieve the last pair of spectacles. These had no rims, the lenses were clear and they felt weightless on his frog nose. The Leap Frog Prince couldn't believe the change in his perception this time. The sky was blue, but there was a storm brewing to the west. As soon as he noticed this weather condition his body made a rapid adjustment — his breathing was easier and his legs began to relax. The Leap Frog Prince looked at the other frog competitors. Some were hard muscled and mean looking, others were pudgy and meek and some were absolutely magnificent. Again his body began to magically regulate. The Leap Frog Prince was mystified, but he felt better, lighter. Turning slowly he peered at the judges. One seemed to be daydreaming, or having a daytime nightmare. He seemed to be very uncomfortable. One judge was highly interested and seemed to enjoy watching and writing. The last judge was looking at the girls up in the crowd. Abruptly, the Leap Frog Prince felt his body and senses making minute corrections all on its own. When he looked at the crowd each individual person seemed to be unique. All were doing slightly different things — some of these would have bothered him before, but now his body shifted. His heart rate had modified, his breathing was deep and full and his muscles felt relaxed and responsive. When the Leap Frog Prince looked at the Flower Backed Turtle, he noticed the most amazing lines of wisdom on his face and there was even a hint of tears in his turtle eyes. The Leap Frog Prince knew he had a very caring companion and his body and senses now made their last correction in one ripping spasm. He was ready to jump. There were several quantum leaps in his round and he jumped his all time best. There was a three-way tie for first place and Leap Frog Prince was in it.

Again the Leap Frog Prince and the Flower Backed Turtle walked on the narrow forest road. The Prince had no trouble entering the reverie of the turtle . . . drifting . . . listening to the forest chirps and flutters . . . walking effortlessly . . . floating . . . relaxing . . . enjoying the safety . . . now stopping . . . now sleeping . . . now dreaming.

It wasn't long before the Siren Below the Pond appeared . . . filmy, delicate and fragile. Her voice in the most caressing whisper said, "Well done, my fine Leap Frog Prince. May you always be blessed with a companion like the Flower Backed Turtle. You may keep this fine leather bag and the spectacles enclosed within the three tiers. I have thousands of leather bags with similar contents for all who dive to find me. Perhaps you will bring the next young leaping frog."

THE MUSE BEMUSED:
PRODUCTIVE AUDIENCES FOR WRITING AND PERSONAL CHANGE
by
Thomas E. Malloy and Janus Daniels

"Mirror, mirror on the wall, who is the fairest one of all?" Some answers are a pleasure to hear, others are not. The question, of course, does not ask for particularly useful information.

Once, when children were poets, a child discovered a magical glob of silvery, crystanine clay that shone like starlight, a delight to hold and behold. Musea was her name, and she discovered that she could stretch the clay into great sheets that were as soft as cobwebs but reflected like mirrors. And when she looked into the special mirrors that she devised from this substance she could see things no normal mirror could show.

She stretched a huge sheet of the stuff across one wall of her room and looked at it. It danced with color to a musical beat. She regarded herself in it. Her image seemed real; she could make it act independently of herself. She made her image bow and smile and dance to the music that filled the mirror. She made it speak and have feelings. This delighted her and she spent many hours watching herself do whatever she wanted herself to do. But the longer she spent with the mirror, the more real her mirror-self became and the less real her real self seemed. Soon her mirror-self acted beyond her control. It did things she didn't ask it to do, it said things she sometimes wasn't comfortable hearing, and it felt things that she sometimes wasn't comfortable feeling. Some essence flowed out from her into the magical mirror and animated her image so that it was no longer completely in her control. And this somehow made her feel as if she were no longer completely real.

This disturbed but also delighted her, and she continued to play with it. She stretched the clay into great sheets that she used to cover all the walls of her room. She covered the ceiling and floor. She covered the windows and the door. She even covered her desk — even her papers. There seemed no end to what she could do with the clay. Her room sparkled and hummed.

She laughed when she saw that where the clay covered portraits on her walls, the portraits took on a life of their own. They spoke to her and changed expressions; they even made gestures.

   She thought she would write a poem about all of this and went to her desk. She began to write on her paper which was coated in silvery gossamer. She had hardly written a word when the portrait of the cleaning lady shouted across the room that her writing was too messy. She wrote a few more lines when the portrait of the kingdom's Chief Minister of Referees of Games in General shouted that she wasn't following the rules of poetry. "The rules of poetry?" she asked herself. All the portraits began such a din of shouting that she couldn't hear the music of her words. When she looked down at her paper she only saw reflections of portraits shouting at her. So she threw down her pen, tore the gossamer off her door, and went out to play in the garden.

FIRST COMMENTS

   In this paper we address processes by which humans construct and respond to internal audiences. We see audience as a crucial piece in the writing process. And it is crucial to more than writing since audience affects all the little performances everyone gives each day. In a sense, audience is a pervasive backdrop to which socialized humans relate. It is how our models of other humans react that provides much of the motivation, many of the limitations, and a great deal of the meaning in life. Since audience so profoundly colors our experience it is important to generate internal audiences that are useful and functional and that move us in the directions we want to move. So the strategy outlined in this paper, while specifically designed to improve college students' writing, has personal implications far beyond that.

   Human experience is profoundly affected by moving among three perceptual positions. Changing perceptual positions had been called perspective taking (Piaget and Inhelder, 1956, pp. 209-246; Flavell, 1977, pp. 131-134). From the first perceptual position you experience the world simply as yourself. From the second perceptual position you experience the world as if you were some other person. Possibly you might hear their voice within your mind making comments. Or, you might "see their point." Or, you might understand how they would feel (as in response to "How would you feel if you were in my situation?").

   From the third perceptual position, which was developed formally by Grinder and DeLozier (1986) and described in written form by DeLozier and Grinder (1987), you experience your relationship to the other person(s) from the outside, from a different logical level, looking down, as it were, from a meta-point-of view at yourself and the other person(s) interacting.

   While the first perceptual position remains our fundamental way of experiencing the world, severe limitations result if it is the only perceptual position a person can occupy — as in early childhood. In Piagetian terms (e.g., Piaget, 1962 pp. 72-74), a developing child must transcend the "egocentrism" of this single point of view in order to engage in normal social relations and develop social values (Ginsberg and Opper, 1969. p. 109). While every child learns to take the second perceptual position to some degree as a natural part of social development, often people reach adulthood without using this cognitive process in specific situations, such as writing college papers.

It is important for writers to have the option of identifying with their readers. It is also important for writers to step back to the third perceptual position and perceive the patterns in their relationships with their readers. Identifying with an audience can be powerful, even overwhelming. For example, we found an art student who had to give up her scholarship and drop out of school for half a year because she was so identified with how each of her professors felt about any art that she literally did not know how she felt, even about her own work. Every strong identification has similar dangers. Since communication requires identifying, the solution is to learn to take a meta-position to relationships as proposed by DeLozier and Grinder (1987). An important and largely neglected skill in writing is the ability to evaluate and change relationships to audiences from the meta-position, for example, by well formed negotiations.

CASE DESCRIPTION

Our audience in this section is someone who is familiar with NLP and who consequently wants to know the context in which we developed our audience package.

In a sense there are two levels of case to describe, a class and particular student in the class. The class is a generic Writing 101 Freshman level introductory composition class required of all students during their Freshman year at the University of Utah. All Freshmen write a standard essay as part of their admission to the University. This writing sample is read by two faculty, who then route students into Writing 50, Writing 101, or Writing 110. Writing 101 receives the bulk of students and is designed for students who are not exceptionally poor nor exceptionally good writers. Each section of Writing 101 has about 21 students.

The section of Writing 101 taught by the senior author is unlike most introductory writing courses. The focus is on installing strategies elicited from expert writers. Usage is approached like any other process, as a matter of learning a strategy for learning standard usage. The emphasis is on important strategies such as a creativity strategy, several idea-integration strategies, a motivation strategy, and an audience strategy, among others. The classroom atmosphere is relaxed and noisy; we have fun. As much as possible we violate the dreary demands of the typical classroom architecture by moving seats around to meet our needs. Students work in groups of four who read and comment on each other's work to ensure that every draft of every assignment has a real audience that is on an equal level with the writer.

The audience strategy described in this paper was elicited from Susan, a student in one class taught by the authors. Susan always did her assignments correctly; that is, her writing always met the spirit of an assignment's demand, and almost always met the letter of its demand. Furthermore, when other students appeared confused about what was wanted from an assignment (or confused about anything in the class, for that matter) Susan would often interrupt the authors' explanation with an "What he means to say is . . ." and then proceed to give a more succinct and direct explanation than the authors were doing.

It seemed to us that she was onto something, so we elicited her strategy. We decided to use her strategy, rather than, say, a professional writer's strategy, to instill in students for two reasons. First, it is nicely tuned to the needs of college students. More importantly, it is a good strategy; in fact, the identification process is very similar to the New Behavior Generator (Dilts & Epstein, 1983).

A final word about case description. The general case of concern for the authors is the introductory writing courses. Nearly every college or university requires that every student take such a course prior to graduation. Nationwide, that's a lot of students every year. Furthermore, the general picture that we have of college students writing skills can be summarized by the saying, "Johnny can't read, or write." College level writing is approached with dismay. Writing teachers need as many new choices in their teaching techniques as possible.

THE ELICITATION OF THE AUDIENCE STRATEGY

In this section we present the text of the elicitation of Susan's audience strategy by the second author. Our audience is people knowledgeable in NLP strategy elicitation techniques since they will be able to discover more than just an audience strategy in the text of our interview with Susan. For those who aren't familiar with these techniques an excellent discussion is presented by Dilts, Grinder, Bandler, and DeLozier (1979).

In the interview text we will use the conventional NLP shorthand for eye movements, but with parentheses rather than superscripts. Right and left are from the subject's point of view. V(c) [5] up and right; V(r) [5] up and left; K [5] down and right; A(d) [5] down and left; A(r) [5] horizontal left; A(c) [5] horizontal and right.

Strategy elicitation. This is the text of the relevant part of our interview with Susan. It took place with her permission during a regular class session. She was aware that we were interested in parts of her writing process and she had a general idea of what to expect during the interview.

"You write fairly quickly, easily, and enjoyably?"

V(r), smiles, "Yes, pretty much."

"I wouldn't necessarily take your word for that, but I have Tom's as well. I think there's something worth finding here. So I may ask some strange questions. First, how do you decide what to write?"

V(r), A(d), "I have an assignment," smiles.

"Yes, and many different ways to fulfill it. How do you decide which one to do?"

V(r), V(c), "I take a look at what I might write."

"You make a bunch of different movies in your head?"

V(r), "Yes, but just of the critical part, the, ahh . . ." A(d), V(r).

"The climax?"

"That's it; they're short."

"So each one is just a few seconds of action. How do you decide which one to use?"

K, "The strongest one."

"Do you choose the one that gives you the most intense feelings?"

V(c), K, "Yes."

"So you have movies. What do those movies include?"

Global access, A(d). "What do you mean?"

"I'll put that another way. Did you see hear, feel, smell, and taste what happened in the movies?"

Slower global access, "Yes."

"Did you normally do that?"

"Yes, all of it."

"Make one of those movies now. Where is it?"

Eyes in center position, "Right in front of me," gestures with fingers pointing in front of her.

"A couple of things; I think this is like looking out through an open window and also if this is a movie of people, a story say, that you can go into any of them, have their viewpoint and experiences, is that . . . ?"

"Yes, yes, like that."

"How do you decide which viewpoint to use?"

V(c), K, "I go with the strongest feelings."

"So you choose on the basis of the peak of action and feeling. I especially like the way you just play the climax instead of whole movies. You keep yourself interested, avoid boring yourself, and also save time by using tiny parts instead of whole movies. I'll steal that. But that doesn't explain what I'm most interested in. I'm told you write differently, that you write well according to the different requirements of each class you take, so much that you write noticeably differently for each teacher."

V(r), smiles, A(d), "I'm pretty good at that."

"How do you know how to write for a particular class?"

V(r), "I don't know, I just do it."

"Sure, but you just do it well. So, have you got a specific class in mind?"

V(r), "O.K., yeah."

"So how do you know how to write for this class?"

V(r), "Ahh . . ."

"I notice you looking up to your left; do you see a picture up there?"

V(r), "Oh, my teacher," smiles.

"You see a picture of the teacher. Do you know where that picture came from?"

V(r), "It's him . . ."

"Does it look like it could be from the first day of class?"

V(r), "Something like that."

"Well, how do you know how to write for this guy?"

V(r), V(c), K, "I don't know, I just"—

"Yeah, but I want to know how that works. You do answer my questions in a useful way; it just doesn't seem to make sense yet. So far you remember, you have an old picture of your teacher up there (gestures) from what you just said I'd like to know if you could start writing for that class right now, can you do that?"

V(r), V(c), K, "Yeah, sure."

"Good. I'd like to know what you see up here," gestures up to Susan's right.

V(r), V(c), "It's him again."

"How does he look?"

"He's sitting at his desk with a red pen."

"How appropriate. How does he know what you're writing?"

V(c), A(d), "He can hear me."

"He can hear what you write?"

"I say it while I write it."

"Do you write in a different tone of voice for each teacher?"

V(r), V(c), A(r), A(c), A(d), "Yes."

"How do you know he likes it?"

V(r), "By the way he looks."

"Most of this actually makes sense now except, how do you know how your professor would react?"

V(r), V(c), K, "I . . ."

"Wait, this looks familiar. I want to make a guess. When you see your professor, do you ever sort of step into his body and get the feeling of what it would be like to be him? To see and hear things his way?"

V(r), V(c), K, "Sure."

"Typically, how far into a class do you start that?"

V(r), "The first day."

"Do you see him when you're proofreading your last draft?"

V(r), V(c), K, "No, not a lot."

"Do you become your professor to read your last draft?"

V(r), V(c), K, "Yes, at least partly."

"Do you ever become your professor to select what to write?"

V(r), V(c), K, "Sometimes it works better that way."

"I'm curious; do you ever mimic people at parties? Presidents and professors and such? Are you good at that?"

V(r), smiles with slight nod, "Don't ask me to do it." Laughs.

"I promise, but you can do it, yes?"

Eyes closed, "Yeah."

"You have a nice system here. Does it ever let you down? What happens when, say, you get a grade lower than you expected?"

V(r), V(c), K, "I turn around and get what I need."

"Meaning?"

V(r), "I look back and try to find what I missed."

"And if you can't?"

"I get back in touch . . . I meet with my teachers and talk to them about it."

"You seem to get to know your teachers very well."

"I know how they would act at the zoo or with their families, at home or anything."

"Do you ever make a movie of yourself sort of dressed like, looking and acting and sounding like your professor? And then go into that?"

"If that's what it takes."

"I think that's enough."

AUDIENCE INSTALLATION PACKAGE FOR CLASSROOM USE

Our specific audience in this section is people who want to teach writers to generate productive audiences. Most of the structure and text of this section is oriented to that audience. To a lesser degree we also address comments to people interested in teaching students better study habits. Finally we have kept in mind anyone who is interested in audience as a central part of human experience and therefore applicable to therapy and personal change.

Later, Musea sat musing to the music of a stream in her garden. She had been unable to write for some time now due to the din of all the portraits in her room. She noticed that an owl in a tree nearby was studying her carefully. They exchanged polite greetings and the owl flew down next to her.

"Amusing isn't it?" said the owl as it held up a magical glob of silvery clay.

Bemused by an owl having some of her precious and magical stuff, she asked, "How did you come by that?"

"Oh, it's everywhere; sometimes I think that the problem is getting away from it, not finding it. Usually it's stretched so thin that you don't notice."

The owl stretched out a charming mirror from its stuff and asked Musea to look into it. He asked her to see many things about herself and she did. And while she was absorbed in her world within the owl's mirror, the owl, quite abruptly and unexpectedly, crushed the mirror into a glob. She gasped at the shock and pain of seeing herself crushed. Then she became angry.

The owl, however, looked at her kindly and said, "You've got to learn the dangers of letting yourself seep out into this stuff." He stretched out a big sheet of the stuff and put it on the ground. Then he flew up to a large tree limb. "Come up here with me. You'll see what I mean."

She still felt angry as she started to climb up next to the owl. By the time she sat on the limb she felt quite relaxed.

"It's a magical limb," said the owl, noticing the changes that came over her. "Look down into the sheet and see yourself writing in it."

This she did, seeing herself at her desk. Soon she saw herself jerk her quill to a stop in response to a nasty comment from the cleaning lady's portrait. She started and stopped writing in a jerky fashion, like a puppet on a string, reacting to conflicting voices from the portraits around her. Soon she saw in her face the frustration that stopped her from writing at all.

"As I said, this tree limb is magical," said the owl. "From up here you can notice the patterns that go on down there. Once you notice, you can make changes." The owl looked at her expectantly.

She wasn't sure what the point was. "What changes?" she asked.

Just look into the mirror and notice . . . and make changes."

The first author generally likes to keep a metaphor running throughout the quarter. This running metaphor is largely improvisational, made up on the spur of the moment in the context of whatever is going on in class. The above metaphor fragment became a bit formal when it was written. It is included as an example of what you might do rather than as a prescription of what you should do. Any metaphor gets boring when told too many times. We have found metaphors fun and useful and suggest that you improvise them utilizing ongoing events. Still, improvisation requires a starting point and Musea and her clay can give you such a starting point.

IDENTIFICATION/PROJECTION EXERCISES

This exercise, which is described in detail by Stevens (1971, p. 227), provides students with a direct demonstration of the power and consequences of their ability to identify with and project themselves onto objects outside themselves. The purpose here is to provide them with a direct experience that we can later relate to their identification with the work they produce and to the emotional impact of their internal audiences.

Take some object that is lying around that is reasonably interesting and hold it up where everyone can see it. Ask people to call out one or two different things even though all were looking at the same object. Then have everyone identify with the various aspects of the object that they noticed. For example (for a piece of wire), "I am flexible," or "I am pointed and sharp." You want them to take the point of view of the object, to see the world as the object does, to hear and speak as the object does, to feel and move as the object does. This foreshadows some of the most important aspects of the audience strategy that they will be learning. Take time and do what is necessary to develop this process.

While people are so engaged, do something to the object that provokes a strong reaction, such as bobbling it, almost dropping it and then catching it. Or, as Stevens suggests, you can crumple it up, which addresses very directly how some audiences give feedback, essentially by destroying the work. This crumpling can be used later to show how to get rid of audiences that are not working effectively.

After this exercise is finished put it into a framework that will give it meaning for the issue of audience. We use this exercise to lay the foundation for changing internal audiences that may be causing students pain and blocking them from writing (among other things). We talk about how humans make up internal representations of themselves and other people. If the metaphor has worked, this discussion can be simple, direct, and largely experiential with a minimum of intellectual abstraction. We can then use the identification/projection experience to anchor just how easy it can be for a human to identify with these internal audiences and so make themselves vulnerable to the crushing comments and actions of the real people represented by their audiences. Finally we make clear that building internal models of people to serve as audiences is a natural and functional process that underlies communication and empathy. It is fine to give people power over you by making them your audience. Those who don't have this as a choice will loose rich feedback in their relationships. The trick is moving to the third perceptual position observing patterns and making appropriate changes.

Universal audiences. Some obvious audiences that are universal — parents, friends, lovers, religious leaders — are worth mentioning to students. This develops clearly that audience is a powerful experience engaged in by everyone. It also can provide a context for discussing just how strong the feelings connected to audience can be.

Stories about audiences. These are set to very short stories that can be told about audiences. The first four illustrate the idea that audiences don't have to be negative, they can give a person nearly unconditional positive regard. The last story illustrates that authors don't have to take too much abuse from their audiences.

1. There is the story about the time Harlan Ellison, in order to help out a failing bookstore, wrote one short story per day in the front window of the store. Passers-by could come in and make suggestions. People stood outside the plate glass window and were in awe that they were actually watching a real author writing and that he might actually allow them to make suggestions. This story illustrates an audience that is impressed by the fact of writing at all. The people outside the store window could not tell anything about the quality of Ellison's writing.

2. Of course we've all seen the enormous crowds on television that the Pope draws when he visits some country. One can imagine people way in back who can barely see the white figure of the Pope. Yet these people are deeply moved just because he is there.

3. There are many small-time bands in every city that do not play well, yet receive an enthusiastic response from their audience.

4. There are many stories of people who run marathons, not to win, but to finish. The very fact of being able to do it elicits admiration from

bystanders, friends, and family. To put the accomplishment of being able to write at all in perspective, we can remember that once it was a magical source of power. Those few scribes who could write records on clay tablets rose to power in ancient civilization.

5. The final story is about Harlan Ellison again. Once he was called into the office of a movie producer to discuss a script he had written. The producer sat at one end of a long table which was lined on both sides by flunkies. Harlan was bade to sit at the other end. The producer took his script and flung it down the length of the table to Harlan, who thumbed through it, noticing numerous changes marked in red. The producer began to explain to Harlan the changes he wanted. Harlan interrupted him and asked just what made the producer think he would make any of the changes. The producer sneered back that of course Harlan would because writers were just toadies. Harlan bowed his head, stood up to his full five feet five inches, shuffled obsequiously to the head of the table, and punched the producer so hard that he flipped over the back of his chair onto the floor. Harlan started to kick the producer and three flunkies dragged him away.

These stories address various issues about the audience, such as the fact that people don't have to sit there and be abused by the voices in their heads; they can respond however necessary to whip the voices into shape, and ecologically balanced responses require three perceptual positions (described below). These are not particularly special stories and we do not recommend necessarily telling them. If they suit your needs use them. They are an example of something you can do to address whatever issues you want about audience. For example, one of NASA's Voyager missions sent a satellite out of our solar system with messages for any intelligent life forms that might find it. It is fun to start students thinking about how NASA approached this very general audience and then discuss the issues that are brought up by that mission as they relate to the students.

Positive Set. This section addresses a good audience strategy as a desirable outcome. Why would students want to install a strategy that allows them to create and alter audiences?

Writing well is one reason. Skilled writers have a productive audience, one that makes writing not only possible but desirable. Usually this audience is positive, although a few writers require adversity to write. The strategy will allow students to invent and try out audiences until they find one that is productive.

There are academic reasons as well. We will show how the audience strategy can be used to study effectively for tests, and even to predict questions on tests. The audience strategy is also useful in careers after schooling is complete, especially for those who work in a hierarchical organization. For example, a woman we know used the audience strategy to great advantage in her work. She was working at a middle level of organization in a large company, and, naturally enough, her audience was her boss, a highly skilled and largely technical thinker. Since his concerns were her concerns she addressed these technical issues at organizational meetings. This seemed so natural as to be without choice for her. When she learned the audience strategy she realized that she could build audiences of the people several levels up the organization; there was no reason that she had to limit her subjective reality to addressing the concerns of her boss. She constructed audiences of people higher in the organization and was able to address their concerns at meetings and was soon promoted, leap frog, over her boss. She had already known how to get applause. It was a matter of being able to construct the right audience so that she could get the right applause.

Perhaps more important than success to most people is personal evolution. Sometimes personal growth is limited by who it is we spend time chatting with inside our heads. If we don't think about this issue, these pervasive audiences seem natural; they are just there. We have no choice about them. Conscious control of an effective audience strategy allows people to choose audiences that will move them in the direction they want to move.

The Audience Strategy. Up to this point it's been our purpose to provide students with:

(1) a framework through the Musea metaphor;
(2) a powerful experience of the basic processes by which they can identify with and model even an inanimate object;
(3) universal examples of audiences;
(4) a series of stories about their potential relationships to audience; and
(5) a positive set to motivate them to want to learn a new and effective strategy for generating audiences of their own choosing.

The next step in the classroom package is the audience generation strategy itself. For the next several paragraphs we will change our audience from teachers to students. It should be noted that by the time we teach this audience strategy our students have a basic vocabulary that includes representational systems (Grinder & Bandler, 1976), submodalities (Dilts & Epstein, 1983; Bandler, 1985), and the difference between an associated and dissociated point of view (DeLozier & Grinder, 1987). All this is not necessary to teach the strategy, but it helps to make it clear and to answer questions.

The following is Susan's strategy for generating audiences. Remember to use it to suit your own needs. In some sense the empathy that you build up by making a person your audience gives that person some power in relation to you. It also gives you some power in relation to that person. The steps below are pretty much tailored to a university classroom (though you can easily modify them to fit any situation). Susan expressed that she used the audiences to help her in the classroom. She had been a poor student and one day decided to be a good student. One of the things she did was to start identifying with teachers to get their point of view. But she indicated that she did this playfully, like a game, and didn't take her teachers' points of view too seriously.

In the same way, we recommend that you use audiences with a sense of fun for your own purposes, which, in the classroom, might be learning interesting ideas and getting good grades. Whenever an audience no longer suits your needs you can crumple it up, like a piece of clay, like the thing I crumpled up earlier, and start over. Discard professors who aren't useful, keep ones that are.

In the following steps you will learn to take three distinctive points of view, that of yourself, that of your audience, and that of a director watching the interaction between yourself and your audience.

1. The Director. Create a perspective from which you can review your relationships, first, to your audience and, second, to your work. You might imagine yourself as a director of a play, sitting in the balcony above the stage, watching yourself playing to the audience. For the purpose of writing, imagine yourself looking down at a scene which contains yourself, the audience you have in mind (often a professor), and the work that you plan to do for your audience. From this point of view, practice changing various aspects of the relationships between you, your audience, and your work. Like the director of a play, make changes in the scene until it has the qualities and quality that you want. Start with simple things: change the color of the clothing people wear, or the posture of you or your audience. Be sure to remember that you can change things about your work — its style, content, etc. — to fit the relationships.

There are many things you can change from the position of the director. For example, in the theater of the mind you can send players on and off stage. So when writing, you can change the audience whenever you want. For example, you can write for an encouraging audience during early drafts and a more critical audience when proofreading for the final draft. You can imagine yourself writing for yourself. You can make the audience disappear and imagine yourself unselfconsciously writing.

2. Gathering Information. Begin by gathering information about the model so that you can construct accurate internal representations. This is done from your own point of view. Watch and listen to the person; read things the person has written (such as the syllabus and assignments). Pay attention to the person's breathing, postures, gestures, voice tones, facial expressions and so forth. It is often the case in the classroom that your purpose in creating an audience is to anticipate how you will be evaluated. If so, carefully gather information on the differences in the person's breath, voice, face, gestures, and posture for things the persons likes and dislikes. This gives information about the person's values.

3. Remembering Information. From your own point of view, make remembered movies of the model. Movies, for our purpose, are internal pictures (especially facial expressions, gestures and postures) with internal sound tracks (especially of voice, most notably voice tones and voice mannerisms). Make sure you can remember the crucial parts of the information you gathered in (2) above.

4. Stimulating. From your own point of view again, construct a movie

with yourself playing the starring role of the teacher (or other model). That is, see the same movie as in (3) above, but with yourself in place of the person you are modeling.

5. Identifying. The next step can be a little hard for some people to do right away since it requires taking the point of view of another person. Children do this with great facility. You may find that you don't want to take the point of view of a particular person. If so, go to position of the director and change things until you can comfortably exchange your point of view with that of the model.

Make up what you would see and hear and feel if you were doing what the model did. For example, pretend you are the professor standing up in front of the class and look out of the professor's eyes at the class and at yourself; be aware of what the professor would experience.

The trick here is first to get an internal movie running using either (3) or (4) above. That is, see either your professor or yourself in front of the class. When you have that in mind, imagine yourself walking up in front of the class, turning around to face the class, and then stepping into either the professor's body or your own body (depending on which movie, (3) or (4), you are watching).

Make sure you have full sensory experience in the movie. Like method acting, include feelings, smells, tastes, along with any other experiences that seem important, such as the sense of balance.

6. Developing your internal representation. Now construct movies of the model in some hypothetical circumstances. What's the person like at home, at the store, on vacation, etc. Practice guessing value choices the person would make, like the brand of cereal or political party the person would choose. Get feedback and make corrections. The more that your movie of the person seems to have a life of its own, the more useful it will be. For example, imagine a person who currently influences you and our values greatly; notice how, in your imagination, that person seems to act autonomously. The purpose here is to learn to make up how the model acts in circumstances where you can't possibly have gathered information about him or her. This gives you practice in the next crucial step.

7. Using your representation. Make movies of how your audience would respond in important academic situations. When you have a draft of a piece of writing, or a part of a draft, see your audience reading your work, line by line. Let this representation of your audience have a life of its own; that way you discover more about its values than if you try to control it. Notice facial expressions and other things that let you know what she or he likes and dislikes.

Watch your audience going over class notes and textbooks making up exams. Jot down the test items the person makes up.

If you are learning values from the model, imagine that person in ethical quandaries and learn to make value judgments as he or she would.

8. Using identification. This technique is even more effective if you "become" the model, rather than watching the model as you did in (7)

above. For writing, step into the person, and read your paper as if you were that person. Hear the model's internal voice commenting on what is good or bad. Feel what the person feels; particularly notice what about your paper feels good and what feels bad. Then revise it according to your audience's values.

When you read your class notes or the textbook while studying for an exam, step into your representation of your professor and read as that person. Notice what seems important and valuable to that person. While you are identifying with that person, you might as well make up the exam. Practice making up the type of question the person uses on exams — multiple choice, essay, or whatever. Students who practice doing this can gain an uncanny sense for predicting what is on exams.

9. Feedback to improve model. Interact with the target person as much as possible. If you get feedback (comments on papers, verbal answers to questions, etc.) that you didn't expect, then go back to (2). Gather more information (talk to professors in person about the feedback you got) and revise your movie. Take a few tries to hone your representation so that it functions well.

If you get feedback that you expect, revise your audience anyway. Make more detailed predictions next time. Fine tune it.

10. Directing the process. Identifying with and modeling other people and their values is a natural and powerful process that is fundamental to social relations. Take the position of the director from time to time to maintain your personal integrity in the process. Regularly review your relationship to your audience and to your work from the original point of view of the director established in (1) above. Make sure that these relationships are meeting your broader needs, values, and goals as a human being.

Remember, in the theater of your mind you are the director and can change whatever you like. If you find that your professor has values and knowledge that you like, keep these. If your professor's values and knowledge do not work for you, then from the position of the director you can discard them.

11. Using the three perceptual positions. Each of the three perceptual positions (or points of view) you've learned to use has great utility in writing. From the position of the director you can change the audience so that you write for a different audience at different points in the writing process or for different pieces of writing. The director can change how you or your audience relate to each other so the task becomes pleasant or at least possible.

From the position of the audience and its values you can discover important things about your writing that you can't notice from your own perspective alone.

From the position of yourself you write. Once you have high quality information from the second and third positions, you can make them disappear and focus solely on writing. When appropriate, you can examine the work you produce from the other two perceptual positions.

12. <u>Using the strategy.</u> Here are a few hints on how to use audience while you write. When you are in place to write (for example, sitting at a desk), imagine remembered movies of things you've actually seen your audience do up and to your left. Imagine movies of things you make up about your audience up and to your right. When you have questions about what you are writing look up to your audience for a reaction.

Use more than one audience for a single writing project. For example, some people like to use easy and friendly audiences early in writing and stricter audiences (like professors) later in writing. Other people like to go back and forth between audiences. They might use a professor audience very early to select a topic, then go to an easy audience to generate some text, and then switch back to their professor to make revisions. There is, of course, no right way. Explore various sequences of audiences to determine what works best for you.

A final note — if you find yourself unable to write, or if you find that you are experiencing a lot of unpleasant emotions, you might stop and be aware of your audience. Sometimes you can remove these kinds of blocks by switching audiences. Put critical audiences off until later where they can do some good.

Those are the main steps of the identification strategy for generating new and useful audiences. Play with these steps and, like a good cook who soon goes beyond a new recipe, alter the strategy to make it more effective for yourself. Also realize that with this strategy, you have choices. You can choose your internal audience. You don't need to be trapped by the audiences that you now have. Remember, the exercise we did earlier with the object I held up. Change any audience that causes you more pain than you want. You don't have to be crumpled up; you can crumple up your internal audience.

EXERCISES FOR AUDIENCE STRATEGY INSTALLATION

Now the authors of this paper would like to change the audience back again from students to teachers who want to impact their students' audience strategies. In this last section of the classroom audience package, we will give some examples of the kinds of activities that you can do with your students to ensure that they will install useful audience strategies. Of course, you will want to make up exercises that fit what you are doing.

AUDIENCE CLINIC

If you have two people available, this demonstration can be a lot of fun. It is based on Monty Python's television skit, Argument Clinic. In case you are unfamiliar with this skit, its essence is that a person comes into the argument clinic, pays some money to a receptionist, and goes into a small room where a person argues with whatever he says.

For example, as the person enters the room he says,

"Looks like you are the one who's going to argue with me."

"Actually, I'm not."

"Of course you are. I just paid my fee."

"No you didn't. I didn't see you pay a fee."

"That's because I paid the receptionist."

"No you didn't."

"Yes I did."

"No you didn't."

"I'll just step out the door and ask her."

"No, you won't. If you go out the door you forfeit your fee and the session's over."

"No it's not."

"Yes it is."

And so on. We act out an example of Argument Clinic for students who are unfamiliar with it and to warm up our audience. Then we role play Audience Clinic with the same sense of comic absurdity. In Audience Clinic, one person plays the Performer, the other plays the Audience. The Performer acts out a series of things (we like to include a kinesthetic, auditory and visual activity such as making waving motions with the hands, humming, and drawing pictures on the board). At first, the Audience reacts to each thing the Performer does in an absurdly comical exaggeration of all the worst ways for an audience to give feedback: "Only a person as worthless as you could wave your hands that poorly; surely you are genetically deficient. Your baby sister always does better." The Performer becomes discouraged with each task attempted and eventually decides to quit.

Next the Performer suddenly and unexpectedly tells the Audience that he is a terrible audience. "I'm paying you after all. You're fired! In fact, you do something. And I'll show how to be a good audience." The crestfallen audience agrees. Here we are reinforcing the idea that a person can crumple up an audience and remake it to her or his own specifications. Next the Audience performs and Performer gives feedback, in a useful and constructive way. Model what you think are useful feedback skills such as the Feedback Frame, the Outcome Frame, etc.

In the final stage of the skit, the Audience asks to have another chance, which the Performer grants. This time the Audience does better, although a few comic slips can keep up interest.

The idea of this exercise is to help the student experience the ridiculousness and universality of the terrible events that sometimes happen in our heads when we look to others to see, "How am I doing, so far?"

PAIRS EXERCISES IN AUDIENCE GENERATION

Have students pair up and practice generating audiences. The idea is for one person to pick a current professor or otherwise significant person and go through the steps of the strategy. The person's partner then asks questions to make sure that the person has constructed a well-formed audience. Since students are not likely to be expert at asking such questions we include here a list of questions that we hand out that they should ask their partners.

Questions for your partner about his/her audience:

Describe the professor you chose. Can you see his or her facial expression? gestures? posture? Make sure you can see each of these.

Can you see the differences in expressions, gestures, postures, voice tones and so on between things he or she likes and dislikes?

Can you hear his or her typical words? It would be good if you could make up at least one sentence (two to three would be better) that is either a direct quote or very much like a sentence that s/he would utter. Can you hear voice tone? Can you hear speech mannerisms ("ahs," clearing throat, etc.)?

Pretend that you can observe the professor reading your first draft. Now see the movie in your mind's eye as s/he reads it. Can you see her or his facial expression (sentence by sentence)? How does the facial expression look when s/he likes a sentence? When s/he dislikes a sentence?

How do gestures and postures differ for what s/he likes and dislikes?

Can you hear any comments s/he makes, either aloud or in her or his mind? How do these differ for what s/he likes and dislikes?

How are speech tonality and mannerisms different for what s/he likes or dislikes?

How does s/he feel in general? How do her or his feelings differ when reading something that she or he likes or dislikes?

While students do this exercise walk around and take the opportunity to help people when they can't do various parts of the strategy. Some people will catch on quickly, others will need things cleared up before they can do the strategy. Remember, it is not enough to describe a strategy; people need experiences which help them to install it.

MIMICKING

Ask students to mimic people. In order to mimic someone, a person needs a good representation of that person, and then needs to step into the representation and act it out.

Have students work in small groups so each person will have a real audience when it is time to mimic. Explain how you can mimic by going through the audience strategy, emphasizing the importance of stepping into your representation of the person you are mimicking. Let people mimic anyone they think will be fun to mimic (yourself as the teacher, John Wayne, Ronald Reagan, Charo, Katherine Hepburn, Mick Jagger, Madonna, a friend, a professor). Make this a high energy, fun exercise.

Some people will have difficulty mimicking, mostly due to embarrassment. Embarrassment is an excellent opportunity to work with the audience strategy because it is an audience issue. You can't be embarrassed without reference to an audience. So you can use the strategy to change the audience of students who are embarrassed to mimic. This can be a very convincing experience for them since it demonstrates how the strategy can be used to get rid of exactly the kind of limit that blocks writing (and other performances).

WRITING EXERCISES

Of course, students need to practice the strategy *in vivo*. Since we teach a writing class, we use the strategy in writing exercises. If you are using it for some other performance, design your exercises around that performance. Below is an example of a writing assignment given after the students went through the classroom package. The Jerry and Lily story referred to is a murder mystery without an ending that we had previously told in class. The students had to make up an ending that solved the mystery when they were practicing a creativity strategy.

Number 3 below produces excellent class discussions.

1. Write an account of the Jerry and Lily story for three audiences: a close friend (in personal letter form), a local newspaper audience (in news-article form), and a professor you have in a current class who seems difficult to communicate with (in the form you would use to answer an essay test question that asked for the solution to a difficult problem). We will practice the audience strategy on this professor. [Note: Here we are practicing three common audience types: a friend, a general reader who is not known to you, and a technical audience with specific demands and a strong sense of evaluation.]

2. Choose some professor from a current (or, if necessary, past) class who seems difficult to relate to (s/he can be the same as in #1 above). Practice the audience strategy with this person. Then, pretending you are this person, go through your materials for the class and make up two midterm test items (two essay questions, or two multiple choice items).

b) Now go through your material for this professor's class and find some concept or selection of material that is especiallv difficult.

c) Now write a few paragraphs explaining this difficult material to a good friend, family member, or other "easy" audience. Name and briefly describe (in a sentence) your relationship to this person.

d) Now write a few paragraphs explaining this difficult material to the professor.

3. Pick someone in your life that you will interact with a lot in the next several days. Pick a particular type of interaction (between that person and you) that occurs frequently (asking them to do you a favor, making a decision, trying to get something done, etc.). For your first few experiments, choose an interaction that is not too important. Choose an interaction that you want to improve with this particular person.

As a lab type project imagine this interaction with that person from the three perceptual positions. Make changes on the basis of experiencing the relationship from these three positions. Remember to choose a minor issue to change while you are learning these techniques.

Now go have the interaction. Write up your observations from this project. Take between one and two pages. We will discuss them next class.

RELATED WORK

We have developed other packages that address other parts of the writing process specifically and performance in general. Malloy (1987a) has developed a series of techniques for utilizing chaotic thought processes to organize and integrate ideas in writing. These techniques can be applied to personal organization and the integration of personal "parts" (Dilts, personal communication). Malloy (1987b), following the work of Dilts (1983), has demonstrated the effectiveness of teaching strategies for spelling in classroom. Malloy and Daniels (in press) use the three perceptual positions (DeLozier & Grinder, 1987) for teaching people to develop ecologically valid values. Malloy, Mitchell and Gordon (1987) have developed and demonstrated the effectiveness of techniques for teaching problem solving strategies that increase intelligence as broadly measured by nonverbal IQ tests and Piagetian cognitive tasks (Inhelder & Piaget, 1964). Currently, based on the work of Dilts and Epstein (1983), packages have been developed and are being evaluated for teaching creativity and idea generation in writing and in general. Finally, packages are under development for teaching scientific theory construction using the work of Dilts (1983), DeLozier and Grinder (1987), Bateson (1972, 1980) and Polya (1968).

FINAL COMMENT

The audience strategy develops and sharpens students' skills at taking three perceptual positions when they write. They write while fully associated in the first perceptual position. They create audiences while identifying with people in the second perceptual position. And they balance their ecology from the third perceptual position. We recommend that you rearrange and evolve the audience strategy and the classroom package to improve it and to suit your own needs. We certainly don't plan to be limited by what we've written down here; and we hope that you won't be either.

Don't take anything of this article too seriously. Take it seriously enough, though, to . . . provoke you . . . to . . . Do SOMETHING . . . just a little bit — or a lot . . . DIFFERENT.

So Musea took the portrait of the Referee and re-hung it in a closet. When she needed to know about rules, she opened the closet door. She also took the cleaning lady's portrait down and replaced it with that of her favorite poet.

"Mirror, mirror on the wall, show me your uses, tell them all."

REFERENCES

Bandler, R, (1985). *Using you Brain—for a CHANGE*. Moab, UT: Real People Press.

Bateson, G. (1972). *Steps To An Ecology of Mind*. New York: Ballantine.

Bateson, G. (1980). *Mind and Nature: A Necessary Unity*. New York: Bantam.

DeLozier, J. & Grinder, J. (1987). *Turtles All The Way Down: Prerequisite To Personal Genius*. Santa Cruz, CA: Grinder, DeLozier and Associates.

Dilts, R. (1983). "Applications of NLP in Education." In R. Dilts, Applications of Neuro Linquistic Programming. Cupertino, CA: Meta Publications.

Dilts, R., Grinder, J., Bandler, R., & DeLozier, J. (1979). *Neuro Linguistic Programming Volume I*. Cupertino, CA: Meta Publications.

Dilts, R. & Epstein, T. (1983, March). *The Dynamics of Creativity*. A Workshop presented in San Francisco, CA.

Flavell, J. (1977). *Cognitive Development*. Englewood Cliffs, NJ: Prentice-Hall.

Ginsberg, H., & Opper, S. (1969). *Piaget's Theory of Cognitive Development*. Englewood Cliffs, NJ: Prentice Hall.

Grinder, J. & Bandler, R. (1976). *The Structure of Magic*. (Vol. 2). Palo Alto, CA: Science and Behavior Books.

Grinder J., & DeLozier, J. (1986). *Prerequisite to Personal Genius* (Cassette Recording). Santa Cruz, CA: Grinder, DeLozier and Associates.

Inhelder, B. & Piaget, J. (1964). *The Early Growth of Logic In the Child*. New York: Norton.

Malloy, T.E. (1987a). *Chaos and order: Teaching the deep structure of organization*. In K. Spear (Chair), Teaching and Researching Cognitive Processes. Paper session presented at the Conference on College Composition and Communication, March 19, 1987.

Malloy, T.E. (1987b) *Principles for teaching cognitive strategies: The Case of Spelling*. Resources in Education (ED281228). Urbana, IL: ERIC, Clearinghouse on Reading and Communication Skills.

Malloy, T.E., Mitchell, C. & Gordon, O.E. (1987). *Training Cognitive Strategies Underlying Intelligent Problem Solving*. Perceptual and Motor Skills, 64, 1039-1046.

Malloy, T.E. & Daniels, J. (in press). Discovering values through identification and perspective taking. *Perspectives*.

Piaget, J. (1962). *Play, Dreams, and Imitation In Childhood*. New York: Norton.

Piaget, J., & Inhelder, B. (1956). *The Child's Conception of Space*. London: Routledge and Paul.

Polya, G. (1968). *Patterns of Plausible Inference*. Princeton, NJ: Princeton University Press.

Stevens, J.O. (1971). *Awareness*. New York: Bantam Books.

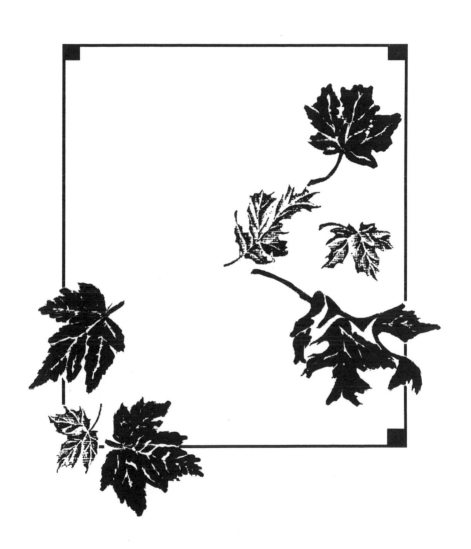

CHAPTER IV

NEW GROUND

NEW GROUND
by
John T. Grinder

Very early in the modeling work in which Bandler and I involved ourselves in the mid 70's in Santa Cruz, we found ourselves shadowed by a very earnest young man who appeared to have appointed himself to the position of our Boswell. He was relentless in his insistence that he capture each in a series of innovations which we generated in our explorations of topics, such as, representational systems, and anchoring. Initially I thought him to be rather presumptuous in assuming this role of scribe. My perceptions shifted over the months as I noted with a mixture of surprise and mild alarm that what to me was simply another example of a reasonably explicitly coded pattern was perceived by him, let's call him Don for convenience, as an entirely new pattern. This difference between Don and me can no doubt be understood in part, at least, as the difference between an explorer and a cartographer, the creator of a process and the user of a product of that process. Yet as important as these distinctions may be, there is still a residual question: How is it that some fellow organisms generalize from structured experiences (sometimes called training) to other contexts while others do not? This difference is rapidly floating to the top of my personal (and ever expanding) list of patterns (and patterns of patterns) to explore.

In this section of *Leaves Before The Wind*, we have three quite different examples of this difference. Mike Kollar's contribution is brilliant in its simplicity and as the reader will discover, non-trivial in its consequences for the health and well-being of workers in industrial settings: my sincere compliments. Eric Oliver's representation is an interesting example of multiple logical levels of generalization within an individual. Cecile Carson's article serves as both an invitation and a challenge to the readers: the invitation is to expand the beginnings of an exploration of this "sixth" representational system; and at the next higher logical level to begin a search for other representational systems without falling into the muddle-headedness of some current forms of mysticism.

Don was, by the way, when last heard from, headed to some destination in the Midwest with four truck loads of filing cabinets.

NLP AND
INDUSTRIAL ACCIDENT PREVENTION
by
Michael Kollar, Ph.D.

During the summer of 1981, I was approached by Doris Jenkins, an employee of E.I. DuPont De Nemours and Company, a major textile producing plant located near Charleston, S.C. The management of this particular plant, the Cooper River plant, had been quite concerned about the number and kind of accidents that had been occurring during the early months of 1981. Specifically during 1981, most of their employees' serious injuries plus most of the injuries requiring first aid were accidents involving hands.

Most of the product work at this plant requires that people use their hands around equipment that could be hazardous if proper care is not taken or if recommended procedures are not followed. It was explained to me that February, 1982, had been declared "Develop Your Safety Attitude" month in hopes of motivating employees to more efficiently follow recommended safety procedures by changing or improving their safety attitudes and practices.

I submitted a written proposal describing a lecture/presentation that would be delivered to the entire plant membership of over 1100 employees. The presentation was one of a five point program developed by the plant's safety committee. It was hoped the presentation would give employees greater insight into how their psychological attitudes could affect their safety attitude, thereby reducing, the number of employee injuries.

Prior to the presentation, in December, 1981, I toured the plant to familiarize himself with the work setting. The written proposal was a series of six separate presentations during the month of February, 1982. With 1100 employees working alternating shifts, six separate presentations appeared to be the most efficient method to insure that everyone was able to attend.

During the plant tour, it was observed that employees interact continuously with production machines that move very fast (high R.P.M.'s) and make fairly consistent sounds. When a machine malfunctions, it sounds different than when functioning properly. When a malfunction occurs, workers had been trained to initiate the "lock, tag, clear, and try" sequence. First, the machine is turned off and "locked" into the off position; second, a small red "tag" is placed on the machine for everyone to see; third, the machine is "cleared" of obstructions; leading to removal of the tag, reactivating the machine, and giving it a "try."

It was during January, 1982, that I attended my first seminar on Neuro-Linguistic Programming (NLP), and the seminar resulted in a major shift in my method of presentation delivery. The four-day NLP workshop, Patterns of Organization, was led by John Grinder and sponsored by the Southeast Center of Neuro-Linguistic Programming, a division of the Center for Professional Development, in Raleigh, N.C.

I decided to incorporate two NLP components during the body of my presentations. The first was an auditory sensory acuity drill. As stated earlier, when a machine malfunctions it sounds different from the consistent sound of a properly running machine. The auditory acuity drill was chosen to assist employees in improving their auditory discrimination abilities in hopes of them becoming more auditorily aware and therefore able to react in a more timely and efficient fashion to the different sounds of a malfunctioning machine.

The second NLP component was a combination visual and internal-external digital anchor. It was my assumption that too much time passed between when a worker saw or heard a malfunction and when the "lock, tag, clear, and try" sequence was initiated. Additionally, the hands of workers are at approximately eye level when having to interact with the machines, so when workers tried to clear their machines of debris or obstruction instead of following the required procedures, injuries to the hands could easily happen.

The anchor was placed between when the workers first perceived a malfunction (visually or auditorily) and when they initiated their "lock, tag, clear, and try" sequence. I instructed the employees to put their hands (tops of hands) in front of their face at approximately eye level (visual anchor) and saying "stop, think" (auditory digital anchor) three times. This exercise was repeated a few times and then more lecture followed about how other plants around the country had reduced their accident rate by initiating similar safety education programs.

From March 1981, through November of 1981, there were approximately 49 accidents to the hands. After the presentation and anchor implementation, from March 1982, to November, 1982, there were 27 accidents resulting in a 55% reduction of hand-related accidents.

It may be assumed that the reduction in the rate of accidents was primarily the result of the workers having anchored the words "stop, think," to whenever their hands appeared in front of their eyes, as they would if they had attempted to clear an obstructed machine without having initiated the "lock, tag, clear, and try" sequence. In addition, by having them practice becoming more auditorily aware, they were more quickly able to discriminate between a properly and improperly functioning machine, thereby decreasing the chances of putting their hands near the machines during unsafe periods.

It is most important to mention that a strong base in NLP theories, techniques and skills is to be used as a vast tool bag from which needed and applicable tools can be plucked. By touring the plant I was able to see, hear and feel what the plant workers saw, heard and felt as they interacted with their machines. After the tour I was able to look into my tool bag and pack those tools which would most efficiently assist me in reaching my outcome, i.e., preventing accidents to the worker's hands.

In closing, I strongly recommend that consulting be a four-pronged approach:

1. Observation and evaluation of current situation;

2. Deciding which NLP technique would be most efficient and how to incorporate the chosen skill or technique into a presentation;

3. Make the presentation; and

4. Evaluate at a future date to determine results.

FIVE YEARS ON THE NLP LIMITED
by
Eric Oliver

For a long time I didn't understand Will Rogers. He remained a mystery until I began to utilize communication and not just conversation. I knew several folks whom I roundly disliked until I found out I could meet their "other-than-conscious"[1] parts as well. That made a big difference.

I met a likeable lawyer once. Years before he met me, Ray had heard a talk presented about Neuro Linguistic Programming (NLP) at a legal conference. This individual decided to tell Ray and his colleagues absolutely everything about NLP in just two days. Ray's resulting confusion and frustration helped keep him leery of NLP for years. However, when he found himself in a tight spot a few years down the road, he looked me up anyway. Despite a successful practice in corporate and contract law, my client the lawyer had a secret; he was a little afraid to work in a courtroom. He had learned criminal law in school and, following graduation, won his first nine cases in a row. He lost the tenth. He continued practice in those areas which did not require courtroom work. Nine years later, here he was, sitting across from me looking for some magic one week before he had to return to court, not once but twice. In one case he was up against an opponent he very much respected who had had a little more practice over the previous nine years.

John Grinder once told me something like "never overlook the obvious." Ray had heard about this anchoring stuff, and thought a little push-button miracle was just what he needed. It seemed my task was to let the part of him in charge of his performance prove there was more to anchoring than just talk. After we got acquainted and he introduced me to his world a little more I asked him to reminisce a bit. We talked about his best work in law school and some of his finest moments years before that. We even talked about those nine wins in a row. We wondered how he might have those moments at hand in the future. He had had difficulty grasping the resources available to him in spite of the most rational perspective he could project.

I asked him to describe, in exquisite detail, the courtroom in which he would be working. He pictured the bench, the jury box, his opponent's table, and his own. He rehearsed exactly where he would place his briefs, his case, his water, everything. He then devised a gesture he could utilize unobtrusively to get his feelings to line up with his perspective, a gesture like holding the edge of the table with his fingers on top and his thumbs along the inside edge. He could use it sitting or standing and by ostensibly checking his notes, lean over and grab his resources. We then rehearsed the process with a deep breath accompanying the anchor for each previous effective performance as we placed it on the imaginary table. At first, he thought it was a little silly sitting there with his hands on a make-believe table in mid-air. However, when he sat there in court with his opponent to his side, and laid out his briefs, his case, and his water just so, and then grabbed the table, some part of him remembered to breathe deeply. Seeing this, as the judge was still in chambers, his opposition leaned over and remarked that he looked "loaded for bear." Ray slowly turned, met his gaze, and intoned softly, "Watch out." Effectively, the case was over.

A year and a half later, having learned a little more about words like disassociation and incongruence, my client the lawyer was arguing in front of a three judge appellate panel. His opponent went first, hammering out a long chain of facts and evidence. Ray noticed all three judges simultaneously pull back at one particular point during his adversary's presentation. He also noticed a shift in each of them which he interpreted to be disagreement with the same point. When his turn came, instead of refuting each point in that long list from his typically exhaustive notes, Ray gathered his courage and framed his argument around that single point. He declared it to be the salient issue and devoted all his effort to that. He observed the three judges' reactions closely, and emphasized anything in his presentation which got a different response than his opponent received. He won. It wasn't until later that he noticed the deep breath he had taken as he placed his hands just so on the table when he rose to speak.

Unnoticed changes, implemented out of our awareness, seem to be the hallmark of elegance. I had the opportunity to see this principle demonstrated by a reluctant student in a two-day seminar. Jill came to my training with her husband who had read the literature and was personally very intrigued with Neuro-Linguistic Programming. It was apparent that his wife in no way shared his enthusiasm. She provided herself with a chance to re-anchor an old internal calibrated loop[2], a phenomenon my friend Dave Dobson calls "Sub-jective Reversal."[3]

Jill was brought to my attention by another participant during the first exercise. She had become quite upset with her attempts during the first exercise. I approached and turned her from the direction she had been facing and moved quite close to her. After some preliminaries, we tacitly; established the anchor "anxious" to replace the tone and word "fear," which she had been using to maintain her predicament. I then helped her build a broader perspective on anxious feelings, which she used to call fear. At my request she drew upon her history and relived several experiences which had produced anxiety responses. She then compared the feeling ("just the feeling") among all the experiences and determined that fear of loss of life felt different than the anxiety of talking in front of class as a child, and that that in turn felt different than the anxiety of deciding what to eat when everyone else at the table had already ordered. She noticed that the feelings all shared similarities, but varied in intensity. All these historical feelings seem to attach themselves to the dilation of the pupils and a particular tone of voice.

I then asked Jill if she knew what a rollercoaster ride felt like. When she said yes, I asked if she might describe that feeling as "excitement," and if she could find any similar sensations there with the ones she had just been reviewing. When she said yes, I suggested she pretend she could sit in the front seat of the rollercoaster, hearing the clack-clack as it climbed the first hill, pressing her back in the seat, hearing the excited voices behind her, and feeling that "excitement" and holding it for just a moment. I then had her compare "anxious" and "excitement" for similarities in just the physical experience of those feelings. I asked if she noticed any similarities, and as she answered yes I asked if she was sure; and as she answered yes I dilated my pupils and said, "Look, as long as you're going to be anxious, you might as well be excited too." By noon the next day she was the first to work in each group she was in, and her groups consistently requested extra work as well.

Another point about calibrated loops might be made by Jill's husband's response. It seemed that the more enthusiasm she showed for NLP, the more he lost interest. And when she decided to come up to the North Woods for our Personal Revolution Weekend (PRW) despite her anxieties, he wound up unable to attend although he had the interest in NLP.

The PRW is often the occasion for some of my favorite encounters, and this was no exception. In addition to Jill, the weekend was attended by several folks schooled in NLP, some of whom teach NLP to earn their living. Among these was a guy I'll refer to as Chief Loon. Calibrated loops again were significant when we engaged in our mental tug-of-war. But presupposition was crucial, especially when it came to reversing or reframing the Chief's status within the group, and mine inside his head.

Chief Loon is a business trainer in a large city. He also is quite an active presence within the NLP network of seminars, symposia, and like gatherings. I was informed at the outset of the weekend by some friends who had had the Chief as a participant in workshops of their own that he often made his presence known in unusual ways. It seems he had a unique method of challenging his hosts to perform at their peak proficiency; that is, he often encouraged members of training groups he joined to polarize to the presenters. The Chief is what some folks might call a provocateur. That alone is nothing new, but the Chief has a delivery which is truly challenging. After setting his main frame within the group, he apparently shuns the spotlight, preferring instead to work in the halls, on breaks, before and after sessions, but rarely in the middle of a session.

At this point a little background on the Personal Revolution Weekend might be helpful to appreciate what happened later. I believe it was Scout Lee Gunn in connection with John Grinder who first brought outdoor

retreats into NLP lexicon. At her suggestion, I borrowed a little from
her experience in constructing the PRW. The PRW is a four-day residential
seminar in a wooded setting consisting of several physical and mental
experiences designed to take maximum advantage of the creative potential in distraction, and paradoxical situations. The experiences, exercises,
and games are arranged to engage people both in and out of awareness
to focus simultaneously on their past, present, and future; their bodies
and their minds; the woods and their homes; their inner world and the
group; and so forth. By providing very different external surroundings,
we often help distract participants from their internal worlds, the actual
sight of all potential Personal Revolutions. The weekend is designed to
bring out-dated patterns in communication and behavior into clear relief
while establishing opportunities to supplant or alter any limitations imposed by those patterns. Bringing limitations into clear relief is rarely
a conscious phenomenon, as parts of Chief Loon and I eventually agreed.
This came to pass during a game called Count Coup, originally borrowed, but later tailored specifically to match the PRW approach.

The first day during an introductory group, Chief Loon established
his major argument with my efforts, stating his opinion that I was neglec-
ting to operate within a "real cooperative frame." This was the last open
challenge he made. For the next day and a half, after each break, as I faced
the group, I discovered a knot of confusion over there, a bit of defiance
over here, a little reluctance in the back, constant editorializing up here,
and, sitting in the center, arms crossed with a close-lipped grin, the Chief
himself. I realized we had begun a kind of contest, with the quality of
a number of participants' experiences balanced on the outcome of our
efforts. Within his pattern, there were no open challenges; however any
pattern can be utilized to help build others, and Count Coup provided
an opportunity.

Count Coup reportedly originated as a Native American means of
testing skills in stealth, honor, and bravery outside of combat. The idea
was to enter enemy territory, and without engaging in combat, steal some
personal effects, or better yet, touch the bravest opponent with a
ceremonial Coup Stick, or best of all, touch him bare-handed. The PRW
version has two tribes crossing the same territory toward opposing goals,
shortly after nightfall. A touch (coup) requires a brave to give up his/her
token of honor to the marauding brave. The group is given a few instructions, each tribe receives additional instructions, and each brave is
given a role to play along with several (sometimes conflicting) personal
instructions to carry out. By simply stating that some folks may have
secrets, we insure that paranoia soon runs rampant.

The Chief's first move was to station himself below the window of
the room in which we were briefing the individual braves so he might
hear and outflank our discussions. After being discovered and shooed
away, the Chief eventually had his turn in the room. I informed him that
this night the two tribes were called the Geese and the Loons, after the

most prevalent waterfowl in the area. I then told him his overt role was to be the chief of the Loon tribe, or Chief Loon. His covert task was to establish a real, cooperative frame throughout his tribe and to do whatever necessary, using all his skills, to overcome any real or imagined obstacles they might have to successfully cross the territory without losing a single brave's token to an opponent's coup. That special rule was nothing special; it was simply a reiteration of the main instruction for the group.

He set off to exert his influence on his tribe, and as I learned later, used every story, anchor, and suggestion he had already set up to accomplish his end. What he did not know was how fond I am of double entendres. His name became very important to every member of his tribe, for, while I set the mood for each and every one of them, I sadly informed them that two years ago, their illustrious Chief had been wounded in the head while acquitting himself heroically in battle. The blow had quite addled his senses. Consequently, while it was incumbent on each of them to pay the Chief the honor and deference due his station, listening attentively to everything he said, they must disregard everything he said the instant the game actually began.

I hoped his pattern would stay consistent and that he would try to sabotage a direct instruction presented to him as his "special role" and already presented publicly to the group. As indicated above, he followed my instructions to the letter. He did everything he could to arrange for his whole tribe to ignore any conflicts and line up with his direction to meet their objectives. According to some observers, he was successful. Several folks in his group had their own independent aspirations in addition to my instructions, yet he managed to overcome all that through his ardent ministrations. Then, seemingly inexplicably, he over-played his hand while establishing his "real cooperative frame." For insurance, after he had general agreement from almost everybody, he insisted they take an oath that anyone who broke the trust would have his/her sleeping bag "personally dampened" by every other tribe member before retiring. That seemed to be the straw that broke the camel's back. At the signal for the game to begin, Chief Loon's braves scattered like rabbits to the four points of the great Medicine Wheel. My challenge was now at hand.

As the game ends, the participants all return to a central indoor location for one of only two group discussions over four days. I hoped that the Chief would give me the opportunity to suggest some things to the group as well as to his "other-than-conscious" parts. A few minutes into the session, someone from Chicago brought up the confusing array of suggested rules. Chief Loon rose as if on cue and berated me loudly and at length for again failing to structure things cooperatively. I watched the group and, sure enough, about half indicated non-verbal agreement with him. To me, this was the last chance; these folks were sitting on a fence, leaning away from the next two days of intense work for their own stated and unstated goals. I edged my attention back to the Chief and, using every term he had marked out as a highly or lowly valued criteria, said this to him: "Chief, I'll be happy to assist you in understanding how the rules can help you learn more personally in a cooperative way, just as soon as you tell me exactly which rules you mean. Was it the rules I gave the group, the rules I gave each tribe, the rules I gave you, the rules I gave your opponents, the rules I gave each person individually, or the rules you all came with in your heads? Give that to me alphabetically, chronologically, typewritten and single-spaced, and I'll be happy to cooperate with you."

The whole group sat back in their chairs and sighed at the moment I did. Then they went inside and stayed . . . momentarily. So did the Chief. The next day, and through almost every other activity that took place the rest of the weekend, Chief Loon turned up but failed to participate. Everyone tried to convince and assist him to join them, and in the process forged an even stronger group. Polarity ceased to be a major factor. An interesting footnote on out-of-conscious functioning was delivered to me a little less than nine months later. The Chief, as do some people I've seen, dropped me a line. It seems that immediately after returning home the Chief redesigned a good deal of what he was presenting to business people. He began repeating several exercises he had experienced at the PRW, with some productive results for him and his clients. Those kinds of cards and letters are really gratifying to receive.

This travelogue through my map of NLP territory would be incomplete without one of my favorite stories. On this occasion I worked without consciously working (as it should be); and my friend Ann changed without aid of a traditional "the-rapist," also a desirable state of affairs. I met Ann in a restaurant shortly after the Personal Revolution Weekend. She had heard of me from some New York folks who had just attended the weekend. She arranged to meet me for dinner during a visit west. It wasn't long into our conversation before she let me know one of the things some part of her had come to discuss.

She told me she was blind on the inside. This woman had, for several years, managed a successful career as a business consultant. She had recently completed an NLP credentialing program at a prestigious NLP institute. And now here she was, sitting across from me over a plate of fish, confessing to a distressing lack of ability to "form internal pictures." This became doubly amazing to me when I discovered that, prior to becoming a consultant, this woman had been quite a successful photographer.

I had to laugh a little when she offered me Freud's loony legacy as a possibility for her lamentable condition. She mentioned, among several potential explanations of the deep hidden meaning beneath her inner darkness, that perhaps she had seen something distasteful or horrible when younger, was "blocking it out," and consequently "blocked-out" all inner pictures as a way of avoiding any "negative" feelings those images might generate. Some part of me heard the implied dynamic and later utilized the perception after a fashion. I began to tell her about a story I was going to tell her, but interrupted myself at the point she appeared to visualize what I was saying, and wondered out loud.

I looked up and wondered how, when she was working on an award-winning collection of photographs, and she had a particular subject framed in her viewfinder, her finger poised on the shutter release, just exactly how she knew when to snap the picture. I salted the conversation visually and paid close attention to all apparent patterns of agreement. I began interrupting the story at less frequent intervals while she seemed to visualize more frequently. The story I finally found myself starting was an involved description of a portion of Joseph Heller's Catch-22. I suggested she might "see what I say" as I began to describe poor old Havermeyer, of whom I told her she strongly reminded me.

"Havermeyer was crazy. He was driven crazy by the flies in his eyes. He was the only one who knew he had flies in his eyes for sure. Havermeyer would spend his afternoons cutting grooves in his 45 caliber ammunition with his bayonet. This is called dum-dumming. A dum-dum bullet. as it leaves the gun barrel in a blaze of fire and smoke, begins to flatten and spread thin as it speeds through the air toward its target, so that upon arrival it forms a sheet of metal instead of a slug. You might imagine the damage that could do. Havermeyer would spend his nights sitting on a crate in pitch darkness in the middle of the supply tent. In one hand he held his 45 trained on a remembered spot in the dark. On one upraised finger of the other hand was a ring attached to a banjo wire which ran through a couple of pulleys all the way up to the only light bulb in the tent. The wire was pulled so tight that a strong breath would flick it on and flood the darkness with light. Over near the back of the tent was a spot he pointed his gun at with a half eaten Baby Ruth on it. Havermeyer would sit, straining to hear in the darkness, until the sound of a mouse nibbling a candy bar reached his ears . . . then he'd turn on the light. The mouse would freeze and scan the room, looking for the source of the light, and, as their eyes met, Havermeyer would blast away. The back of the tent was decorated with tiny bits of mouse pelt and candy from his nightly vigil."

"You see, Havermeyer was crazy, but not as crazy as you. He was driven crazy by the flies in his eyes. He knew that not only did he have flies in his eyes, but everybody else had flies in their eyes too. He'd tell them he had flies in his eyes and they'd look to see, but because of the flies in their eyes, they couldn't see them. It drove him crazy. And that's still not as crazy as you, because if all it took was showing you the flies in your eyes, you'd see them easily. But, you're sitting there listening and not really hearing. If you could hear me, you could see what I'm saying. But you can't 'cause you've got bananas in your ears. If you'll just pull out the bananas, you'll be fine."

She looked at me. She looked up and right, and then straight up. She found that pretty funny, and she nodded as we laughed. Then she looked up, nodded, and laughed again.

Helping someone bring perceptions into awareness that weren't there before makes Will Rogers a lot more understandable to me. When I met Ann for dinner a few months later, I was over-enthusiastically discussing perception at length, until she interrupted me and asked, "Eric, just exactly how do you define perception?" After some thought, I said, "Reality."

NOTES

1. I have begun adopting D.R. Dobsons's term "other-than-conscious" over sub-, or un-conscious. Understanding that consciousness seems to be a gift of those portions of the mind outside of awareness, it strikes me as more accurate to represent awareness as in and out of consciousness, rather than subservient to it.

2. For information on re-anchoring calibrated loops read Grinder, John and Bandler, Richard, Reframing: Neuro-Linguistic Programming and the Transformation of Meaning. Moab, UT: Real People Press, 1982.

3. For information on subjective reversal see *Hypnosis & Other Mythical Kingdoms Of The Mind* by Dave Dobson.

THE VESTIBULAR (VS) SYSTEM
IN NLP
December 1, 1987
by
Cecile A. Carson, M.D.

The vestibular system is one of the special sense organs of the nervous system that has not been specifically delineated as a "representational system" in Neuro Linguistic Programming (NLP). It allows living forms to interrupt space without losing their balance or connection with their previous position — its function therefore is to maintain equilibrium, i.e., *whole body position in space.*

Other special sense organs for taste, smell, vision, hearing, and touch have been well-described in NLP. Touch (from sensory nerve endings in the viscera) are presently categorized as "kinesthetic" in NLP usage. Although neurologically this label is incorrect, it has served well to organize observations and interventions within the NLP framework. Kinesthesia (also termed "proprioception") consists of nerve endings which do not receive external physical stimuli directly, but rather modify our sensations of position change of body parts through stimulation of nerve endings in the muscles, tendons, and joints. Thus, *"kinesthetic"* relates to *part body position in space.*

Kinesthetic and vestibular input complement one another, the former matching its somatic hologram of muscle position with the latter's hologram of vertical and horizontal spatial position and movement in any of the spatial planes. Because it is phylogenetically, anatomically, and functionally distinct from the kinesthetic system — and has a distinct set of predicates — the vestibular system has useful applications in communication and change work.

PHYLOGENY

"All creatures are connected to the earth by gravity and inertia. The pull of gravity and the resistance of inertia are constant and unyielding, and yet we do manage to rise up and move. The mastery of gravity has been the central issue in evolution from fish to human being."[1]

The Vestibular system is more primitive than the special sense organs of smell, taste, hearing, and vision, and as such, tends to be more out of conscious awareness. Its earliest form was as a gravity receptor called a statocyst in primitive jellyfish of the late Precambrian era more than 600 million years ago. From this simple statocyst, a continuous increment in anatomic complexity occurred which evolved into the vestibular system in humans described in Figure 1.[2] Embryologically, the human vestibular system develops from our fetal ectoderm and the proprioceptive system from our fetal mesoderm, distinctly separate origins for the complementary functions.

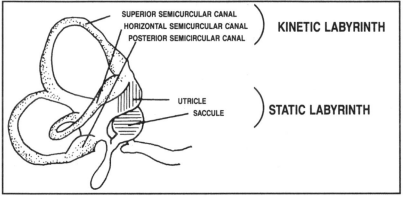

Figure 1. Anatomy of the Right Vestibular Apparatus

The vestibular system consists of a *vestibular apparatus* which sits deep in the inner ear surrounded by cranial bones. There is a left vestibular apparatus and a right vestibular apparatus. Along with the eyes and proprioceptive nerve endings throughout the body, it constitutes the sensory information used by the nervous system in maintaining equilibrium. In addition, hearing functions in an orienting and localizing way, but its input is not as primary as that of vision and proprioception.

The vestibular apparatus consists of two major parts:

a) The *static labyrinth*, made up of two large chambers called the *utricle* and the *saccule*, which detects the position of the head with respect to gravity and also detects linear acceleration; and

b) the *kinetic labyrinth*, made up of three semicircular canals (each at 90-degree angles to each other), which detect angular acceleration and angular velocity (e.g., rotation). The kinetic labyrinth also has a special role in coordinating movement of the eyes with movement of the head.

Each of the structures of the static and kinetic labyrinths contain highly sensitive hair cells connected to the vestibular nerve which are stimulated by flow of a gelatinous material in the semicircular canals or in the utricle and saccule. This gelatinous material flows when the head changes position in relation to gravity or to changes in acceleration. After a particular group of hair cells are stimulated, the vestibular nerve carries this information to other parts of the brain stem and cerebellum to coordinate reflex corrective movements of the eyes, head, trunk, and limbs to maintain equilibrium.[3]

Thus the vestibular system can be thought of as having an important *integrative* function among the various sensory inputs, primarily visual and proprioceptive. "Unlike those sensory organs that respond to energy sources external to the body, the labyrinths respond to self-generated forces within the head. During natural head movements these forces are not under voluntary control and therefore the vestibular responses are more automatic than those of the other sensory modalities. For example, one can remove vision simply by closing the eyes, whereas one cannot suppress vestibular stimuli during head movement."[4] Excessive stimulation of the vestibular system can produce a syndrome known as *motion sickness* consisting of perspiration, nausea, vomiting, increased salivation, yawning, and generalized malaise. Persistent visual stimulation can also produce the syndrome.

The following examples illustrate this interrelatedness of input:

a) Have you ever become dizzy or nauseated watching a film of a chase scene with the camera mounted on the pursuit car bumper as it careens around corners at a high rate of speed, even though your head and body are comfortably seated in a chair watching the movie and not moving at all? You may find yourself actually putting out a hand to keep from falling because the visual input is so compelling; and

b) Conversely, in the "Mad House" at carnivals, proprioceptive input in the form of pressure in the joints and muscles of your legs tells you that you are on an incline leaning forward — but the room has been painted to trick your vision into thinking that you are on a horizontal plane in a "normal" room.

A key word for the vestibular system is balance. Any movement of the whole body sets up immediate and powerful compensatory reflex actions to maintain equilibrium for protection and survival of the organism. Since these reflexes are so critical for our well-being, they occur extremely quickly and usually out of conscious awareness.

The following diagram illustrates these interactive processes:

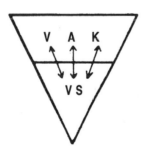

VS: VESTIBULAR
V: VISUAL
A: AUDITORY
K: KINESTHETIC

The arrows flow in both directions, since primary stimulation of the vestibular apparatus can lead to corrective actions by the eyes, muscles, and joints — and stimulation of muscles, joints, or of eyes (as in the previous examples) can cause the vestibular apparatus to compute being "off balance" and initiate corrective reflexes.

ACCESSING CUES

Not surprisingly, there is no one characteristic eye movement or whole body position that is indicative of vestibular access in the moment. Eye direction and body direction are determined by: a) direction of rotation (clockwise, counterclockwise); b) direction of fall (off vertical axis); and c) deceleration. Basically, the *eyes* go in the *opposite direction* of the movement and *whole body* in the *same direction* for a) and b), as in the following diagrams:

A) ROTATION CLOCKWISE:
EYES MOVE COUNTERCLOCKWISE
BODY MOVES CLOCKWISE

ROTATION COUNTERCLOCKWISE
EYES CLOCKWISE, BODY
COUNTERCLOCKWISE

B) FALLING FORWARD
EYES MOVE UP INITIALLY

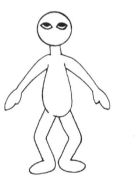

FALLING BACK:
EYES MOVE DOWN INITIALLY

For changes in acceleration c), if the head remains static on accelerating, the eyes move up.[5]

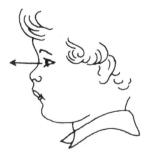

During rotation of the head in horizontal (spinning) or vertical (tumbling) planes, a physiologic condition known as *nystagmus* occurs. This manifests as involuntary jerking movements of the eyes when the person is stopped and staring straight ahead after spinning or tumbling around several times. The person experiences this as "vertigo" or as the room "spinning" when he stops. It results from the lag period of the gelatinous material in the vestibular apparatus, after being set in motion, to finally coming to rest.

Of note is that the eye movements and body movements described in this section also occur when the subject *imagines* or *remembers* that he is moving his body in these ways through space.

SUBMODALITIES

The characteristics of the vestibular representational system (VS) are: a) *orientation* — position with respect to gravity or axis of reference b) *acceleration* — (deceleration or absence of acceleration) change in velocity over time (velocity being speed in a given direction) c) *torque* — angular (rotational) force d) *inertia* — resistance to change of the motion (or motionlessness) of a body.

PREDICATES

The predicates of the vestibular representational system (VS) are quite distinct, though a number have been grouped under the "kinesthetic" category in the past. The following predicates relate to whole body movements in space, as well as to spatial relationships. Prepositions, in particular, communicate spatial relationships as they form the linguistic scaffolding of space and time. In fact, our spatial predicates tell us what it is like to exist as an entity that is separate from, and yet related to, other things. "Our experiences of location, distance, connection, and of self and other gain meaning and coherence through their spatial representation."[6]

a) VERBS	b) PREPOSITIONS	c) EXPRESSIONS
balance	over	off balance
suspend	under	in suspense
center	around	on the edge
position	up	shift your position
orient	down	turn around
stabilize	off	dizzy
shift	on	upside down
rotate	through	flipped out
gyrate	beyond	hung up
spin		spacey
whirl		off the wall
spiral		hanging out
accelerate		going in circles
whip		over and over

a) VERBS	b) PREPOSITIONS	c) EXPRESSIONS
careen		rolling along
loop		in orbit
lean		topsy turvy
catapult		over a barrel
somersault		in a tailspin
flip		upstanding
tumble		laid back
fall		out of kilter
dive		looped
plunge		banking the curves
sink		wound up
learn		out on a limb
tilt		laid back
sway		gravity of the
swing		situation
rock		rocking the boat
trip		slipping away
circle		slipped up
unwind		spinning around
float		tripped up
stuck		teeter-totter
stalled		free-floating
		can't get rolling

EXPLORING THE VESTIBULAR SYSTEM

Children are wonder models for re-discovering a more direct sense of the vestibular system. Unfortunately, as we move from childhood to adulthood, we tend to increasingly limit the variety of ways we choose to move our bodies through space, frequently narrowing our selection to standing (walking) and sitting (driving) in the vertical plane, or lying (sleeping) in the horizontal plane. As a result we may fear "new directions," "slowing down" the fanatic pace of our lives, or "plunging" into the unknown for what we want.

The following simple exercises are designed to help you begin a playful exploration of this system that has become largely unconscious and to use it in creative and innovative ways for pleasure and for therapeutic work.

RECAPITULATE PHYLOGENY

1. The jellyfish is like a floating umbrella, so it is only interested in interrupting the vertical plane. In this exercise, begin with upright posture and walk in a flat open area with your eyes closed. Then, on a more varied topography, try to maintain balance (still with eyes closed) just using the vertical aspects of the static portion of your vestibular system. Notice how the posterior portion of the muscles of your extremities extend themselves and stiffen: this uses your more primitive extensor muscles for balance.

2. Again in the vertical plane, you can block the ears, wear odd thicknesses of sandals or shoes, and experience how you maintain your balance.

3. To experience the vestibular portion of orientation as separately from proprioceptive input as possible, go underwater with minimal breath-holding. Then close your eyes, turn your body in a number of directions, and notice if you can figure out which plane your body is in.

4. Turn your head sideways while riding in a car to experience speed in a new way, by stimulating a semicircular canal generally not used in the usual upright (vertical) seated position.

5. Any other activities which may remind your body of movements it enjoyed as a child would be appropriate here, such as rolling down a hill (with and without eyes closed), standing on your head, cartwheel, roller skating, swings, and see-saws. The adventurous may want to try a trampoline or break dancing!

6. Martial arts and body movement exercises such as Feldenkrais[7] allow more intricate explorations. When utilized on a regular basis, they improve posture and body alignment, which quite literally results in a change of perspective in moving through life.

7. One can experience the impact of visual stimuli on the vestibular system with books of artists such as M.C. Escher.[8] In his works, as illustrated in the following graphic, his drawings refuse a conformable stationary point and thus make us dizzy by continuously changing perspective:

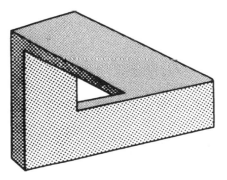

APPLICATIONS

With accessing cues and a set of unique predicates, the vestibular system can be utilized in much the same way as the standard representational systems now described in NLP (V, A, K, O, G). Because it serves an important integrative function among several of the other special senses, and is a more primitive sense organ and more out of conscious awareness, it also has the potential to facilitate very powerful and rapid change work by addressing a deep need persons have to bring more balance into their lives. (Conversely, some of the strategies can be used in reverse as off-balancing techniques when a pattern has become too restrictive or protective and the needed change work relates to beginning to move in new directions.)

1. *rapport* — *body sway* is a very compelling lead out of the subject's awareness, much like the snake in the basket of the Near East. This rocking or swaying, either upper body or whole body, is reminiscent of early mother-infant interactions and can communicate powerful feelings of support and comfort. A wonderful "prop" is the porch *swing or slider* which quickly establishes effective rapport between the riders. Also dancing, by joining music/rhythm/others, establishes a fluid, balanced movement through space into which changes can be introduced.

2. *spatial dissociation* — a variant of visual dissociation, this technique physically places the subject in different positions to attenuate the visual experience with a vestibular one as well. This can be used in Change History, strategies, or in dealing with intense feelings from trauma, phobias, etc.

3. *spatial squash* — analogous to the "visual squash," the subject is placed alternately in two polarity positions. In each position, she talks about/enacts the issue for that pole. With each alternation, the poles are brought closer together until they are "squashed" in the center point, the integration being observed both physiologically and in the subject's language:

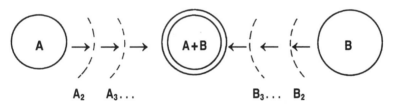

4. *spatial cues* — a prominent feature of observing John Grinder training a group is his spatially marking out pieces of information or resources as he paces back and forth. He then moves back to the spot he has marked out when he is ready to retrieve the material he has "stored" there earlier.

5. *somatic (whole body) change work* — these techniques assume that the body is an absolute somatic metaphor of how we move through our lives, and that the vestibular system is a key representational system in this process. The "dance" of our lives — or the "play" of our lives — is reflected quite literally in how we intersect and sequence our movements through the space around us.

   a) *utilizing somatic metaphors of language* — expressions from a person of, "I just can't let go," can be utilized in somatic change work by: (1) finding a convenient branch or a playground gym set,

(2) having the person hold on to it while mentally placing in the
   bar or branch each thing he feels he can't let go of, and
(3) when he is ready, releasing the bar.
Another example would be "That's a line I can't cross."

b) *"trust" activities* — these include trust falls, trust circles, trust lifts,
   etc., which require a person to surrender ("trust") his own
   maintenance or equilibrium to another (or to others). This activity is quite a stretch for many persons, as a basic fear we all
   have is fear of falling. It is a powerful stimulus to one's vestibular
   system, and rapidly produces a deeply altered state. If, in addition, the person holds in his mind something in life he wants to
   trust will be there for him, a collapse of anchors occurs which
   repatterns the "software" of his neurological computer.

c) *physical challenges (obstacle or ropes courses)* — these challenges consist of physical elements on, near, or high above the ground that
   offer a way to gather information about an individual's patterns
   in life, as well as a way to reinforce or reprogram these patterns.
   Observations include how a person sets an outcome, initiates a
   task, negotiates space and obstacles, and achieves an outcome.
      In order to reprogram patterns, subjects are placed in a physical
   state of resource or "excellence" (whole body balanced, generous
   stance, upper body out over buttocks, eyes relaxed and focused

on an outcome to move toward, and diaphragmatic breathing). This physically begins to free them up from limited ways of moving in their lives. If they are simultaneously holding an outcome in their minds they had felt "stuck" or "unbalanced" about achieving, it allows a collapse of anchors through "rewiring" the soma-to-psyche loop.

High and low elements ropes courses are structures utilized in Project Adventure activities in high schools across the country. It is possible to utilize these elements to bring streamline and individualized NLP technology to bear on an already stimulating and learning-filled environment as long as the "bottom line" is physical safety. For example, a "balance beam" may be a specifically built structure, or may consist of a broad, low wooden fence of large logs which bound the parking spaces of a park. Or it may even be walking a curb in balance.

6. *unwinding* — For people who experience themselves as "wound-up" or "going in circles," first identify the direction of rotation in which they experience these circumstances. Then ask them to slowly begin to rotate in the opposite direction with suggestions to "unwind" or "discover a new direction." You can then invite them to continue this opposite direction of rotation until they reach what they experience as the "balance point" for themselves.

7. *time distortion* — Our time is measured by the movement of whole (celestial) bodies in space through the attraction of gravity. All time distortion change work is related to acceleration or deceleration of time and is congruent with the essence of vestibular submodalities. A particular clinical application of time distortion may be in the person with Type A behavior characteristics, a primary feature of which is time pressure, i.e., not enough time. Typically, these persons are taught stress reduction through relaxation exercises which they quickly master, do for the requisite number of times each day, and then rush off to the rest of their busy day's activities feeling deprived of the 20-40 minutes of time the relaxation exercise required! More appropriate for them might be a time distortion experience in which it is slowed down to allow them the experience of "lotsa time!"

8. *spatial mapping* — This technique is useful in marking out boundaries of a process, which then allows a subject to locate him/herself spatially within the appropriate place of this process. Steps in the process behind her/him and ahead of her/him are not only seen visually but have an additional impact on her/him through vestibular input.

9. *ritual acts* — Ritual can be understood as a conscious, symbolic act to help us move from one state to another. A ritual act moves us through both literal and highly symbolized space toward our desired outcome.

10. *trance induction* — Utilizing primarily vestibular predicates in a trance induction is experienced by many as going quickly into a very regressed state (back to the womb?). The following induction utilizes

only vestibular predicates, but I would recommend a strong pre-induction orienting to the here-and-now of where they are in the room, etc., in representational systems (V, A, K) before proceeding:

Let's *suspend* the present moment and *float back* to time when you were in a delightful playground . . . And as you begin to *orient* yourself to this delightful playground . . . *circle over* to the children's swings . . . as they move *back and forth* . . . sometimes *faster* . . . and sometimes *slower* . . . *swinging* . . . *swinging* . . . *swinging* . . . now *slowing* . . . *slowing down* . . . to *hang* . . . *suspended* . . . in *mid air* . . . And *turn around* to *re-orient* yourself . . . *circling* . . . once again . . . *over* to the *edge of the playground* where the *teeter-totter* is located . . . *moving up* . . . *down* . . . *up* . . . *down* . . . coming *slowly* to rest at this *center* point of *balance* . . . *poised* . . . developing even more *equilibrium* now to *shift* with changes . . . to trust that whatever *shifts* occur . . . you can know where the *balance* point *lies* . . . and this knowledge can help you move to the *edge* of new ideas . . . and *tumble* into new understandings . . . to *plunge* ahead in your own growth and development . . . only as *fast* as you maintain your point of *balance* . . . Now begin to *float back* to the present time-space *coordinates* . . . *slipping* easily . . . into full *orientation* to your present surroundings . . . and your alert state.

11. *other* — Once we have a sense of balance and a "reference" sense of ourselves, a conceptual "stretch" might be to move beyond boundaries of self-and-other relationships to "jump into the abyss" (in Carlos Castaneda's terms) or become one with a point of reference so there is no distinction or separateness (as Einstein did in conceptualizing the theory of relativity).

There are probably hundreds or thousands of possible other applications utilizing the vestibular system in change work. The reader is invited to launch into discovering these for her/himself.

Case 1

A writer was "stuck" in finishing a paper due the next day. While holding her outcome in her mind, she put on music and began free-form dancing for 5-10 minutes. Ideas began to flood her mind, which she quickly jotted down. She continued dancing until the major pieces of the next section of her paper were in place.

Case 2

A young woman was referred for onset of panic attacks when she became engaged. She explained, "The problem is, I've never been married before!" The therapist told her to bring her fiance with her the next visit, and the therapist would perform a mock wedding and marry them. At this point the woman both laughed and broke out in a sweat — a sign of the presence of both humor and fear. Humor was integrated into the carefully planned ritual one week later. The couple wore their tackiest clothes, had a "double ring ceremony" (a tiny bell tied to a small leather thong which they tied to each other's finger), threw "wild" rice, and toasted afterward with Coke — to the "real thing." There were visible signs of integration as she proceeded spatially down the corridor, into the room, and made the final step forward for her vows after being invited to "leave any unnecessary fears behind." The woman's panic attacks disappeared, and five months later she was married.

Case 3

A 41-year-old woman with advanced metastatic breast cancer wanted psychological strategies to help her cope with the disease's progression as well as to combat it emotionally as much as possible. She was in a relatively weakened condition physically, and so was invited to walk a "balance beam" in the form of a curb alongside one of the driveways to the office. Using her body as metaphor, she realized that it was extremely difficult for her to put an outcome ahead of her toward which to walk. When she was able to achieve this and hold her attention on it, she was then asked to share what might knock her "off balance" in getting that outcome. She offered three things. Then as she began to walk toward her outcome, she was challenged verbally with each of the three (husband, bad medical reports, mother). Her body's response (in degree of loss of balance) to the challenges ranked them hierarchically in terms of emotional difficulty for her, a ranking which held consistently over two more tries. She was then coached in how to maintain balance during each of the challenges while continuing to walk toward her objective. This she was able to do. Over the next four months, she resolved each of those difficulties in her emotional life: first husband; then bad medical reports (which kept coming in as her disease progressed); finally, mother. With the healing of the relationship with her mother, she lapsed into coma within two days and died a few hours later. Medical staff and her friends alike were amazed at the quality of her life the last few months, the emotional energy and joy of living she shared with all around her, and the centered way she dealt with each piece of news. In the last few weeks, instead of becoming progressively isolated as many are in the terminal stages of an illness, she had a steady stream of visitors from both hospital staff and community that she was able to relate to in a very calm and genuine way.

CONCLUSION

It is my hope that the addition of the structure and potential uses of the vestibular system (VS) in NLP work may help us all move through life in a wider-based, more flexible stance that allows us to increase our responsiveness to our work, our risk-taking, and our playfulness.

ACKNOWLEDGEMENTS

Special thanks to Jim Shafland, who first wondered about a missing system; to Pat Palmer for playing with predicates; to John Grinder for strategies to my unconscious which opened much of this up; to Steffi Lahar for going in circles with me; to Scout Lee for physically moving me through it; to Dave Gordon for "orientation;" and to Michael Livesay, the "Vestibular Man!"

REFERENCES

1. Robbins, J. "Vestibular Integration: Man's Connection to the Earth, *Somatics*, Autumn, 1977, p. 28.
2. Baloh, R. and Honrubia, V., *Clinical Neurophysiology of the Vestibular System*, Philadelphia, F.A. Davis Co., pp. 6-7.
3. Guyton, A., *Textbook of Medical Physiology*, 6th Ed, Saunders.
4. Baloh, Op. cit., p. 86.
5. Baloh, Op. cit., p. 66.
6. Jones, R., *Physics As Metaphor*, New York, New American Library, 1982, pp. 51-52.
7. Feldenkrais, M., *Awareness Through Movement*, N.Y. Harper & Row, 1977.
8. Escher, M.C., *The Graphic Works of M.C. Escher*, New York, Ballentine Books, 1960.
9. Lee, Scout, et al., *The Challenge of Excellence, Vol. 1: Learning the Ropes of Change*, (Stillwater, Oklahoma, Excellence, Unlimited, 1984).

Invitation

Artistry in the use of NLP is, of course, not restricted to the broad areas of interest explored in this book. We invite those of you who practice the art of Neuro Linguistic Programming to submit manuscripts describing your unique and valuable applications of NLP. We look forward to reviewing them and publishing the best in a second volume.

Submit Articles to:
Grinder, DeLozier and Associates
1077 Smith Grade
Bonny Doon, California 95060
408-475-8540